Risk Management and Error Reduction in Aviation Maintenance

MANOJ S. PATANKAR
Saint Louis University, USA

JAMES C. TAYLOR
Aviation Consultant, Los Altos, USA

ASHGATE

Published by
Ashgate Publishing Limited
Gower House
Croft Road
Aldershot
Hampshire GU11 3HR
England

Ashgate Publishing Company
Suite 420
101 Cherry Street
Burlington, VT 05401-4405
USA

Ashgate website: http://www.ashgate.com

British Library Cataloguing in Publication Data
Patankar, Manoj S.
   Risk management and error reduction in aviation maintenance
   1.Airplanes - Maintenance and repair - Management
   2.Airplanes - Maintenance and repair - Safety measures
   3.Airplanes - Maintenance and repair - Standards
   4.Airplanes - Airworthiness 5.Risk management
   I.Title II.Taylor, James C.
   629.1'346'0684

Library of Congress Cataloging-in-Publication Data
Patankar, Manoj S., 1968-
   Risk management and error reduction in aviation maintenance / Manoj S. Patankar and James C. Taylor.
        p. cm.
   Includes bibliographical references and index.
   ISBN 0-7546-1941-9 (alk. paper)
    1. Airplanes--Maintenance and repair--Quality control. 2. Risk Management. 3. Airlines. 4. Aircraft accidents. I. Taylor, James C. (James Chapman), 1937- II. Title.

   TL671.9.P38 2003
   629.134'6'0685--dc21

                                                              2003050035

ISBN 0 7546 1941 9

Printed and bound in Great Britain by MPG Books Ltd, Bodmin, Cornwall

Contents

List of Boxes

List of Figures

List of Tables

Preface

This book is aimed at both aviation maintenance students as well as practitioners.

It is now a widely accepted fact that about 12-15% of all commercial airliner accidents are attributed to maintenance errors. The Maintenance Resource Management (MRM) programs that have been implemented across the world over the past 13 years have raised the awareness about the error-causing factors among the maintenance community.

Now, as we look forward, we are faced with the challenges to both implement the results from past research as well as continue to advance the profession through programs aimed at actively mitigating error-inducing conditions.

In this book, we attempt to bridge the past and the future of MRM programs by using the concept of *risk management*. Thereby, we acknowledge the human fallibility as well as the systemic ability to control effects of errors. We hope that upon reading this book, you will come to accept that risks, although inherent in the maintenance process, are manageable through appropriate interventions at both individual as well as organizational levels.

The key concepts presented in this book include what we are calling the 'Hawkins-Ashby' model of risk management, the emerging Concept Alignment Process for risk management, the under-rated concept of interpersonal trust in risk management, the under-used principle of professionalism and the under-used practice of return on investment calculation for risk management. Through these concepts, we try to bring forth the ideas for the next generation of MRM programs—behavior-based, proactive, beyond regulatory compliance, and truly embracing the systemic elements discussed in Chapters 3 and 4.

Finally, we use eight accident cases that had maintenance error as either the primary cause or a contributing factor. Through these cases, we illustrate some of the common risks that maintenance professionals take.

Chapter 1 provides a general overview of the safety statistics in the aviation industry and leads the readers into thinking about some theoretical concepts such as the Hawkins-Ashby model and some practical issues such as the cost of an accident.

In Chapter 2, we discuss three different components of safety culture: national, professional, and organizational. Here, we demonstrate that aviation maintenance personnel are more individualistic than pilots and hence it will be even more challenging to implement team concepts in the maintenance environment.

In Chapter 3, we present an introduction to ergonomics, human factors, and MRM. The research and development activities under MRM are explored further. In this chapter, we introduce the readers to fourth generation MRM programs.

In Chapter 4, we discuss the application of sociotechnical systems to aviation maintenance. Together, these two chapters provide the "bridge" between the past and the future of MRM programs.

In Chapter 5, we present a very troubling issue—mutual trust in the maintenance community. As we experience another round of turbulence in the global aviation industry and as we continue to witness the development of virtual organizations, the concept of *mutual trust* will become even more significant.

After reviewing the safety and risk issues at a rather macroscopic scale in the preceding chapters, we discuss the role of an individual in Chapter 6; specifically, we discuss the different types of risks that are taken by maintenance professionals and how simple habits could be developed to mitigate those risks.

In Chapter 7, we present a slightly quantitative perspective of risk management. In an attempt to discuss human reliability without the use of reliability models, we present simple probabilistic data that could be used to (a) understand the relative importance of certain causal factors and (b) apply the concepts of systemic reliability to human-centered systems.

In Chapter 8, we present a formula that could be used to calculate the return-on-investment for MRM programs, especially training. As it is becoming increasingly important to justify the financial viability of programs that are not mandated by regulations, the application of the MRM ROI formula will be invaluable.

Finally, in Chapter 9, we discuss eight maintenance-related accident cases. In this chapter, we discuss the chain of events of each accident as well as the causal factors associated with those accidents. We also draw upon the preceding discussions of different types of risks and risk management.

We sincerely hope that you find this book useful in understanding the field of MRM: its development, challenges, and prognosis. Furthermore, as the Federal Aviation Administration and Transport Canada move toward a comprehensive and systemic approach toward safety management, we hope that you will be able to use the fundamentals of MRM in measurement and management of a comprehensive safety management system.

We encourage you to reflect upon your personal experiences as you read this book and continue to be more proactive in your quest for safety.

Respectfully,

Manoj S. Patankar
Chesterfield, MO

James C. Taylor
Los Altos, CA

Acknowledgements

Research in aviation maintenance is not possible without generous help from numerous practitioners—the hardworking and genuinely caring individuals like yourselves. Over the years, literally thousands of mechanics, inspectors, managers, maintenance engineers, and support personnel have entrusted us with very valuable information. They have taken the time to respond to survey questionnaires, participate in interviews, and allowed us to observe their work practices. We are eternally grateful to them for their hospitality and openness.

We would like to extend our special gratitude to the following individuals for their relentless support and encouragement: David Driscoll, Scott Gilliland, John Goglia, Jay Hiles, Barbara Kanki, Kevin Lynch, Robert and Gordon Mudge, Ken Peartree, Michael Peate, Zoe Sexhus, Deepak Sharma, Robert Thomas, III and Jean Watson.

We would also like to acknowledge our universities for their support: Saint Louis University—Parks College of Engineering and Aviation, San Jose State University—Department of Aviation and the Institutional Review Board and Santa Clara University—School of Engineering.

We thank John Hindley and his staff at Ashgate Publishing Limited for providing excellent help in bringing this project to fruition in a timely manner.

Finally, we thank our family members for their support, and encouragement to pursue this project: Kirsten and Sanjeevani Patankar and Ellen Jo Baron.

Chapter 1

Defining Risk in the Aviation Maintenance Environment

Instructional Objectives

Upon completing this chapter, you should be able to:

1. Explain the critical need to reduce the number of aviation accidents.
2. Explain the concepts of *risk* and *safety* in the aviation maintenance environment.
3. Discuss the effects of poor operational and maintenance practices on the design safety of an aircraft.
4. List some specific ways in which maintenance personnel can minimize risk.
5. List some of the different types of costs associated with a typical aircraft accident.

Introduction

Risk is the probability of an unfavorable outcome. If we consider the classic example of tossing a fair coin, each side of that coin represents an equally likely event. Hence, the risk of such a coin not landing on its "head" or "tail" is 50 %. In the aviation industry, risk could be expressed in terms of number of accidents per x-number of flight hours. The lower the number of accidents per x-number of flight hours, the lower the probability of accidents. Therefore, in ideal terms, the safest activity would have a zero probability of accidents. In reality, however, safety is dynamic as well as relative because it is the probability of an accident that is acceptable to a given society. In other words, as long as a society perceives the benefits of a certain activity to be greater than the risk of failure in that activity, that activity will be considered "safe" in that society. As that society learns more about the advantages and disadvantages of that activity or the means to minimize the risks, it will redefine the acceptable level of risk, and consequently "safety".

This chapter presents a general overview of aviation safety data, a summary of maintenance-related aviation accidents in the past decade, and a discussion of how risk is introduced into a particular flight. We use the concept of normal operating envelope (NOE) to define the criteria upon which safety of flight depends. When any of the parties concerned with the safety of flight commits errors, they compromise the design safety of that flight and increase risk. We have connected the SHELL model developed by Hawkins (1987) with Ashby's law of requisite variety (Ashby, 1956) to form a Hawkins-Ashby model of risk management. The chapter concludes that this combined model could be used to understand and manage risks such that the requisite degree of safety is maintained.

Aviation Safety Data

Aviation safety data are available through several reliable sources such as the Federal Aviation Administration (www.faa.gov), the National Transportation Safety Board (www.ntsb.gov), the Boeing Commercial Airplane Company (www.boeing.com), the International Air Transport Association (www.iata.org), the Flight Safety Foundation (www.fsf.org), and the Air Transport Association (www.airlines.org). Safety data from other countries is somewhat difficult to obtain; however, Internet sites such as *aviation-safety.net* provide worldwide airliner accident reports and some general safety data. In this chapter, we present data to illustrate the magnitude of aircraft operations and the corresponding levels of safety.

Accident statistics released by the Air Transport Association (ATA, 2002) indicate that the number of accidents of U.S. registered 14 CFR § 121 operators (scheduled air carriers) beginning in 1932 have decreased dramatically. Table 1-1 presents some NTSB's standard terms and their definitions. Figure 1-1 illustrates a stable accident rate since 1982 while Figure 1-2 illustrates the concurrent increase in the number of passenger enplanements.

The net result of these changes is that if the accident rate does not decrease beyond the 1999 level, the number of § 121 accidents in the future would increase dramatically. The forecast accident rate is one § 121 aircraft per week by the year 2010. Therefore, the present accident rate, although substantially lower than any other modes of transportation, will probably not be acceptable as the passenger enplanements continue to increase. In other words, the society is likely to expect a much lower level of risk for air travel for it to continue to be safe in the year 2010.

Table 1-1:   Some NTSB's terms and their definitions

Accident: an occurrence associated with the operation of an aircraft that takes place between the time any person boards the aircraft with the intention of flight and all such persons have disembarked, and in which any person (occupant or non occupant) suffers a fatal or serious injury or the aircraft receives substantial damage.

Fatal injury: any injury that results in death within 30 days of the accident.

Serious injury: any injury that requires hospitalization for more than 48 hours, results in a bone fracture, or involves internal organs or burns.

Substantial damage: damage or failure that adversely affects the structural strength, performance, or flight characteristics of the aircraft and would normally require major repair or replacement of the affected component.

Incident: an occurrence other than an accident associated with the operation of an aircraft that affects or could affect the safety of operations.

Level of safety (or risk): fatality or injury rates. Only past levels of safety can be determined positively. Accident rates are closely associated with fatalities and injuries and are acceptable measures of safety levels. Fatality, injury, and accident rates are benchmark safety indicators. Current and future safety levels must be estimated by other indicators or by extrapolating past trends.

Primary, secondary, and tertiary safety factors and indicators: these safety factors and indicators describe the relative "closeness" between the measured safety factors and the fatality, injury, and accident rates. Theoretically, primary indicators provide the best measures of changes in safety, followed by secondary and tertiary indicators. In practice, some tertiary indicators are more readily available and more accurate than primary indicators.

Primary factors: these factors are most closely associated with fatalities, injuries, and accidents. Accident/incident causal factors, such as personnel and aircraft capabilities and the air traffic environment, are examples. Incidents and measurable primary factors are primary indicators.

Secondary factors: these factors influence the primary factors. Airline operating, maintenance, and personnel practices, along with federal air traffic control management practices, are examples. Quantifiable measures of these factors, such as aircraft or employee utilization rates, are secondary indicators.

Tertiary factors: these factors include federal regulatory policy and individual airline corporate policy and capabilities that influence the secondary factors. An example of a tertiary indicator is the result of federal air carrier inspection that quantifies the extent of the carrier's regulatory compliance.

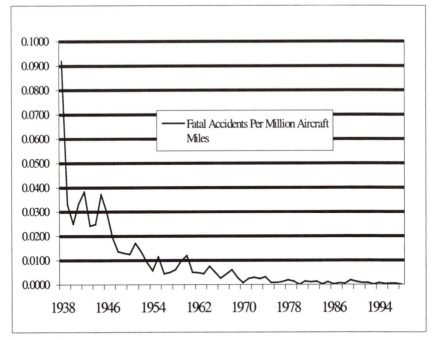

Figure 1-1:   Decline in fatal aircraft accidents since 1938

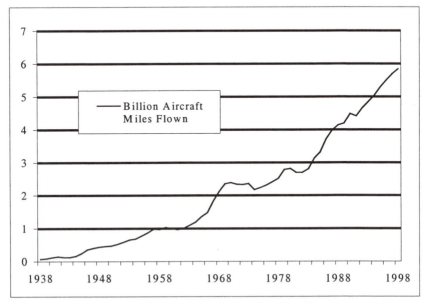

Figure 1-2:   Dramatic increase in aircraft miles flown

Now, if you review Figures 1-3 and 1-4, you will realize that aircraft damage and passenger injury are on the increase while serious accidents have diminished. Next, figure 1-3 shows year- by- year accident rates from 1990 through 1999 for 14 CFR §121 Air Carriers. Figure 1-4 shows Passenger injuries and injury rates for recent years. Finally Tables 1-2 through 1-6 support those figures with numbers of crashes, injuries, fatalities, and aircraft destroyed sorted by NTSB classification of accident severity.

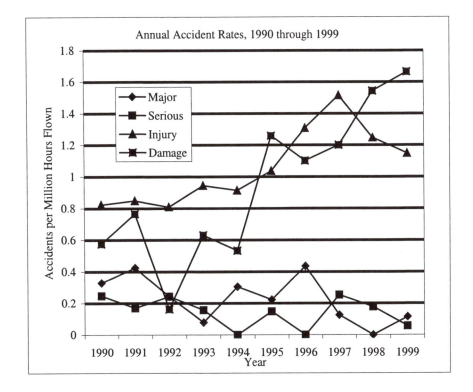

Figure 1-3: **Annual accident rates from 1990 through 1999 for 14 CFR 121 Air Carriers**

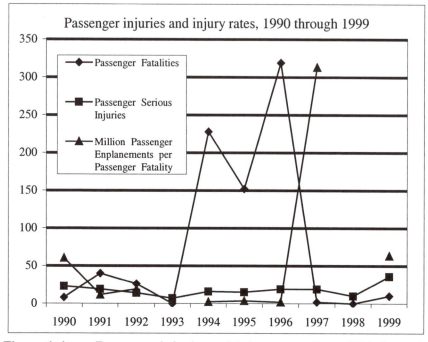

Figure 1-4:   **Passenger injuries and injury rates from 1990 through 1999**

Table 1-2:   **Accidents and accident rates by NTSB classification, 1990 through 1999, for U.S. air carriers operating under 14 CFR § 121**

					Aircraft Hours Flown				
		Accidents				*Accidents per Million Hours Flown*			
Year	*Major*	*Serious*	*Injury*	*Damage*	*(millions)*	*Major*	*Serious*	*Injury*	*Damage*
1990	4	3	10	7	12.150	0.329	0.247	0.823	0.576
1991	5	2	10	9	11.781	0.424	0.170	0.849	0.764
1992	3	3	10	2	12.360	0.243	0.243	0.809	0.162
1993	1	2	12	8	12.706	0.079	0.157	0.944	0.630
1994	4	0	12	7	13.124	0.305	0.000	0.914	0.533
1995	3	2	14	17	13.505	0.222	0.148	1.037	1.259
1996	6	0	18	14	13.746	0.436	0.000	1.309	1.018
			See note below						
1997	2	4	24	19	15.838	0.126	0.253	1.515	1.200
1998	0	3	21	26	15.838	0.000	0.178	1.247	1.543
1999	2	1	20	29	16.846	0.115	0.057	1.148	1.664

Note: Effective March 20, 1997, aircraft with 10 or more seats must
conduct scheduled passenger operations under 14 CFR 121.

Definitions of NTSB Classifications

Major - an accident in which any of three conditions is met:

· a Part 121 aircraft was destroyed, or

· there were multiple fatalities, or

· there was one fatality and a Part 121 aircraft was substantially damaged.

Serious - an accident in which at least one of two conditions is met:

· there was one fatality without substantial damage to a Part 121 aircraft, or

· there was at least one serious injury and a Part 121 aircraft was substantially damaged.

Injury - a nonfatal accident with at least one serious injury and without substantial damage to a Part 121 aircraft.

Damage - an accident in which no person was killed or seriously injured, but in which any aircraft was substantially damaged.

Table 1-3:   Passenger injuries and injury rates, 1990 through 1999, for U.S. air carriers operating under 14 CFR § 121

Year	Passenger Fatalities	Passenger Serious Injuries	Total Passenger Enplanements (millions)	Million Passenger Enplanements per Passenger Fatality
1990	8	23	483	60.4
1991	40	19	468	11.7
1992	26	14	494	19.0
1993	0	7	505	No Fatalities
1994	228	16	545	2.4
1995	152	15	561	3.7
1996	319	19	592	1.9
See notes below				
1997	2	19	626	313.0
1998	0	10	631	No Fatalities
1999	10	36	634	63.4

Notes: 1. Injuries exclude flight crew and cabin crew.

2. Effective March 20, 1997, aircraft with 10 or more seats must conduct scheduled passenger operations under 14 CFR § 121.

Table 1-4:   **Number and rate of destroyed aircraft, 1990 through 1999, for U.S. air carriers operating under 14 CFR § 121**

Year	Hull Losses	Aircraft Hours Flown (millions)	Hull Losses per Million Aircraft Hours Flown
1990	3	12.150	0.247
1991	5	11.781	0.424
1992	3	12.360	0.243
1993	1	12.706	0.079
1994	3	13.124	0.229
1995	3	13.505	0.222
1996	5	13.746	0.364
	See note below		
1997	2	15.838	0.126
1998	0	16.846	0.000
1999	2	17.428	0.115

Note: Effective March 20, 1997, aircraft with 10 or more seats must conduct scheduled passenger operations under 14 CFR § 121.

Table 1-5:   **Accidents, fatalities and rates, 1990 through 1999, for U.S. air carriers operating under 14 CFR § 121**

Year	Accidents All	Accidents Fatal	Fatalities Total	Fatalities Aboard	Flight Hours	Miles Flown	Departures	Accidents per 100,000 Flight Hours All	Accidents per 100,000 Flight Hours Fatal	Accidents per 1,000,000 Miles Flown All	Accidents per 1,000,000 Miles Flown Fatal	Accidents per 100,000 Departures All	Accidents per 100,000 Departures Fatal
1990	24	6	39	12	12,150,116	4,947,832,000	8,092,306	0.198	0.049	0.0049	0.0012	0.297	0.074
1991	26	4	62	49	11,780,610	4,824,824,000	7,814,875	0.221	0.034	0.0054	0.0008	0.333	0.051
1992	18	4	33	31	12,359,715	5,039,435,000	7,880,707	0.146	0.032	0.0036	0.0008	0.228	0.051
1993	23	1	1	0	12,706,206	5,249,469,000	8,073,173	0.181	0.008	0.0044	0.0002	0.285	0.012
1994	23	4	239	237	13,124,315	5,478,118,000	8,238,306	0.168	0.030	0.0040	0.0007	0.267	0.049
1995	36	3	168	162	13,505,257	5,654,069,000	8,457,465	0.267	0.022	0.0064	0.0005	0.426	0.035
1996	38	5	380	350	13,746,112	5,873,108,000	8,228,810	0.276	0.036	0.0065	0.0009	0.462	0.061
See notes below													
1997	49	4	8	6	15,838,109	6,691,693,000	10,313,826	0.309	0.025	0.0073	0.0006	0.475	0.039
1998	50	1	1	0	16,846,063	6,744,171,000	10,985,904	0.297	0.006	0.0074	0.0001	0.455	0.009
1999	52	2	12	11	17,428,000	6,793,000,000	11,636,000	0.298	0.011	0.0077	0.0003	0.447	0.017

Notes: 1. The 1999 data are preliminary. Flight hours, miles, and departures are compiled by the Federal Aviation Administration.
2. Effective March 20, 1997, aircraft with 10 or more seats must conduct scheduled passenger operations under 12 CFR § 121.

3. The 62 total fatalities in 1991 include the 12 persons killed aboard a Skywest commuter aircraft and the 22 persons killed aboard the USAir airliner when the two aircraft collided.

Table 1-6:   Accidents, fatalities, and rates, 1990 through 1999, U.S. general aviation (14 CFR § 91)

	Accidents		Fatalities			Accidents per 100,000 Flight Hours	
Year	All	Fatal	Total	Aboard	Flight Hours	All	Fatal
1990	2,215	443	767	762	28,510,000	7.77	1.55
1991	2,175	433	786	772	27,678,000	7.85	1.56
1992	2,073	446	857	855	24,780,000	8.36	1.80
1993	2,039	398	736	732	22,796,000	8.94	1.74
1994	1,994	403	725	718	22,235,000	8.96	1.80
1995	2,053	412	734	727	24,906,000	8.23	1.64
1996	1,908	360	632	615	24,881,000	7.67	1.45
1997	1,853	353	643	637	25,464,000	7.28	1.39
1998	1,909	365	623	617	26,796,000	7.12	1.36
1999	1,908	342	628	622	27,080,000	7.05	1.26

Notes: 1. The 1999 data are preliminary.
2. The 1998 flight hours are preliminary.
3. Flight hours are estimated by the Federal Aviation Administration.
4. Suicide/sabotage cases included in "Accidents" and "Fatalities" but excluded from accident rates in this table are: 1990 (1, 0); 1991 (3, 2); 1992 (1, 1); 1993 (1, 1); 1994 (2, 2); 1995 (4, 3)
5. Since April, 1995 the NTSB has been required by law to investigate all public use accidents. The effect upon the number of general aviation accidents has been an increase of approximately 1.75 percent.

Considering that since March 20, 1997, aircraft with 10 or more seats had to conduct scheduled passenger service under 14CFR § 121, Figure 1-3 illustrates a significant jump in the number of passenger enplanements per passenger fatality since 1997. Passenger fatalities spiked in 1994 and 1996 largely due to a US Air B737 accident and a TWA B747 accident. Relatively, 1997 and 1998 had fewer fatalities. Although Swiss Air flight 111 resulted in the death of 217 passengers and 14 crew members, it does not register in Figure 1-4 because it was not a U.S. registered aircraft.

Overall Statistics

A comparison between the total accidents and fatal accidents presented in Table 1-3, shows, on an average, a ratio of about one fatal accident to every 4.5 reportable accidents. The average reportable accidents for scheduled and non-scheduled air service in the United States went from 26 during 1990-1996 to 50 during 1997-1999 because from March 20, 1997 onward aircraft with 10 or more seats had to conduct scheduled passenger operations under 14 CFR §121.

Safety: A Case of Elephant and the Blind Men?

Since we are addressing an international audience, the elephant and blind men story may not be familiar to everyone. Let us digress a bit to explain this use of 'elephant and the blind men'. We will return to our safety discussion shortly.

As the story goes, a few blind men were sent out to identify an item. One of them felt it and said it is a tree. He had touched a rather large and solid pillar and could be certain that it was a mature tree. Another one refuted and said that he had felt a rope: it was strong and slender with some sort of a brush attached to one end. Basically, different people had touched different parts of an elephant and so although each was telling the truth, nobody knew the whole story and it was very difficult to determine that they were in fact describing different parts of the same item.

Now, how does it relate to safety? In our experience, we have found the use of the term safety to be significantly different among different professional groups and contexts. In aviation, there are three categories of safety—personal safety, aircraft safety, and flight safety. Typically, when people talk about personal safety, they are referring to personal injury issues such as injuries to *individuals* while at work. Several examples such as eye injuries because of not wearing appropriate protective glasses, falling-off the wing because of not wearing a safety harness, etc. can be cited under this category. Aircraft safety issues encompassing *incidents* (see NTSB's definition in Table 1-1) such as incorrect or incomplete repairs, incorrect documentation, or ground damage to *aircraft* outside of the chocks-off to chock-on period. Flight safety includes events that occur between chocks-off and chocks-on—essentially, that is the duration of a flight (see NTSB's definition of *accident* in Table 1-1). Hence, such events affect both *aircraft* as well as *individuals*. Because of such differences in the use of the word 'safety', the implications differ. For example, a Flight Safety Committee is focused on issues that affect *flight safety*; an

Airworthiness Committee is focused on issues that affect *aircraft safety*; and a Ground Safety Committee is focused on issues that affect *personal safety*.

Another way of looking at these differences is to think in terms of regulatory compliance. Personal safety and ground safety are typically handled from an industrial accident perspective—personal injury occurred because the individual was not wearing protective gear or ground damage occurred because the individual did not follow company procedures. Flight safety is typically handled from a more systemic perspective—a particular chain of events led to the accident. Also, remember that accidents are investigated by the FAA or the NTSB; while, incidents and personal-injury cases are investigated by the company. An FAA Letter of Investigation (LOI) can also result from a lack of maintenance regulatory compliance. Aircraft safety or airworthiness is increasingly viewed as a chain of events as well as a matter of regulatory compliance. The recent introduction of MEDA, ASAP and BASIS programs underscore this systemic view. In the United States, the Occupational Health and Safety Administration (OSHA) may be involved in personal health or injury cases. Typically, OSHA does not get involved in accident cases because those are in the FAA's jurisdiction.

Getting back to our analogy with the elephant story, how do we "see the elephant"? The answer lies in being able to move from a compliance-based perspective to a beyond-compliance model—addressing behavior-change, proactive assessment of safety performance at both individual as well as organizational levels, and truly embracing the sociotechnical elements discussed in Chapter 4.

Eight Maintenance-related Accident Cases Between 1990-1999

We have selected eight maintenance-related accident cases that occurred between 1990 and 1999. These cases, from both the U.S. National Transportation Safety Board (NTSB) as well as the British Air Accidents Investigation Branch (AAIB) databases, are discussed in greater detail in Chapter 9. The following synopses give a brief introduction to these maintenance-related accidents.

Single-engine Airplane

NTSB Report ID# SEA95FA213: On September 10, 1995, a Cessna P210N was destroyed when it collided with terrain during an emergency descent after the loss of engine power. The commercial pilot, who was the sole occupant of the aircraft, was fatally injured. The aircraft had departed Eugene, Oregon, about 0930, with a company flight plan, and was expected to return to Harrisburg, Oregon, at the end of the aerial photography flight.

Probable Cause: The pilot was unable to maintain glide speed and land the airplane safely. Contributing factors to this accident were the loss of engine power due to oil starvation at the crankcase main bearings and crankshaft main journals, resulting in the separation of four connecting rods due to thermal stretching and breaking of their rod bolts.

Helicopter

AAIB Report ID# 2/98 (EW/C95/9/4): On September 27, 1995, an Aerospatiale AS332L Super Puma (tiger) helicopter departed from Aberdeen at 0702 hrs for a flight to the Tiffany Platform, 136 nm to the north-east, with the first officer as the handling pilot. At 0729 hrs, while cruising at 3,000 feet ASL and 120 kt, there was a sudden onset of severe airframe vibration. The commander diverted to Longside Airfield and, after transmitting a MAYDAY call at 0752 hrs, the helicopter landed at 0821 hrs. The passengers were evacuated without injury. Subsequent examination of the helicopter revealed that a tail rotor blade flapping hinge retainer had fractured on one side.

Causal Factors: (1) Maintenance inspections conducted over a period prior to the incident flight did not detect a developing surface crack in the Blue tail rotor blade flapping hinge retainer, despite additional work on the associated tail rotor drive shaft assembly to rectify a tail rotor vibration problem, which was detectable as a trend recording within the Health and Usage Monitoring System about 50 flying hours previously and was the subject of an associated alert 5 hours before the incident; (2) the undetected fatigue crack extended during the flight, fracturing one side of the flapping hinge retainer and causing excessive and potentially critical tail rotor vibration; (3) the fatigue crack had been initiated by fretting and corrosion of the flapping hinge retainer bore induced by abnormal cyclic loading of the retainer, which was attributed to the effects of a defective flap needle-roller bearing during some previous period of the tail rotor drive shaft's life; and (4) the inspection provisions within the aircraft Maintenance Manual associated Maintenance requirements did not specify periodic visual inspections of such retainers, since they had been designated and certificated on a 'safe-life' basis.

Turboprop Airplanes

NTSB Report ID# NTSB/AAR-92/04: On September 11, 1991, Continental Express EMB-120 experienced a structural breakup in flight and crashed in a cornfield near Eagle Lake, Texas. Two flight crew members, one cabin crew member, and eleven passengers aboard the airplane were fatally injured.

Probable Cause: Failure of Continental Express maintenance and inspection personnel to adhere to proper maintenance and quality assurance procedures for the airplane's horizontal stabilizer deice boots that led to the sudden in-flight loss of the partially secured left horizontal stabilizer leading edge and the immediate severe nose-down pitchover and breakup of the airplane. Contributing to the cause of the accident was the failure of the Continental Express management to ensure compliance with the approved maintenance procedures, and the failure of FAA surveillance to detect and verify compliance with approved procedures.

NTSB Report ID# DCA95MA054: On August 21, 1995, an EMB-120RT airplane operated by Atlantic Southeast Airlines, Inc. experienced the loss of a propeller blade from the left engine propeller while climbing through 18,100 feet. The airplane then crashed during an emergency landing near Carrollton, GA, about 31 minutes after departing the Atlanta Hartsfield International Airport.

Probable Cause: The NTSB determined that the probable cause of this accident was the in-flight fatigue fracture and separation of a propeller blade resulting in distortion of the left engine nacelle, causing excessive drag, loss of wing lift, and reduced directional control of the airplane. The fracture was caused by a fatigue crack from multiple corrosion pits that were not discovered by Hamilton Standard because inadequate and ineffective corporate inspection and repair techniques, training, documentation, and communications.

Business Jet

NTSB Report ID# NTSB/AAR-95/04: On December 14, 1994, Phoenix Air's Lear 35A crashed in Fresno, California. The flight crew declared an emergency inbound to Fresno Air Terminal due to engine fire indications. They flew the airplane toward a right base for their requested runway, but the airplane continued past the airport. The flight crew was heard on Fresno tower frequency attempting to diagnose the emergency conditions and control the airplane until it crashed, with landing gear down, on an avenue in Fresno. Both pilots were fatally injured. Twenty-one persons on the ground were injured, and twelve apartment units in two buildings were destroyed or substantially damaged by impact and fire.

Probable Cause: (1) Improperly installed electrical wiring for special mission operations that led to an in-flight fire that caused airplane systems and structural damage and subsequent airplane control difficulties; (2) improper maintenance and inspection procedures followed by the operator; and (3) inadequate oversight and approval of the maintenance and inspection practice by the operator in the installation of the special mission systems.

Domestic Air Carrier

NTSB Report ID # NTSB/AAR-96/03: On June 8, 1995, ValuJet flight 597 suffered an uncontained engine failure. As the flight began its takeoff roll, a "loud bang" was heard by the airplane occupants and the air traffic control personnel. The right engine fire warning light illuminated, the flightcrew of a following airplane reported to the ValuJet crew that the right engine was on fire, and the takeoff was rejected. Shrapnel from the right engine penetrated the fuselage and the right engine main fuel line, and a cabin fire erupted. The airplane was stopped on the runway, and the captain ordered the evacuation of the airplane.

Probable Cause: Failure of the Turk Hava Yollari maintenance and inspection personnel to perform a proper inspection of a 7th stage high compressor disk, thus allowing the detectable crack to grow to a length at which the disk ruptured, under normal operating conditions, propelling engine fragments into the fuselage. The fragments severed the right engine main fuel line which resulted in a fire that rapidly engulfed the cabin area. The lack of an adequate record-keeping system and the failure to use "process sheets" to document the step-by-step overhaul/inspection procedures contributed to the failure to detect the crack and, thus to the accident.

AAIB Report ID# 3/96 (EW/C95/2/3): On February 23, 1995, a British Midlands Airways aircraft was climbing to cruise altitude after a departure from East Midlands Airport en-route for Lanzarote Airport in the Canary Islands. Following an indicated loss of oil quantity and subsequently oil pressure on both engines, the crew diverted to Luton Airport; both engines were shut down during the landing roll. The aircraft had been subject to borescope inspections on both engines during the night prior to the incident flight.

Causal Factors: (1) The borescope inspections for both engines were signed-off as complete in the aircraft technical log although the HP rotor drive shaft covers had not been refitted; (2) during the borescope inspections, compliance with the requirements of the aircraft maintenance manual was not achieved in a number of areas, most importantly the HP rotor drive covers were not refitted and ground idle engine runs were not conducted after the inspections; (3) the operator's quality assurance department had not identified the non-procedural conduct of borescope inspections prevalent amongst company engineers over a significant period of time; and (4) the CAA, during their reviews of the company procedures for JAR-145 approval, had detected limitations in some aspects of the operator's quality assurance system, including procedural monitoring, but had not withheld that approval, being satisfied that those limitations were being addressed.

International Air Carrier

AAIB Report ID# 5/2000(EW/C98/1/3): On January 9, 1998, a United Airlines B767, operating as flight 965 was on its way from Washington, DC to Zurich. While in cruising flight near Paris during an ETOPS flight, abnormal warnings appeared on the flight deck instrumentation and circuit breakers began tripping. The captain, in consultation with the airline's maintenance control center at Heathrow, decided to divert and land at Heathrow. The aircraft subsequently landed safely, but during the landing ground roll, the right thrust reverser failed to deploy fully and smoke appeared at the forward end of the passenger cabin.

Causal Factors: (1) multiple circuit breakers were tripped because of electrical arcing and associated thermal damage to a wiring loom adjacent to the aft/upper inboard corner of the forward galley chiller unit within the Electronic and Equipment bay, with resultant thermal damage to an adjacent loom and smoke generation; (2) prior damage to the wiring loom insulation adjacent the aft/upper corners of the chiller unit had occurred due to contact with such units during associated removal and installation; this chiller unit had been replaced on the day before the accident; (3) aluminum alloy swarf was present within the E&E bay prior to the accident and had probably assisted the onset of arcing between adjacent damaged wires in the loom; (4) incorrect installation of the chiller unit, with its heat exchanger exhaust fitted with a blanking plate, would have caused warm exhaust air to discharge from an alternative upper vent which was capable of blowing any aluminum swarf around the wiring loom; (5) the crew were unaware of the potentially serious arcing fire in the E&E bay during the flight due to failure of the bay smoke warning system to activate on the flight deck, because the density of smoke emitted by the arcing wiring in the bay was apparently insufficient to be detected by the only smoke sensor, which was located in the card and rack cooling system exhaust duct; and (6) the jamming of a severely worn latch, associated with the right off-wing slide compartment, prevented that escape slide from operating during the evacuation; such latches exhibited vibration induced wear on other aircraft.

Human Reliability and Risks

After reading the above synopses of accidents, you might wonder if any of them were avoidable. Some people, called the high-reliability theorists, believe that all accidents are avoidable; while others, called normal-accident theorists, believe that at least some accidents are unavoidable. According to the high-reliability theorists, if appropriate processes and redundancies are implemented such that systemic weaknesses are rectified and failures are contained, accidents can be avoided. On the other hand, normal-accident theorists believe that in complex, tightly-coupled systems accidents are unavoidable. A key factor in these two theories is human reliability. Fundamentally, the high-reliability theorists believe that although individual humans are not very reliable, the system can be made highly reliable by incorporating appropriate redundancies and safety nets. The normal-accident theorists believe that systemic redundancies and safety nets are not always effective, especially over a long period of time. Well, the debate between high-reliability theorists and normal-accident theorists is further explored in Chapter 7. For now, it is enough to recognize that strong theoretical foundation and empirical data exists on both sides.

In order to minimize risk, aircraft designers envision the life and environment of the aircraft and design it such that it will have a very low probability of failure within its projected lifespan, within its anticipated environment. When either the life expectancy or the environment is altered, risk is increased: the greater the alteration (assuming life *extension* of the aircraft or *deterioration* of its environment), the greater the risk. Risk is introduced into the system due to errors committed by every entity connected with aircraft operations. Earlier in this chapter, we defined safety as management of risk within the society's expectations; to achieve total safety, either errors must be avoided completely or the systemic redundancies must accommodate all possible errors. Unfortunately, we often find that the systemic redundancies are either deficient at their inception or they deteriorate over time.

In the aviation industry, risks are controlled largely by specifying the minimum acceptable standards through both national as well as international regulations. Such regulations prescribe the minimum standards for aircraft—design, manufacture, operation, and maintenance, personnel certification; airport—design, operation and maintenance; and air traffic control. Together, these regulations define the normal operating envelope (NOE) for the aviation industry. In practice, however, the designers, operators, maintainers, and air traffic controllers may not be able to contain their aircraft within its NOE at all times. When an individual or an organization causes an aircraft to be pushed out of its NOE, the risk is increased—possibly beyond the society's acceptable limits. For example, if a flight instrument that is required for Instrument Flight Rules (IFR) is inoperative, a mechanic may return the aircraft to service after discussing the operating limitations with the owner/operator. However, such a discussion does not guarantee that the operator will not fly this aircraft in IFR conditions, and if the operator does fly the aircraft in IFR conditions, the operational risk is increased, legal issues aside.

The NOE concept further illustrates the compliance-based safety discussed earlier in this chapter. The Hawkins-Ashby model, discussed below, is aimed at helping maintenance professionals transition into the beyond-compliance model.

The Hawkins-Ashby Model

Hawkins (1987) presented a systemic model, called the SHELL model, consisting of four interfacing components: software, hardware, environment, and liveware (by which he meant the human factor). Software includes procedures, manuals, checklists, as well as computer programs; hardware is the actual aircraft and all its parts; environment in the original SHELL model consisted of atmospheric aspects, but in the Hawkins-Ashby model, we have included organizational factors as well; and the liveware-liveware (for L-L) include pilots, mechanics, and air traffic controllers. If these SHELL components are used to represent an aircraft operation, we can apply Ashby's law of requisite variety to manage the dynamics of aircraft operation. The law of requisite variety states that the variety within a system must match the variety outside the system—in other words, any variation outside the system must be matched by appropriate variation within the system (Ashby, 1956). For our application of Ashby's law to the SHELL model, we use the previously introduced concept of normal operating envelope (NOE) to be our 'system', and we place the SHELL component that changes first to be temporarily outside the system and the rest to be within the system. Therefore, if the weather changes from VFR conditions to IFR conditions, the environment is outside the system and changes will have to be done to one or more of the other components within the system to bring the external SHELL component back within the NOE. Similarly, if a new aircraft is being operated, there is a change in the hardware and so the hardware will be outside the system and changes will have to be made to one or more of the other components within the system. If changes that are made to one or more of the SHELL components that remain in the system are timely and appropriately matched with variations outside the system, the aircraft operation can be maintained within its NOE. Thus, the Hawkins-Ashby model's statement is as follows: when one SHELL-component changes, at least one of the remaining components must change timely and appropriately to maintain the aircraft operations within the normal operating envelope.

The ability to recognize which one of the SHELL components has been placed outside the system and which other ones need to change to maintain risks within the acceptable levels will take individuals as well as organizations to safety beyond compliance.

Operations- and Maintenance-related Compromises to Design Safety

Now, let us consider the Hawkins-Ashby model from the perspective of the hardware's interaction with the liveware and the environment. Aircraft manufacturers are required to demonstrate the safety of their design to their regulators in accordance with the local aviation regulations such as the Code of Federal Regulations (in the U.S.) or the Civil Aviation Regulations (in the U.K.) in order to receive a type certificate for their design. The type certification process is exhaustive in every detail. It includes evidence from the manufacturer that their design meets all the requisite safety and performance criteria, including flight tests that actually demonstrate the aircraft's capabilities. Thus, the design safety of an aircraft is established. Once an aircraft is type certificated, its continued airworthiness depends on proper operation and maintenance—a certain level of performance from the liveware (people) and stability in the environment (organization) is assumed. Therefore, when the regulators approve a particular aircraft's design, they expect that it is operated and maintained within its NOE. Once again, this means that the pilots will fly the aircraft within its performance parameters and the maintainers will maintain the aircraft in an airworthy condition. If the liveware or the environment introduces a change in the system, that change must be compensated by a requisite change in the appropriate SHELL component. Otherwise, the design safety is compromised by either an out-of-NOE operation or maintenance action and the risk of an accident is increased.

Operations-related Compromises to Design Safety

Operational compromises to design safety occur when the flight crew's performance degrades and thereby places the hardware outside the normal operating envelope. Since this book's emphasis is on maintenance-related accidents, the operations-related compromises to design safety are discussed only briefly. Consider the following two cases:

NTSB Accident Report AAR-94/07: On January 7, 1994, a Jetstream 4101 operated by Atlantic Coast Airlines crashed 1.2 nautical miles east of runway 28L at Port Columbus International Airport, Columbus, OH. The flight had been cleared for an ILS approach to runway 28L and was in contact with the local tower controller when it crashed into a storage warehouse. Pilot, co-pilot, flight attendant, and two passengers were fatally injured, two passengers received minor injuries, and one passenger was not injured. The airplane was destroyed. Instrument meteorological conditions prevailed and the airplane was on an IFR flight plan.

Probable Cause: The NTSB determined the probable cause to be (1) an aerodynamic stall that occurred when the flight crew allowed the airspeed to decay to stall speed following a very poorly planned and executed approach characterized by an absence of procedural discipline; (2) improper pilot response to the stall warning, including failure to advance the power levers to maximum, and inappropriately raising the flaps; flight crew inexperience in "glass cockpit" automated aircraft, aircraft type, and in seat position, a situation exacerbated by a side letter of agreement between the company and its pilots; and (3) the company's failure to provide adequate stabilized approach criteria, and the FAA's failure to require such criteria.

NTSB identification CHI90FA193: On July 24, a student pilot and an instructor pilot were flying a Piper PA-38 aircraft. This aircraft was new to both; furthermore, the student had never flown with this instructor before. Shortly after arriving in the training area, witnesses observed the airplane spin to the ground. The airplane was over maximum gross weight at takeoff and at accident. No mechanical discrepancies were found. Elevator trim was full nose up. Both pilots had flown a majority of their flight time in another make and model for which the spin recovery procedure and the useful load above full fuel are different.

Probable Cause: The instructor pilot's inability to recover from a stall/spin. Contributory factors were aircraft weight and balance exceeded, and the instructor's and student's lack of familiarity with the aircraft.

In the case of the Atlantic Coast accident, both pilots were unable to exercise appropriate stall recovery procedures even after the warning systems had provided the appropriate warning. One of the presumptions in achieving the design safety of an aircraft is that the flight crew is proficient in operating the aircraft within its envelope under reasonable operating conditions. The flight crew's proficiency includes manipulative skill as well as conservative judgment. In this particular case, the organization and the FAA (both part of the environment) were also responsible for the accident because they were ineffective in preventing latent conditions (cf. Maurino et al., 1997) such as lack of training, ineffective oversight, or inadequate hiring standards from setting-up the individual pilots to take risks. Thus, per the Hawkins-Ashby model, deterioration in the environment—the lack of training, ineffective FAA oversight, or inadequate hiring standards—was not adequately compensated for by the other systemic components, thereby compounding the risk.

In the case of the PA-28 aircraft, the first component to change was the hardware. The pilots' unfamiliarity with the aircraft, led to violations of the weight and balance limits and inability of the pilots to recover from the stall/spin condition. In this case, the aircraft operation was outside its NOE because a variation in the hardware was not matched with appropriate variation in either proper training of the flight crew (liveware) or changes in the operating procedures (software change) of the organization (environment) such that they could prevent two inexperienced pilots flying together or prevent the coexistence of both a liveware change as well as an environmental change.

Maintenance-related Compromises to Design Safety

In maintenance, two inherent safety features tend to be compromised. First, *aircraft design* safety tends to be compromised because people believe that the multiple redundant systems aboard most airliners are designed to allow for occasional malfunction of one of the systems. Consequently, over a period of time, airliners are dispatched with more and more items inoperative—the Minimum Equipment List of an aircraft that has been in operation for a decade or so tends to be much larger than when it was first introduced into service. Second, the *procedural design* feature, called duplicate inspections, tends be compromised. The concept of duplicate inspections was designed to detect complacency-based errors and make sure that at least the safety-critical items are inspected thoroughly. Over a period of time, this process tends to be compromised because (a) the mechanic knows that it is going to be inspected twice before dispatch, (b) the first inspector knows that it is going to be inspected one more time before dispatch, and (c) the second inspector knows that both the mechanic as well as the previous inspector are very reliable and so he need not be as concerned. Then, of course there are economic pressures that tend to minimize the inspections because inspection costs!

Let us consider the previously-introduced case of Atlantic Southeast Airlines (ASA) Flight 529 as an example of compromise to the aircraft design safety. Under the design safety considerations, the EMB-120 aircraft was capable of withstanding only propeller blade-tip damage and the Hamilton Standard (HS) propeller had demonstrated to have an unlimited life when maintained in accordance with FAA-accepted HS maintenance instructions.

Hamilton Standard discovered that at least two similar composite propeller blades had failed in March 1994 and initiated a thorough ultrasonic inspection program. Blades that were found to be defective based on an on-wing ultrasonic inspection were to be sent to HS. In accordance with AD 94-09-06, a HS contract inspector removed the accident blade from service on May 19, 1994. The subsequent HS shop ultrasonic inspection confirmed the rejectable indication; however, upon examination of the taper bore, the technician concluded, 'No visible faults found, blend rejected area'. The blade was blended and returned to ASA on August 30, 1994. It was reinstalled on the left propeller assembly of the accident airplane on September 30, 1994. By the time of the accident, the blade had accumulated 2,398.5 hours and 2,425 cycles since the HS blend repair. In this case, the maintenance compromise to design safety was committed at the manufacturer's site and it took almost eleven months for the problem to lead to an accident.

The Hawkins-Ashby model can be applied to maintenance situations as well. In the above case, the environment consists of ASA's maintenance facility and Hamilton Standard's repair facility; whereas, the liveware consists of the HS contract technician who inspected the propeller on the aircraft and decided to send it to HS' facility in East Windsor as well as the technician who inspected the propeller at the East Windsor facility and performed the blend repair. There was no apparent deterioration of either the liveware or the environment at the ASA facility. The organization at the HS facility had deteriorated because there was confusing information regarding the inspection technique, damage tolerance, and repair scheme. Since the HS technician did not compensate for this deterioration, the liveware was affected at this stage and the risk was compounded.

Compounding Nature of Risks in Maintenance

In aviation maintenance, compared to flight operations, flaws are likely to remain dormant for a longer time. This dormant period could serve as an opportunity to solve the problem or a means (inadvertently) to mask the problem. For example, in the ASA case above, Hamilton Standard had known of two other similar propeller blade failures and the FAA had issued an Airworthiness Directive (AD) almost one year prior to the ASA accident. As of July 1996, there were 15,000 suspect blade types in the industry, worldwide. So, it seems like both Hamilton Standard and the FAA were trying to address this problem such that the faulty blades could be identified in time and removed from service. However, an HS technician interpreted the propeller flaw as a false positive (test indicated a fault when it did not exist) and returned it to ASA. ASA mechanics must have assumed that the propeller was airworthy because it was cleared by the manufacturer. So, in this case an error made by the HS technician was not detected in time. Later, HS discovered that the technician had used similar judgment on ten other propeller blades.

Per the Hawkins-Ashby model, this is a case where the hardware had deteriorated and so one or more of the other three components had to compensate. However, a more detailed look at the case also reveals that the liveware and the environment had deteriorated as well. The environment had deteriorated because it was a newly certificated facility, therefore many of its employees had limited experience. The liveware had deteriorated because the technician had worked between 8 and 26 hours of overtime and therefore was probably not at his best performance capability at the time of the accident blade inspection and repair. Overall, it seems like the hardware deterioration was not compensated because the environment as well as the liveware had deteriorated, compounding the risk.

As a result of the ASA accident, the FAA and Hamilton Standard researched the blade problem in great detail. The FAA then released an AD that mandated ultrasonic inspection of the blades every 500 cycles and refined the inspection procedures. Hamilton Standard improved its inspection procedures by providing a more consistent calibration block set. From the perspective of compounding the risk, it seems like the HS technician, the HS engineers, and the FAA inspectors each took small risks, and together, placed the hardware in a compounded risk situation.

The Cost of an Aircraft Accident

Cost is another dimension of risk. It helps managers and insurance agencies quantify risk in terms of compensation. Such cost-accounting of risk also makes it convenient for executives to view the positive effects of safety programs in terms reduction in costs rather than increase in costs. The cost of an aircraft accident is difficult to determine because it involves several inter-related aspects. Besides the obvious direct cost of human life and damage to property, an aircraft accident affects indirect costs like (a) damage to the company's reputation, (b) environmental damage, (c) litigation costs, (d) productivity loss, and (e) loss of highly-skilled personnel. According to Mathews (2000), the average insured cost (mostly direct costs) of an aircraft accident per year is $1.0 Billion, worldwide. Mathews estimates that the indirect costs to be about four times the direct costs per accident. See Table 1-7 for a list of typical direct and indirect costs presented by Mathews. In an example of direct versus indirect costs, Mathews states that if a catering truck were to hit an airplane, it could cost the company $1,700 in direct costs and up to $230,000 in indirect costs.

Table 1-7:   Direct and indirect costs of an aircraft accident

Direct Costs	Indirect Costs
Loss of life	Litigation costs
Damage to equipment	Lost productivity
Damage to property on ground	Additional training investment
Damage to environment	Accident investigation costs

Consider the following data regarding workers' compensation (Table 1-8) as an example of the cost of lost time injuries in aviation.

Table 1-8:   Workers' compensation costs

Company	$/Injured Worker	Injured Workers	Costs per Year
Airline "A"	173	Over 10,000	$1.7 Million
Airline "B"	521	Over 60,000	$31 Million
Airline "C"	571	Over 60,000	$34 Million
Average	422	Over 43,000	$18 Million

Additionally, Mathews (2000) estimates $50,000 per event such as ground damage that can be attributed to airline processes or personnel.

Chapter Summary

The aviation safety data, presented in this chapter, indicate that the rate of hull loss accidents in the past two decades has remained stable. If the air traffic continues to grow at an exponential rate over the next ten years, the extant accident rate would yield a staggering rate of one airliner accident per week. Such an accident rate—or risk—may not be acceptable to the society and hence it must be controlled. The Hawkins-Ashby model presented here suggests that changes in any one component of a system must correspond with timely and appropriate changes in the other component(s); otherwise, the systemic risk will increase.

Review Questions

1. Why does the aviation industry need to reduce the *rate* of major accidents?
2. Define *safety*.
3. Describe the concept of a normal operating envelope for your aircraft or automobile.
4. As a maintainer, how do your actions ensure that the normal operating envelope of your company's aircraft is respected.
5. Identify, from your experience, a case of operational and/or maintenance compromise to design safety of an aircraft, automobile, or any household appliance.

6. Explain the Hawkins-Ashby model with an example.
7. List the direct and indirect costs associated with an event such as the loss of (a) mechanic certificate, (b) pilot logbook, (c) driving license, (d) credit card, or (e) computer data.

Chapter 2

Personal, Professional, Organizational and National Perspectives

Instructional Objectives

Upon completing this chapter, you should be able to:

1. Identify your personal definition of safety.
2. Recognize the personal defining moments which build character.
3. Recognize the significance of high professional standards and etiquette.
4. Describe the effects of personal, professional, organizational, and national perspectives on the definition and practice of safety.
5. Recognize and list typical organizational norms.
6. Discuss the relationship between an individual and his/her organization.

Personal Definition of Safety

In Chapter 1, we discussed two definitions of safety: in the first definition, safety was freedom from risk; while in the second definition, it was management of risk within a value that is acceptable to the society. Now, let us consider safety at an individual level. Personally, how would you define safety as it relates to your job? How does your definition relate with the minimum standards prescribed by your regulator? As a pilot, you may consider a flight without an undesirable outcome as a safe flight; as a mechanic, you may consider maintenance actions that do not result in an undesirable outcome to be safe actions; and as a manager, you may consider a flight or a maintenance operation that does not result in personal injury or property damage to be a safe operation. In any case, these definitions assume absence of a loss to mean presence of safety: they are passive definitions of safety. Additionally, these definitions fall under the paradigm 'end justifying the means'. If we, as an industry, do not want to have one airliner accident per week by the year 2010, we must practice an active definition of safety. Such a definition should include specific actions that improve the process of maintenance, flight, or management and thereby have a positive effect on the overall safety.

Now, let us try the personal definition of safety one more time. This time, the pilots may consider a flight to be safe when (a) prior to the flight, the pilots discussed the strengths and weakness of their flight, (b) the planned flight was executed in accordance with the applicable aviation regulations, (c) the flight did not exceed pilot or equipment capabilities, and (d) after the flight, the pilots discussed at least one event, irrespective of whether it was a positive or a negative event, in order to keep improving their performance. Mechanics may consider a maintenance action to be safe when (a) the mechanic was appropriately qualified to perform the action, (b) the mechanic used all pertinent data and appropriate tools, (c) the mechanic did not exceed his/her physical or intellectual capacity while performing the work, and (d) neither signed for a job that he/she did not perform, nor performed a job that was not supported by appropriate documentation. Furthermore, when mechanics work as teams, they could conduct pre-task briefings and post-task briefings to improve their maintenance quality and effectiveness. Examples of this approach are presented in the next chapter, under *Fourth Generation MRM Programs*. Managers may consider an operation to be safe when (a) the operation does not set-up either the pilots or the mechanics to perform beyond their legal or ethical responsibilities, (b) they do not reward risk-taking behaviors, (c) they do not punish people who either disclose their own mistakes or report a systemic failure, and (d) they recognize that safety does not cost: it pays.

What else can we do to improve our personal definition of safety? Although the second set of definitions is active and better than the first set, it could be made more proactive. For an individual to push the definition of safety one step further, he/she must practice 3Ps: Persistent Pursuit of Perfection. If pilots, mechanics, and managers persistently pursue perfection in their professional responsibilities, they would proactively, improve safety by solving problems that are precursors to accidents rather than by post-accident resolution of select issues.

Let us consider the following case (Box 2-1) reported by us in *SAE Transactions* (Patankar & Taylor, 2000a) to illustrate how pilots, mechanics, and managers in one aviation organization practiced the 3Ps. In this case, pilots, mechanics, and the managers demonstrated extraordinary persistence to actually find out why the aircraft read lower hydraulic system pressure, went through the trouble to seek approval from the manufacturer to operate the aircraft under the extant conditions until the problem was resolved, and also sought the concurrence of their FSDO. Under similar circumstances, another operator was likely to rely on the judgment of one mechanic who was willing to sign-off the aircraft and return it to service without jeopardizing the schedule. After all, it was just a matter of 100 psi after the first engine start. The operation of hydraulic components did not seem to have been affected. Moreover, neither the flight manual nor the maintenance manual specified which engine was to be started first.

One way to incorporate the 3Ps in your personal definition of safety is as follows:

> My maintenance action is safe when (a) I am appropriately qualified to perform the job, (b) I use approved and most current data, tools, and procedures, (c) I seek second opinion prior to final release of the aircraft while performing complicated procedures or when I work more than 10 hours on the job, (d) I never sign for a job that I did not complete nor do I leave any job with incomplete documentation, and (e) I make conscious efforts to minimize discrepancies in data or rules as and when I encounter them in order to prevent myself and others from committing errors.

Personal Defining Moments: Choosing Between Right and Right

First of all, we are indeed talking about choosing between 'right' and 'right'. These, according to Joseph Badaracco (1997), are the tough decisions that are responsible for shaping one's character. Unlike the 'right' versus 'wrong' decisions where the wrong choice could be unethical, illegal, or both, the right versus right decisions are based on personal values and priorities. Komarniski (2000) reprinted a story about a young mechanic who had to face such a defining moment. In that story, Doug, the mechanic, had the opportunity to do one of the two 'right' things.

Doug was the lowest man on the totem pole...he made 20 cents an hour, swept the floor, performed all odd jobs in the hangar, and helped out on the flight line, once in a while. Jobs were scarce during those times and Doug was fortunate enough to have one. One night, he was helping a couple of other mechanics fuel a Ryan on the San Diego Flats. As they finished pouring the last gallon into the tank, Doug dropped the rubber hose attached to the funnel into the tank. Nobody else noticed. Doug reasoned that the hose was probably not going to block the fuel supply and if he told his boss about the hose, he could lose his job. It was right (at that time, of course) for Doug to say nothing about the rubber hose because *he did not believe* that it would have affected the safety of the flight and he knew that disclosing his action would certainly result in him getting fired. It was also right for Doug to disclose his action to his boss because *he did not want to be responsible for putting the only non-perfect part on the aircraft.* Doug struggled with this dilemma. He could not sleep. Finally, he woke-up his boss and told him about the hose. The boss was furious, but knew about the importance of the next day's flight and the implication of not removing the hose from the tank. He gathered the three mechanics and went to the aircraft. Through the early hours of the following morning, they drained all the fuel and removed the hose.

Box 2-1:   Low hydraulic system pressure on an Astra SPX Jet

The flight crew of a routine flight verbally reported to a mechanic that the hydraulic system pressure was low after engine starts. The pilots wrote the squawk in the aircraft logbook as, "Hydraulic system pressure reads 2800 psi after engine starts." In a maintenance team meeting that followed between the liaison mechanic, two other mechanics, and the chief of maintenance, it was noted that the same discrepancy had been reported about a year earlier. At that time, one of the mechanics had swapped the indicator, tested the indicator, swapped the transmitter wiring, etc. but was not able to duplicate the problem. He made a note of the verbal squawk and the maintenance actions he had taken while attempting to diagnose the fault. Another mechanic reminded the team about the direct reading pressure test conducted the previous year which indicated 3000 psi at the pump, but for some unknown reason indicated a drop of at least 100 psi at the indicator. A follow-up brief with the flight crew clarified the squawk: the hydraulic pressure was noted at 2800 psi after the first engine (number-1) start and 2900 psi after the second engine start (both engines running).

   To further investigate the matter, one of the mechanics researched the Aircraft Flight Manual (AFM) and discovered that the manufacturer called for a minimum of 2900 psi after the first engine start. If the pressure read less than that, the aircraft did not meet dispatch criterion. Upon referring back to the squawk, the mechanic questioned as to why they were not informed about this problem prior to the departure. He requested a meeting with the chief pilot, the line pilot in question, and the chief of maintenance. In a discussion that followed, the line pilot stated that he had observed that he could get 2900 psi if he started the number-2 engine first, but it dropped to 2800 psi after the number-1 engine was also started. Because the checklist did not state the minimum pressure requirement with both engines running, he operated the aircraft. Furthermore, it was also discovered that the AFM did not specify as to after which engine is started, the pressure should be 2900 psi. The pilots normally started the number-2 engine first; if they were to start the number-1 engine first, would the pressure readings have to be any different?

With the problem clarified, the maintenance crew decided to brainstorm regarding the possible solutions to the problem. The criticality of the issue was that the Department had sustained a complete hydraulic system failure on the same aircraft the previous year; the management was very concerned about an impending failure. Also, if this issue could not be resolved, the Department would have had to ground the aircraft and cancel its flights until the system read 2900 psi after the first engine start.

In the brainstorming process, the mechanics identified several different approaches, analyzed each approach, and developed a strategy. They decided that they would switch the gages between the two similar jets, search for any extraneous influences on the gage, and test the wiring more thoroughly. In the meantime, the chief of maintenance was to try to secure a letter of authorization from the manufacturer to operate the aircraft with 2800 psi pressure while the problem was being investigated. To relieve the pressure on maintenance, the chief pilot had already agreed to cancel the next day's flight, if necessary.

The extensive wiring checks and the extraneous influence checks did not identify any problems, but the swapped gage now read 50 psi higher than the original gage. So, the system pressures were reported as 2850 psi after the number-1 engine was started and 2900 psi with both engines running. The chief of maintenance was able to get the authorization letter faxed-in from the manufacturer and get concurrence from the local Flight Standards District Office (FSDO). Therefore, the Company was able to release the aircraft on schedule.

At that time, the boss fired Doug, but asked him to come see him later in the day. In the meantime, he asked Doug to store the hose in a glass bottle with some gasoline.

Doug's boss had the opportunity to do one of the two right things. He would have been right to fire Doug to "teach him a lesson" and he would have been right in rewarding Doug for being forthright.

The next day, everyone watched the gleaming Ryan—*The Spirit of St. Louis*—take-off from the San Diego flats. Doug's boss rehired him with a 5-cents raise.

Ten days later, the *San Diego Times* reported the story of Charles Lindbergh taking-off from New York for Paris. On that day, Doug's boss had him bring back the bottle that stored the hose. The hose had disintegrated into a thick sludge. Everyone knew that if they had left the hose in that tank, the airplane would never have made it to Paris.

Doug chose to disclose his actions and consequently learned about implications of maintenance action on aviation safety while earning a raise. Doug's boss chose to reward Doug's forthrightness, but also chose to go one step further and illustrate to Doug the likely effects of his actions. By so doing, he solidified the long-range effects of Doug's defining moment.

Whether you are a practicing aviation maintenance professional or a student, we are certain that you have had your share of defining moments. By way of Doug's story, we just want to point out that if you are a maintenance manager, your response to your subordinates will shape their character as well as their perceptions about you and the company.

Professional Culture: Standards and Etiquette

The professional culture, as defined by the roles, responsibilities, and practices of the aviation maintenance personnel, is somewhat dependent on the certification process and the rights and privileges earned through that process. Throughout the world, aviation maintenance personnel are authorized to perform return-to-service maintenance based on an approval process that is derived from either the United States or the United Kingdom. The regulators in the United States, the Federal Aviation Administration (FAA), provide for an Aircraft Mechanic certificate with Airframe and Powerplant (A&P) ratings and the regulators in the United Kingdom, the Civil Aviation Authority (CAA), provide for an Aircraft Maintenance Engineer (AME) license with a type rating. Let us consider the procedural and philosophical differences between these two parent processes and how they may influence the implementation of human factors principles.

American FAA-based Maintenance Personnel Certification Process

In the American FAA-based maintenance personnel certification process, the individuals are known as aircraft mechanics and are awarded a *certificate* by either the Federal Aviation Administration or the corresponding regulatory authority of the country in which such a process is adopted. These certificates are valid for the life of the certificate holder. If a certificated mechanic has received appropriate training on a specific maintenance item, and has satisfactorily performed that maintenance action under the supervision of an appropriately certificated mechanic, that mechanic is authorized to perform the same maintenance action unsupervised and return the aircraft or its component to service.

To qualify for an Aircraft Mechanic's certificate with both airframe and powerplant ratings (A&P), candidates may either enroll in an FAA-approved training program at a college or university or provide evidence of 30 months of combined airframe and powerplant experience. The FAA-approved training program consists of at least 1900 hours of lecture and laboratory instruction. Upon completion of this training, the candidates appear for three written examinations: general, airframe, and powerplant. Once they pass these examinations, they take an oral and practical examination from a Designated Mechanic Examiner. The oral and practical examination may last anywhere from a few hours to a few days, depending on the candidate's preparation. Once the candidate is successful in all three written examinations, the oral, and practical examinations, the examiner may award the candidate with a temporary certificate. From this point on, the candidate is authorized to perform maintenance on aircraft. Currently, there are no type-training requirements for A&P certification.

At certain companies, the certificated aircraft mechanics prefer the term *Aviation Maintenance Technician* (AMT) because it projects a better professional image. In this book, we have used the terms *aircraft mechanic*, *A&P mechanic*, and *AMT* interchangeably. When we refer to maintenance personnel without the Aircraft Mechanic certificate, we make it very clear.

British CAA-type Licensing Process

In the United Kingdom, and in most countries from the former British Commonwealth, the aviation regulations are based on the British Civil Aviation Regulations. The individual maintenance personnel approved by CAA are called Aircraft Maintenance Engineers (AMEs) and they are awarded *licenses* that need to be renewed. The AME license is type-rated and the engineers have a return-to-service authority.

To qualify for an AME license, candidates undergo a process consisting of practical work experience, written examinations, and an oral examination. Typically, candidates start as apprentices and gain two to three years of practical maintenance experience on airworthy aircraft. After they have gained the requisite practical experience, they are eligible for their first written examination: Paper I (Basic Engineering & Regulations).

The candidates who pass the Paper I examination, then appear for the Paper IIA (Heavy Airframe) and/or Paper IIC (Jet Engine). These examinations focus on the technical details of aircraft and/or engine systems. Then, they must appear for Paper III Airframe Type or Paper III Engine Type. This examination is based on detailed troubleshooting procedures and system specifications on one specific aircraft, such as the Boeing 737-400 or the CFM-56 engine. Upon successfully completing all three papers, the candidates are eligible for an oral and practical examination. The oral examination is usually conducted by the local regulators. It is like a panel interview without a time limit. If a candidate completes both airframe and engine papers and both the oral examinations successfully, he/she is eligible for an AME license with a type rating.

Under an AME license, engineers approve and return to service the work performed by other technicians. Therefore, a disproportionately smaller number of AMEs are responsible for the maintenance work compared to the FAA aircraft mechanics who personally perform and certify their own work.

Professional Conflicts

A review of the primary and contributing factors of several NTSB accident investigation reports since 1975 indicates that a significant number of accidents are being attributed to human attitude and behavior toward safety—human factors issues. This discovery led to the development of Cockpit Resource Management (CRM) training which was later renamed as Crew Resource Management to include flight attendants (Wiener et al., 1993). Significant emphasis was placed on Crew Resource Management (CRM) in order to address the human factors issues in the 1980s, and there was a strong emphasis on Maintenance Resource Management (MRM) programs in the 1990s. The CRM efforts on flight decks have advanced through several generations due to the ready access to flight simulators, relatively closed environment to apply CRM practices, and strong lobbying by pilots to require such training by regulations. MRM programs are currently in their fourth generation of development (cf. Taylor & Patankar, 2001), but this training is not yet mandated by the FAA regulations. Most airlines and some corporate aviation departments are providing MRM training due to either a unique collaboration between airline management, local FAA, and labor union(s) or certain individuals championing these programs within their span of control. Both CRM and MRM programs have also had their effect on accident investigation processes and self-disclosure of hazardous situations by pilots as well as mechanics.

It is quite clear from the presentations at the Human Factors in Aviation Maintenance and Inspection (HFIAM) symposia, sponsored by FAA, British CAA, and Transport Canada, that the human factors efforts in the United States, United Kingdom, and Canada have had a global impact. Together, the training programs, international conferences, and the investigation reports, have laid the foundation for a much safer culture in the aviation industry. Nonetheless, professional conflicts among aviation maintenance personnel exist at two levels: global and domestic.

Global Conflicts: The following discussion is based on our findings (cf. Patankar & Taylor, 1999a) at three airlines: Companies A and B were major U.S. air carriers and Company C was a domestic Indian air carrier. Our field observations at Companies A & B, using A&P mechanics, versus Company C, using AMEs, revealed that AMEs enjoyed a significantly higher professional status, received better compensation, and were more team-oriented in their behavior than A&P mechanics). The AMEs wore uniforms similar to the flight crew: white shirts and blue trousers. They even had epaulettes to designate their rank. Such specialized qualification and the pilot-like uniform lets the AMEs enjoy a higher professional status compared to the A&P mechanics. In terms of financial compensation, the AMEs were found to be among the best paid aviation employees in their country. Helmreich and Merrit (1998) reported that flight crews from many Asian countries had low individualism scores (high collectivism); meaning, the goals of these flight crews did not reflect independence from their organization. Consistent with these findings, the data from Company C indicate that the AMEs hold a higher value for teamwork and they are more likely to set collective goals.

A further analysis of the team-oriented behavior of the AMEs revealed that only one AME was assigned to release the flight at any given time. If other AMEs were attending to the flight, they worked as specialists for either airframe, engines, or avionics. The rest of the maintenance personnel (at times up to 30 people) associated with that flight were unlicensed. Therefore, the group worked as a team. This composition is comparable to that of the flight crews because in a typical cockpit, even if both pilots are certificated to operate the aircraft, only one of them is the pilot-in-command. Therefore, just like the flight crews, the AME-type maintenance crews also exhibit collectivistic behavior.

Domestic Conflicts: Within the United States issues like lack of performance-based incentives, high individual risk, and deterioration of training can inhibit the company-wide implementation of MHF/MRM principles.

Lack of Performance-based Incentives: In Companies A & B, and we suspect similar in most companies in the United States, aircraft mechanics are evaluated only during their probationary period—typically the first six months. After that, there are no periodic evaluations. Consequently, subsequent training and reward structure is based on seniority alone. It may be beneficial for the airline industry to do some introspection and re-evaluate its incentive system. When Southwest Airlines was starting out, Herb Kelleher defended his low-fare strategy by saying, 'We are not competing with other airlines; we are competing with ground transportation' (Freiberg & Freiberg, 1996, p. 54). Similarly, the airlines are now competing not just within themselves, but against other industries, for quality employees. The airlines are not going to be able to obtain professional technicians based solely on the glamour of air travel; instead, they will have to offer performance-based incentives that are competitive against other industries.

High Individual Risk: Through MRM training, both Company A and Company C, seem to be striving for what Helmreich and Merritt (1998) call 'collectivistic culture' rather than an 'individualistic culture'. Yet, both an A&P mechanic certificate as well as an AME license provide most *individuals* relatively *equal* airworthiness approval authority. Therefore, on one hand the airlines seem to want their technicians to work and act like a team, but on the other hand, they also expect the technicians to exercise individual approval authority. As long as an individual technician is capable of returning an aircraft to service, the responsibility for erroneous actions will rest on the individual. Erroneous maintenance actions may lead to a certificate action by the regulators, which in-turn, may prevent the individual from working as an aircraft technician in the future. This is a high professional risk. Arguably, air transportation is a high-risk environment and it follows that the high professional risk may be justified; however, the correlation of high incentives to high professional risk is a strong indicator of an underlying blame culture, especially in the AME-type system.

Deterioration of Training: Since the FAA's A&P mechanic certificate, in a way, requires at least some on-the-job training (OJT) and because both Company A and Company B were faced with reduction in training budgets, they increased their reliance on OJT. The fundamental assumption in OJT is that the new employees are going to be associated with the experienced ones; but, considering that most of the experienced and senior technicians are typically on a different shift than the junior technicians, it is quite probable that the experienced technicians are on day (first) or swing (second) shift and the new technicians are on the mid-night (third) shift. Under such conditions, the OJT at both Company A and Company B was limited to the mechanic's ability to seek appropriate guidance.

At Company A, age versus shift data showed, as expected, that the younger technicians were more concentrated in the afternoon and night shifts while the older technicians are concentrated in the day shift. From a training perspective, this setup created two conflicts. First, since most training was conducted during the day, the younger, less experienced mechanics were brought in (for training) off-shift when they were less likely to be at their peak performance. Second, the very experience of senior technicians that OJT hoped to transfer to the younger technicians was not available to the night or afternoon shifts–the place where it was needed the most. The reduction in classroom training activity has not been sufficiently compensated by OJT. In Company C, the AMEs and technicians worked together consistently: everyone worked on rotating shifts, irrespective of the seniority. So, the experienced AMEs were better associated with the new AMEs and the disconnect in OJT, found in Companies A&B, was not as prevalent in Company C. However, a rotating-shift pattern is not recommended due to inability of the workers to ever optimize their work and sleep cycles.

Organizational Culture

Helmreich and Merritt (1998) defined organizational culture as 'the values, beliefs, assumptions, rituals, symbols and behaviors that define a group, especially in relation to other groups or organizations' (p. 109). In addition to the ethnographic observations of the maintenance personnel at Companies A, B, and C (same companies as used in the previous discussion on professional cultures), the authors also studied the annual reports and public relations documents from these companies to illustrate the organizational differences, and to determine their core values. Most of these documents focused on customer satisfaction. Additionally, they were sensitive to issues such as fleet standardization, employee satisfaction, and technology upgrade. These companies seem to hold safety in high regard; yet, it was not clear whether they instituted it as a *core corporate value*. According to Collins and Porras (1997), core values are 'the organization's essential and enduring tenets—a small set of general guiding principles; and not to be confused with specific cultural or operating practices; not to be compromised for financial gain or short-term expediency' (p.73). It is essential that airlines regard safety as a core corporate value and exercise this value at all levels; otherwise, safety-related programs may be treated as the 'flavor of the month'.

In 1998, when we reviewed the status of the maintenance human factors programs in the United States, we discovered that only four of the seventeen participating (in maintenance human factors symposia) air carriers had implemented maintenance human factors programs. Several airlines started, stopped, and even restarted these programs several times between 1989 and 1998.

In India, Company C was the only carrier that had offered maintenance human factors training. That training did not continue past the first round of awareness instruction.

Fluctuation in the support for MRM programs at the U.S. as well as foreign air carriers is found to be a symptom of several organizational problems such as 'revolving door' leadership, blame culture, low professional status of maintenance personnel, and merger mania.

'Revolving Door' Leadership

At Company A, we observed that senior managers were changing their assignments so frequently, that the employees recorded the organization's management chart in pencil—a strong indicator of revolving door management. Under such conditions, management policies become unclear to the employees and any program started by one particular manager may not be continued by his/her successor. Whenever a change in the senior management brought about a change in the corporate image, employees treated these changes as 'flavor of the month'.

The management at Company B was comparatively stable, but the company had evolved into a mosaic of organizational cultures representative of the past acquisitions of regional airlines. This organizational problem is discussed in detail in the *Merger Mania* section below.

At Company C, we observed that several key management positions were filled by foreign nationals. On the surface, it seemed as if the start-up airline was drawing upon the experience of these foreign management personnel. Field interviews later revealed that although the foreign nationals may have been brought-in to lend their expertise, the company did not make any attempts to develop local talent. Also, if procedural changes were suggested by the local employees, they were not considered. Only foreign nationals were respected and listened to. As a result, the local employees developed a certain degree of discontent against the management.

Blame Culture

Many researchers (Drury & Rangel, 1996; Hobbs & Robertson, 1996; Drury et al., 1997; Marx, 1997; and Wenner & Drury, 1996) are trying to persuade airlines to eliminate blame culture, but most of these efforts seem to be concentrated on the blame for an accident or incident. We discovered that in all three companies (A, B, & C, as above), the blame culture is ingrained much deeper. For example, when a flight is delayed, the person or the department responsible for the delay is required to file a report. Several individuals and departments must interact to produce an on-time departure, all supposedly working as a team. When an official delay report has to be filed, there is competition among these individuals/departments to blame the other for the delay. The team-structure that everyone works so hard to maintain in the working environment, starts to break down when the 'finger-pointing' begins. The fine line between blame and accountability begins to fade.

Another interesting perspective on blame culture is that MRM training could be used by the employees to generate excuses for lack of performance. For example, foremen at Company A stated that following the training, technicians started to use the words like 'fatigue' and 'stress' to get out of tasks they did not want to do. He recognized the importance of human factors, but did not overtly use many of the human factors principles because he was apprehensive that they too could be abused by his technicians.

The term 'blame culture' takes on a different form when viewed from the context of a government-owned airline. In India, the government has partial ownership of two large airlines, and is responsible for investigating all the accidents and incidents. It is understood by the AMEs in India that if there is an accident or a major incident involving their aircraft (the one that they have released for flight) their employment will be terminated. Managers have explained to the unlicensed technicians that the AMEs get paid so well because in case there were any accidents or incidents in which the AMEs were liable, they were likely to be terminated immediately. High-risk equals high-reward. Moreover, since accident investigation reports and safety statistics are not public knowledge, nobody outside the investigating group would ever know the exact reasons behind the accident/incident. In the past, the government has declared certain individuals responsible for accidents and relieved them from their duties immediately after the incident. A high-ranking official such as the Director of Maintenance is quite likely to be suspended or terminated even before the investigation starts. The director may or may not be rehired, even if he was acquitted.

Low Professional Status of Maintenance Personnel

Since most maintenance activities are not accomplished in plain sight of the passengers, management tends to keep the maintenance employees in the background. Ethnographic observations at Companies A & B indicate that many technicians worked in a significantly deteriorated work environment (Company B more than Company A). When asked about the reasons for such poor maintenance of the facilities, technicians at both Company A and Company B felt that they were subjected to poor working conditions because their work areas were not exposed to the passengers. Also, when the airport was being renovated, the technicians knew about several problems with the building, but they were never consulted with by the airport planners or the airport's management prior to making capital improvements to the airports. Consequently, the technicians have to work under extremely cramped, inefficient, and sometimes unsafe conditions.

Another example of maintenance employees being in the background was observed at Company C. The airline, out of fear from its competition, embarked on a splurge of route and fleet expansion. They even added different types of aircraft (ATR 42 & 72) to their existing fleet of Boeing 737s. When the maintenance department suggested that a slower growth would be desirable from a safety perspective, the marketing and operations executives did not slow down. Consequently, certain key maintenance managers resigned from the Company.

Merger Mania

Patankar and Taylor (1998) have used the term *merger mania* to describe a phenomenon associated with 'a forced change in the values, vision, and communication practices of personnel following their entry into another company'. At Company B, the authors found that several of their aircraft mechanics had come from smaller regional airlines that Company B had acquired. These 'expatriates' seemed to be trying to maintain their parent company's culture rather than acclimatizing to Company B's culture.

Similarly, at Company C, there were several senior maintenance managers from other airlines, and they too tried to rebuild the processes and practices from their parent airline, rather than developing new processes that were pertinent to the new airline. Such deep-seated resistance to acquire a new corporate identity affects the implementation of MRM programs because the new employees are not able to work with the older ones as a team. There is a constant struggle of 'us against them'.

If safety is regarded as a core corporate value, the above barriers are less likely to impede the safety initiatives. The organization will have its safety value strong enough that the incoming managers will have to live by those values rather than changing them. Similarly, the blame culture will erode because the organization will be more interested in long-term solutions to safety problems rather than quick identification (and subsequent dismissal) of the last person who touched the aircraft. Aircraft mechanics will be involved in all decisions that affect the operation and maintenance of aircraft and their opinions will be valued by the management. In cases wherein a company acquires another smaller carrier, every effort will be made to ensure that the new employees understand the acquiring company's corporate culture. Of course, this is a vision and not the reality. But unless the vision (whatever it may be) is clearly identified, it is not likely to be achieved.

From an organizational perspective, as long as safety is not a core corporate value and safe behaviors of individuals and groups are not integrated into the reward structure, safety will continue to remain in the back seat. Although, the professional culture at Company C appeared to be better suited for MRM implementation, the deficiencies in the organizational culture at Company C limited the success of their MRM program.

Organizational Norms

Norms are the unwritten rules, the way things are actually done. Some of these norms are positive, but most are negative. Aviation maintenance personnel are quite resourceful and they take pride in being able to do their job. So, when their company is unable to provide them with the ideal equipment or manpower, they improvise. For example a company may have a policy that requires the mechanics to use wing-walkers before they pushback an aircraft from the gate; however, in reality, the company may never allocate enough people to allow for wing walkers. Therefore, the organizational norm is formed: they know the policy says use wing walkers, but they never do. Another example of a norm is the use of belt loaders as ladders or the use of a forklift instead of an overhead crane to lift an engine. In a majority of the instances, these actions may not result in any undesirable consequences; however, such actions do perpetuate the continued use of improper practices and tools.

Consider the case of a torching engine below. It illustrates how in addition to organizational norms, individual complacency and time pressure, especially in a line maintenance environment, can lead to some very dangerous situations. A natural byproduct of experience is complacency. As people get more experienced at doing a specific task, they are likely to be complacent about the task because they have done that task several times. In this case, the mechanic was well-experienced and had performed his duty diligently for several years, but one day he slipped—or did he? Had he been accustomed to doing it that way? Had others also failed to pull circuit breakers when working on borescope inspections? We do not know.

In line maintenance, there is a tremendous emphasis on pushing the aircraft out on time. The maintenance managers are under pressure to keep the schedule and so are the gate agents. In this case, with a fully-loaded aircraft, the mechanics made a good call by asking the pilots to quit trying to start the engine and pull the aircraft back to the gate, but the pilots put the additional pressure because they did not seem to want to wait any longer.

In the case presented in Box 2-2, since the pilots found the circuit breakers pulled-out, it is obvious that someone else must have pulled the breakers without informing the mechanic. Since the mechanic had not pulled the breakers, he did not check if they were pushed-in prior to signing off the job card. Consequently, the mechanic ended-up signing for two tasks that he did not perform. Do you see a norm here? Remember a norm is an unpublished rule or the way people actually do their work. We do not have enough data here to say that more than one person signed off a job card without performing the specified task; however, there is room to question the work practices of other individuals. If additional mechanics have noticed themselves signing off tasks that they did not perform, or not signing-off work they did perform—for whatever reasons, then such a practice would be a norm.

Lessons Learned: Try the following exercise: remove the word 'mechanic' from the above case and insert your name; then read the case over again. Now, what would you do differently? The mechanic, who was faced with this situation, recommended that the company modify the borescope inspection process such that it includes a functionality test of the ignition system after the inspection.

Box 2-2:   The torching engine

A maintenance dispatch crew of a major air carrier pushed back their aircraft and signaled the flight crew to start the engines. After the tug was removed, the flight crew was unable to start the right engine due to low N2, so they started the left engine. Then, they tried to start the right engine again using bleed air from the left engine. The right engine did not start. A mechanic asked the flight crew to check all the circuit breakers to ensure that everything was set. The mechanic then requested the flight crew to shut down the left engine because he would have to tow the aircraft back to the gate to investigate the problem. When the mechanics were about to push the aircraft back to the gate, the flight crew found several circuit breakers out and they told the mechanics that they would reset them and would like to attempt starting the right engine again. The flight crew started the left engine first and then attempted to start the right engine. The right engine started, but due to the previous attempts, there must have been additional fuel than required because the engine spit out a fair size fireball from the tailpipe that lasted about 3-4 seconds. From the time that the right engine "torched" till the pilots shut down both engines the following chain of events took place: (a) a dead-heading flight attendant, occupying a passenger seat, yelled "Fire!" (b) the other flight attendants in the back of the aircraft opened the rear exit doors and deployed the chutes, (c) since the engines were still running, the chutes remained somewhat parallel to the ground, and (d) a woman, with her infant, tried to slide down the chute, but fell. Both mechanics were shocked to see what had happened.

One of these mechanics had prepared the right engine of that aircraft for a borescope inspection. Although the job card called for the mechanic to pull the igniter circuit breakers, he did not think that was necessary because he was not going to connect external power. After the inspection, when the mechanic closed-up the engine, he signed-off on both pulling and resetting the circuit breakers although he had done neither of those tasks.

Challenge Yourself: Can you think of five norms? Write these down and try to change them. In some cases, it may be as simple as taking the time to write clear shift turnovers or it may be as bureaucratic as getting a job card revised. In either case, by changing a norm, you are avoiding an incident/accident.

Striking a Balance Between the Individual and the Organization

The basic question is whether or not there is a good match between the individual and his/her organization. When there is a choice as to which organization one should join, several factors must be considered very carefully. Besides the basic issues of compensation, geographic location, work hours, and advancement opportunities, an aviation maintenance professional has the following additional issues to consider: quality of technical training, quality of safety equipment and processes, maintenance standards, and quality of labor relations.

Considering Hertzberg's (1968) research on factors that satisfy or dissatisfy people with their work, it is fair to say that the dis-satisfiers are more likely to affect the individual's perception of professional dignity and self-worth, thereby influencing his/her quality of work more than the issues of convenience such as compensation, location, work hours, and advancement opportunities.

National Perspectives on Safety

Considering the international nature of the aviation industry, we were curious to know if safety was influenced by differences in national perspectives. In 1984, Geert Hofstede conducted the earliest, and perhaps the largest, cross-cultural research programs ever in a systematic study of work-related values across more than 50 countries. He found that within a given industry certain national differences are seen in hierarchical differences and social distance (he called it power distance), in preferences for individualism or collectivism, and in tolerance for uncertainty (he called it uncertainty avoidance). Later, Helmreich and Merritt (1998) showed the effects of differences in national culture among airline pilots and surgeons. Their results act to confirm the theory and prior findings of Hofstede (1984). We (Taylor & Patankar, 1999) found that some of these differences in national culture reported by Hofstede, and confirmed by Helmreich and Merritt, also affect airline mechanics and their managers.

The MRM/TOQ Survey

Survey questionnaires have been long used by Helmreich and his colleagues at the University of Texas (UT), to measure attitudes, which show acceptance or rejection of Crew Resource Management (CRM) concepts (Helmreich & Wilhelm, 1991). Their Flight Management Attitude Questionnaire (FMAQ) has been carefully developed and tested and is a reliable and valid measure of pilot values (Helmreich, et al., 1993). Helmreich and Merritt (1998) used items from that survey in their cross-national sample of airline pilots.

A version of the FMAQ was developed for airline maintenance personnel by UT researchers (Taggart, 1990). Since 1992 that maintenance survey has been further adapted and applied to maintenance mechanics and their managers throughout the world (cf. Stelly & Taylor, 1992; Taylor, et al., 1997; Taylor & Patankar, 1999). That survey form is called the 'Maintenance Resource Management Technical Operations Questionnaire' or MRM/TOQ (Taylor, 1998). A sizable number of questionnaire items have been retained from the original UT survey, and provide close approximation to the data reported by Helmreich & Merritt (1998). Thus some of the pilots' data on national differences can be replicated in the MRM/TOQ using similar survey items in an airline maintenance environment. Like the FMAQ, the MRM/TOQ (for mechanics and maintenance managers) is also well-tested and established as a reliable and valid measure of work values and opinions (Taylor, 2000).

The Measures: Hofstede's data show that the U.S. culture is highly individualistic and stresses priority for personal goals. The FMAQ 'Command' scale as well as questionnaire items dealing with coordination and assertiveness are shown by Helmreich & Merritt (1998) to be good descriptors of power-distance, and of collectivism, and many of those items are used in the MRM/TOQ reported here. Johnston (1993) has observed that Hofstede's data reveal a strong, inverse correlation between the power distance and the 'individualism' dimensions—countries with large power distances tend to be collectivistic, and vice versa.

The MRM/TOQ 'command responsibility' and 'assertiveness' scales are used to measure Hofstede's 'power-distance' dimension. The MRM/TOQ 'goal setting & sharing' scale, as well as two individual questions from the 'communication & coordination' scale will gauge the degree of 'collectivism' for each region. Those two individual items include one question about the start-of-the-shift meeting's importance for safety and teamwork. The other question examined here, asks about debriefing and critique as an important part of team coordination. Both questions are quite similar to items used in the FMAQ, but are modified to suit the maintenance employees' work situation.

The Sample: A major U.S. based airline has used the MRM/TOQ to measure about 2,350 line maintenance personnel in 48 cities throughout the world.   Although MRM/TOQ was administered at 32 cities in the continental U.S. and 16 cities in the rest of the world, only those cities with more than five respondents (n>5) were included in the sample reported here.   That smaller number of sites includes about 1,800 maintenance workers in 25 cities.   About 1,600 of those maintenance personnel were employed in 15 stations in the U.S. and the remainder were local employees at line stations in 10 foreign cities in Asia and Latin America.

The participants in this study are mechanics, line station maintenance personnel (including licensed engineers as well as unlicensed assistants), and managers. The mechanics in the U.S. stations overwhelmingly hold the FAA Aircraft Mechanic (A&P) certificate.   Foreign respondents in the present sample are also mainly A&P mechanics.   The exception is found in two locations (Delhi and Hong Kong) where only about half hold mechanic certificates; and the rest are either Aircraft Maintenance Engineers (AMEs) with type-certification, or they are mechanical assistants without license or certificate, who are supervised by a licensed person.

Participants completed the MRM/TOQ during the period from January 1996 to November 1997 as part of an ongoing evaluation process to assess the effects of a two-day training program on 'human factors in maintenance'.   These participants responded to an initial survey immediately before their training commenced.

Respondents were given the brief questionnaire (MRM/TOQ) by a training facilitator and were told that there were no 'right' or 'wrong' answers and that all completed surveys would be processed by university researchers who would hold the individual results in strictest confidence. The survey forms contained a set of core questions which included items asking about the value of sharing management command responsibility, the value of assertiveness (power-distance); and it also contained items measuring the value of communication & coordination, and goal-sharing among and within work groups (individualism vs. collectivism). All items were written in English except for a Japanese translation, which was used in two line stations in Japan.

The Cultural Regions: Line maintenance respondents in this sample are divided into three foreign regions or cultural areas and three U.S. regional areas. The six regions and their constituent city stations are shown in Table 2-1.

Research Questions: The presumption that was tested, following both Hofstede and Helmreich and Merritt's results, was that the similarities in national culture found for other occupations, would also be evident for airline mechanics. Specifically the differences between the U.S. and other cultures would be shown in power-distance and individualism scores that were more similar between U.S. regions and different from both Asian regions and from Latin America. To test this notion, and to control the effect of the human factors training on attitudes, survey responses to a pre-training survey were analyzed.

Table 2-1:   Regions, numbers of respondents and constituent line stations

U.S. Regions	Foreign Regions
East Coast (n=417)	Latin America (n=26)
Boston	Rio de Janeiro
New York – Kennedy	Sao Paulo
New York – La Guardia	
Washington – National	SE Asia (n=95)
Washington – Dulles	Singapore
Miami	Bangkok
	Taipei
Midwest (n=735)	Hong Kong
Minneapolis	Delhi
Chicago	
Indianapolis	
Denver	East Asia (n=55)
	Tokyo
West Coast (n=466)	Osaka
Seattle	Seoul
Portland	
San Francisco	
Los Angeles	

Results: It was assumed, for the measures used here, that Hofstede's 'Power-distance' dimension was an inverse function of the MRM/TOQ 'command responsibility' scale. This function was also presumed for the MRM/TOQ 'assertiveness' scale—that is, as power-distance increases, command responsibility as well as assertiveness decreases. Figure 2-1 shows the pre-training survey results, by region, for the command responsibility and the assertiveness scales. The overall test of differences among regions, the Multivariate 'F' Test, was statistically significant for both of the scales measuring power distance (F for Command Responsibility = 20.55, $df = 5$, $p>.000$; F for Assertiveness = 17.48, $df = 5$, $p>.000$).

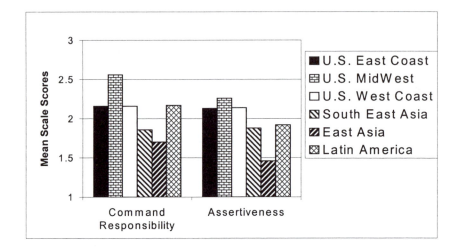

Figure 2-1:   Power distance for airline maintenance: pre-training sample

As Figure 2-1 clearly shows, the higher scores for the U.S. regions and lower scores for the Asian regions are consistent with the expected power distance positions. Although the Latin American region is apparently lower on power distance than the Asian regions, it is not statistically different from either the U.S. regions or the Asian regions. All six mean score difference comparisons between the lesser power-distance for each of the three U.S. Regions and the greater power-distance for each of the two Asian regions prove statistically significant for both scales (.000<p<.03).

Figure 2-1 also shows differences between the two Asian regions on one of the two scales. The power distance for East Asia, as measured by mean differences in assertiveness, was found to be significantly greater than the already high power-distance of the SE Asia region (p<.000)—while the command responsibility difference between the two Asian regions is non-significant. What these findings imply is that the even greater power-distance of mechanics in Japan and Korea is evidenced by their being even less willing than their counterparts in Singapore, Thailand, Hong Kong, Taiwan and India to speak up when it may cause conflict or disagreement with others.

Individualism among Airline Pilots: Helmreich and Merritt (1998) noted an enhanced desire for group harmony among Asian pilots. This was contained within what the authors describe as all pilots' '...strongly individualistic [...desires] to be consulted about their duties and in wanting to talk freely with their peers and superiors as they see fit' (p. 69). Consistent with that finding, those investigators found a universal professional consensus that communication and coordination are as important as technical skills among the pilots they studied. This appeared as little or no different among pilots from different countries in the degree of agreement they placed on matters of communication and communication. Among the set of specific items they analyzed is one that states, 'The pre-flight briefing is important for safety and for effective crew management' (Helmreich & Merritt, 1998, p.67). The investigators found that more than 85 % of pilots in all countries they studied agreed that these briefings were important. Conversely, Helmreich and Merritt report finding large inter-country differences to the item 'A debriefing and critique of procedures after each flight is an important part of developing and maintaining effective crew coordination' (1998, p.77). The U.S. and other Anglo pilots had lower scores on this item than did the others. Helmreich and Merritt speculated that the strongly individualistic American- and British-culture pilots are more reluctant to publicly evaluate their own performance than are pilots in Asian countries (1998, p.77). Although these combined results apparently describe the specific characteristics of the airline pilot occupation, they do little to disentangle the paradox of apparent simultaneous strengths in independence and collectivity (opposite poles) on Hofstede's dimension in the results of that sample.

Individualism and Airline Mechanics: Helmreich and Merritt's results establish the differences in "power-distance" between Asian and western pilots. But their results do not further illuminate the apparent paradox of the absence of a strong inverse relationship between power-distance and independence found by Hofstede and reasonably expected (e.g., Johnston, 1993) among pilots. How different in matters of individualism and collectivism might mechanics be from pilots?

Maintenance versions of items dealing with communication and coordination were also included in the MRM/TOQ. In most cases however the specific questions used with the mechanics do not have a one-to-one correspondence with the communication and coordination items used in the analysis of pilots' national culture. Despite particular differences, two items from the MRM/TOQ can be used as close approximations to those used with the pilots. It was interesting to compare, in this mechanics' study, the differences in the value of maintenance crew meetings between the U.S. and three foreign regions with reference to the pilot's results.

Figures 2-2 and 2-3 compare the different national regions of mechanics on two questions. One question is worded, 'Start-of-the-shift team meetings are important for safety and for effective team management'. A second question states, 'A debriefing and critique of procedures and decisions after the completion of each major task is an important part of developing and maintaining effective team coordination'. The first of these two questions corresponds with the item Helmreich & Merritt found to *not* discriminate among pilots from 22 different countries. The second question is quite close in wording to the highly discriminate one in the earlier study, except that the mechanics' version references larger, less frequent tasks.

Response to question about start-of-the-shift team meetings importance for safety and teamwork: Figure 2-2 shows, first of all, that in all six regions nearly two-thirds of all respondents say they agree that holding shift meetings are important. But Figure 2-2 also reveals substantial differences among them, in the additional strength of that agreement.

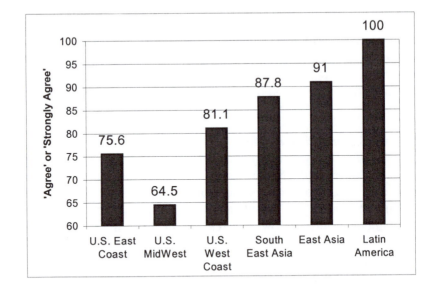

Figure 2-2:   **Start-of-the-shift team meetings are important for safety and for effective team management**

Mechanics are Less Collectivist than Pilots

The result presented in Figure 2-2 is substantially different from the pilots' samples where all responses exceeded 85 % agreement. The differences among the mechanics' in different cultures are significant when tested as expected proportions (χ^2=16.7, df=5, p<.005). Furthermore, while Southeast Asia, East Asia, and Latin America all have over 85 % agreement to this value of crew meetings at the start of the workday, their U.S. counterparts do not. The mean differences among the six regions are significant overall as well (F=22.3, df=5, p<.000). The mean scores for both East Asia and Latin America are significantly larger than all three U.S. regions (.000<p<.001). Although Southeast Asia is significantly below Latin America (p<.01) there is no significant difference between SE Asia and East Asia. The foreign mechanics are all more collectivist than those in the U.S. It is also noteworthy that the mean score for U.S. Midwest region is significantly smaller than either of the other two U.S. regions (4.06>3.76<4.24; p<.000).

Response to question on debriefing and critique as an important part of team coordination: Although an overwhelming majority of all respondents agree with this value, Figure 2-3 shows both diversity of agreement and continued differences among the U.S. regions.   A test for expected agreement for this item shows statistically significant differences among the regions displayed in Figure 2-3 (χ^2=21.6, df=5, p<.001). A test for differences among the regions' mean scores for this item is also significant (F=7.2, df=5, p<.000). The mean scores for both the U.S. East and West Coast regions are significantly larger (p<.000) than the U.S. Midwest region's mean score. Except for the East Asian mean score being found to be significantly larger than the U.S. Midwest region, no other mean differences were found for this item. Despite these overall differences, there is less effect between the U.S. and foreign regions than was found for meetings at the *start* of the work shift (Figure 2-2). Indeed there is much less diversity among the mechanics' scores on this item.

Mechanics are More Uniformly Individualistic than Pilots

Compared with Helmreich and Merritt's results, all mechanics' mean scores are substantially larger than the U.S. pilots and substantially smaller than the pilots from Japan and Brazil. Mechanics, it appears, are less diverse overall than the pilot sample and their mean scores on the debriefing item are lower (less collectivist) than *two-thirds* of the countries in the pilot sample, including all except the Western European, U.S. and Anglo pilots (Helmreich & Merritt, 1998, p.78).

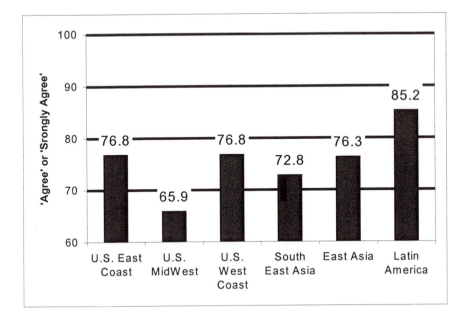

Figure 2-3: **Mechanics' response to a statement regarding the importance of debriefing as a tool to develop and maintain effective team coordination**

Both of the items measuring "collectivist" values reveal that mechanics in the U.S. are more individualist than their counterparts in three foreign regions. Compared with the pilots sampled by Helmreich and Merritt, the U.S. mechanics (and many of the foreign mechanics, especially in Figure 2-3) reported here show lower agreement to the value of work-related crew meetings and briefings.

Collectivism as Measured by the Goal-Sharing Scale

The MRM/TOQ contains six items, which cluster closely together (Taylor, 2000). These six items are answered with the standard five-point response scale used in both the FMAQ and MRM/TOQ. That scale goes from 'strongly disagree', to 'strongly agree'. Combined, these six items form a scale or index of 'goal-sharing'. Following Hofstede's definition of collectivism, this scale's scores should increase as collectivism (or a value for group goals) increases.   In the pre-training MRM/TOQ survey, these items form an index of purposeful, collective behavior, prior to human factors concepts being presented to the respondents.   No similar items to these, or a goal-sharing index, are contained in the FMAQ.

Figure 2-4 presents the mean scores for each of six regions on the transformed goal sharing scale. The overall test of differences among regions, the Multivariate 'F' Test, was statistically significant for the goal sharing scale ($F = 10.77$, $df = 5$, $p > .000$).

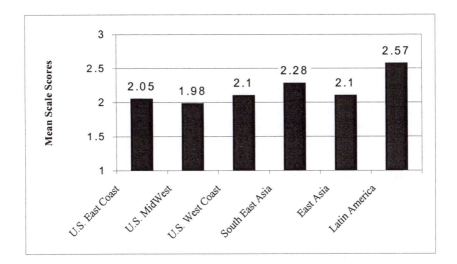

Figure 2-4:   Collectivism in airline maintenance: Goal setting and sharing scale (corrected to culture bias). Pre-training sample

Multiple comparison tests of mean differences reveal that both South East Asia and Latin America are significantly higher on the goal sharing scale than all three U.S. regions ($p < .03$). These differences compare favorably with Hofstede's findings of national cultures (Hofstede, 1984, p. 159). Those original findings graphically depict Japan (a major component of the 'East Asia' region in the present analysis) lying closer to the U.S. on the 'Individualism' dimension, while Hong Kong, Singapore, Thailand and Taiwan (components of the SE Asia region), and Brazil (sole constituent of the Latin American region) lay further distant on that scale. That pattern is replicated in the differences among national cultures shown in Figure 2-4.

Discussion

The same U.S.-based company employs all the maintenance personnel examined in this study. Furthermore, the overwhelming majority of the mechanics in this sample hold the FAA Aircraft Mechanic (A&P) certificate. Despite this homogeneity of employment and certification, the differences among members of different national cultures in this sample confirms others' findings showing that work values in Asia and Latin America are different from those in the U.S.

The results shown earlier in Figure 2-1 reveal that mechanics from the U.S. line stations show a lower "power-distance" gradient than local personnel in Asian and Latin American line stations. Power distance in Figure 2-1 is shown as unwillingness to disagree with others, including the boss. These findings confirm similar patterns of differences found in other aviation occupations and in other industries.

Figures 2-2, 2-3, and 2-4 above, show that line maintenance personnel in the U.S. are uniformly more individualistic than their maintenance counterparts in Asia and Latin America. This result also replicates earlier, well-documented, research in other occupations and industries. But despite that confirmation of national differences within occupations, these maintenance people (as a total group) are more individualistic than airline pilots measured in an earlier study. We believe that this results from an individualistic occupational culture of the A&P certificate holder – a professional designation permitting return-to-service authority to every mechanic – which represents this present sample in nearly its entirety.

National culture and other influences: This study has shown for mechanics, that national culture supercedes organizational and occupational influences. Aircraft Mechanics, working under the same company's rules and policies, but originating from markedly different national cultures will demonstrate their national differences. Attempts to change organizational culture in a multinational company will need to take these national differences into account.

Professional culture and individualism: The above results also showed that mechanics (at least these A&P mechanics) are in several respects more individualistic than pilots from the same countries, who were in turn more individualistic than their national cohort in other industries during previous decades.

Unlike airline pilots who always distinguish a single pilot-in-command, together with the subordinate and coordinated roles of all others in the cockpit, the signatory authority of A&P mechanics causes them to act more like individuals—not very dependent on others to help them achieve their ends. In this environment, the working A&P mechanics (as well as the Lead mechanic providing them with operational guidance) are more likely to focus on satisfactorily completing assigned repair tasks than to consider larger goals or objectives such as production goals, cost, or safety. Those larger goals are left to maintenance foremen and managers to administer. Airline pilots, on the other hand, are likely to see each journey as a set of complex, interrelated tasks to be coordinated among the members of the flight crew in attaining safety and efficiency goals.

If changes to the safety culture of a company are attempted, the influence of national culture and professional culture must be considered. Strongly individualistic national cultures (such as in the U.S.) should increase the difficulty of implementing consciously and actively-shared safety goals. Strongly individualistic professions, such as the A&P mechanic, may further increase the difficulty of implementing such goals. It is possible that where mechanics' work is *structured* to *require* more coordination and cooperation, their ability and willingness to accept and share larger goals will increase. This shift is expected to accompany higher attitudes toward collectivism. Such structural change may be more easily accomplished where licensure requires some mechanics to lead and others to follow.

Chapter Summary

This chapter presented the effects of personal, professional, organizational, and national perspectives on the interpretation of 'safety'. As individuals we are influenced by their environment—organizational and national, and professional standards and etiquette. Most importantly, mechanics tend to be more individualistic than pilots. Hence, future success of MRM programs will depend on the industry's ability to overcome the inherent resistance to teamwork.

Review Questions

1. State your *proactive* definition of safety. How do you ensure that you practice it consistently?
2. How did the Astra mechanics, in the sample case, practice Persistent Pursuit of Perfection (3 Ps)?
3. Think about some of the defining moments in your life and how they may have influenced your character.

4. What is one of the most significant causes of reduction in the enthusiasm for MRM programs in the maintenance community?
5. Discuss some organizational norms. State the norms, describe the company policy, and discuss why those norms exist. How can these norms be changed? If any of these norms are positive, how can they be written into the company policy?
6. In your experience, how have the differences in personal, professional, national, or organizational perspective influenced the practice of safety?
7. Discuss the implications of the cultural research presented in this chapter with respect to your work environment.

Chapter 3

Ergonomics, Human Factors and Maintenance Resource Management

Instructional Objectives

Upon completing this chapter, you should be able to:

1. Differentiate between *ergonomics, human factors,* and *maintenance resource management (MRM)*.
2. Discuss the different strategies used in delivering the MRM training programs and their relative advantages and disadvantages.
3. Discuss some of the most significant barriers to MRM implementation.
4. Describe a few cases of successful MRM implementation.
5. Discuss the importance of an MRM Master Plan.
6. List some MRM targets and the associated evaluation techniques.
7. Explain why MRM programs need to be evaluated.

Introduction

This chapter presents some fundamental distinctions between the terms *ergonomics, human factors,* and *maintenance resource management.* The focus, however, is on maintenance resource management (MRM) because maintenance personnel have the most opportunities to practice risk management in that domain. Four generations of MRM programs, effectiveness of MRM programs, and implementation strategies are discussed in this chapter.

Ergonomics

In fact, the distinction between the terms *ergonomics* and *human factors* is difficult. In England and Europe, *ergonomics* is used rather broadly. The International Ergonomics Association defines *ergonomics,* as follows:

> Ergonomics is the scientific discipline concerned with the understanding of interactions among humans and other elements of a system, and the profession that applies theory, principles, data and methods to deign in order to optimize human well-being and overall system performance. (http://www.iea.cc/ergonomics/)

According to the Ergonomics Society of the United Kingdom,

> Ergonomics is about 'fit': the fit between people, the things they do, the objects they use and the environments they work, travel and play in. So when we talk about 'fit', we don't mean physical fit, we are concerned with psychological and other aspects too. That is why ergonomics is often called 'Human Factors'. (http://www.ergonomics.org.uk/ergonomics.htm)

In the United States, *ergonomics* is more commonly used in its physical sense—as the study of designing equipment to better fit the humans. As a result of such research, safety engineers have been able to provide equipment that is less prone to personal injury. Examples of such equipment include chairs, desks, hand-tools, computer keyboards, as well as various instrument gages.

Experienced aircraft mechanics may think that we have had ergonomic designs in aviation for a long time, and they are correct. If we were to compare the cockpit controls in various piston-engine aircraft, we will notice that the shape and feel of a propeller control lever in all these airplanes is the same. The same will also be true for throttle and mixture control. In such applications, the idea was that if the look and feel of a control is the same in all (almost) airplanes, in an emergency situation, the pilot is less likely to operate the wrong control. Are such controls not considered 'ergonomic'? Well, yes! The idea behind such design goes back to World War II and was implemented simply to minimize the probability of erroneous operation.

As we will see in the following section, the field of ergonomics has the potential to significantly improve the safety in the maintenance environment as well. When appropriate scientific principles are applied, the maintenance workplace will have better lighting, improved procedures, as well as more friendly tools.

Ergonomic Audit

Ergonomic audit is the first step in determining initial or continued compliance with ergonomic standards as well as mismatches between the system and its human workers. Ergonomic standards for a wide variety of applications are discussed in journals and conference proceedings that are published under the aegis of Human Factors and Ergonomics Society (www.hfes.org). The FAA has developed an Ergonomic Audit Program (ERNAP) that serves as a tool for organizations to conduct extensive self-evaluation of the workplace, documentation, equipment, and work processes. The full-version of the ergonomic audit instrument is available at http://hfskyway.faa.gov.

The fundamental purpose of an ergonomic audit is to test the human-machine system for design deficiencies. For example, consider the *Pre-maintenance Documentation* worksheet (from http://hfskyway.faa.gov) in the ERNAP instrument. This worksheet could be used by an aircraft mechanic prior to starting the maintenance task to evaluate the job/task card or maintenance manual. At the individual level, even if the mechanic is not in a position to bring about any immediate corrections to the job card, he/she will at least be aware of some of the deficiencies like missing diagrams or confusing warnings. When the Ergonomic Audit Program is applied at an organizational level, work-process deficiencies can be corrected in a proactive manner.

Human Factors

Human Factors is used as the overall term in the United States. The following popular definitions of *human factors* are accepted.

> Human Factors is the discipline that tries to optimize the relationship between technology and the human. (Kantowitz and Sorkin, 1983).

> The central approach of human factors is the application of relevant information about human characteristics and behavior to the design of objects, facilities, and environments that people use. (Grandjean, 1980).

> The goal of human factors is to apply knowledge in designing systems that work, accommodating the limits of human performance and exploring the advantages of the human operator in the processes. (Wickens, 1984).

Basically, one might conclude that *ergonomics* is used as the umbrella-term in Europe and *human factors* is used as the umbrella-term in the United States—but primarily in terms of human-machine-environment perspectives. Once we get into the discussion about interaction among people in aviation maintenance, the term Maintenance Resource Management is a better choice.

Maintenance Resource Management (MRM)

In the past seven years Maintenance Resource Management, or 'MRM', has become one of the pillars in aviation human factors. The industry creators of a multiparty cooperative program in maintenance to improve communication and reduce errors (reported in Taylor & Christensen, 1998, pp. 48, 105-6) coined the term in 1992. The industry correctly defines MRM as "...an *interactive* [emphasis added] process focused upon improving the opportunity for the maintenance technician to perform work more safely and effectively" (ATA, 1999). In that same ATA document MRM is referred to as a training program, but MRM is much more than training. MRM is a tool to provide individuals and groups with the skills and processes to manage errors that are within their control, such as communication, decision-making, situational awareness, workload management, and team-building. Part of MRM is training, but part of it must be the application and management of the attitude, skills, and knowledge that *training and behavior* can provide.

Maintenance Resource Management (MRM) Programs

The origins of MRM programs can be traced back to 1989, after the Aloha Airlines accident, as a derivative of the extant Crew Resource Management (CRM) programs. Since those early days, MRM programs have evolved into four distinct generations. Today, the two most commonly found programs are attitude-change programs and behavior-change programs. The fundamental difference between these programs is that the former tends to seek safety behaviors via an internal change in the safety attitudes of the participants, while the latter focuses on specific skills that can be used to effect a prompt manifestation of safety behavior, regardless of the attitudinal status.

First Generation MRM Programs

The first generation MRM programs, dating from 1989 through 1994, were intended to reduce maintenance errors through improved interpersonal communication and teamwork. These programs were successful in improving awareness about safety and communication among maintenance personnel. Such changes led to safety improvements. These programs were either limited to a one-shot approach consisting of two days of training (Taylor & Robertson, 1995) or were brought to a premature end for extraneous reasons (Taylor, et al., 1997). The following three cases present the variety in purpose and content of the first generation MRM programs.

Case 1: Flight-based CRM program in maintenance: The very first reported CRM program for maintenance in a large U.S. airline began in November 1989. The purpose of the maintenance CRM training was similar to that of the company's flight crew CRM training—to ensure that teamwork and coordination are optimal and best use is made of all resources, including people, information, and equipment (Taggart, 1990). The training topics were as follows: interpersonal communication, assertion and conflict management, stress, critique skills, value of briefings, situation, awareness, leadership behavior, and case studies.

The program was conducted for small groups over a several weeks and included over 80 maintenance managers and supervisors. Although it was intended that all 750 maintenance managers in the company would be trained, the program was suspended and the company was liquidated before that occurred. But as the first experience, that program set high standards. Participant enthusiasm for the course was very high—over 80% said there would be at least a moderate change in their on-the-job behavior.

Case 2: Assertive management communication skills and performance: Beginning in June 1991 a second airline undertook a CRM in maintenance training course for communication and safety (Fotos, 1991). This training continued for over two years. This early and highly successful version of MRM emphasized open and assertive communication, both in theory and in practice, as well as an awareness of others. The purpose of the course was stated as 'equipping participants with the skill to use all resources to improve safety and efficiency'. Specific objectives, or topics covered were as follows: diagnose organizational 'norms' and their effect on safety; promote; assertive behavior; understand individual leadership styles; understand and manage stress; enhance rational problem-solving and decision-making skills; and enhance interpersonal communication skills.

Time was taken during the two-day training program to role-play giving and receiving assertive communication (Stelly & Taylor, 1992), and participants praised that activity highly (Taylor & Robertson, 1995, p.49). All maintenance management and professional engineering staff (N>2,000) attended the program. Enthusiasm for this program actually exceeded the high marks earlier reported by Taggart (1990) – at the end of the two-day training nearly 90% of the participants said there would be at least a moderate change in their on-the-job behavior (Taylor & Robertson, 1995, p.15). This program was brought to completion by August 1993 (a 26-month period). The post-training attitudes showed improvement in feelings toward participation, stress management, and communication; but no immediate improvement in attitudes about assertiveness – those would come later. These maintenance managers also initially indicated intentions to change in rather passive ways (e.g., 'to be a better listener') than to immediately practice assertiveness and 'speaking-up' Two months following training, however, feelings about assertiveness increased for many of these managers – and their intentions for further steps were more active as well (Robertson, et al., 1995; Taylor & Robertson, 1995; Taylor & Christensen, 1998). For 24 months following the onset of the program, the incidence of lost-time-injuries and aircraft ground damage decreased (Taylor & Robertson, 1995), and the former was highly correlated with the improvement in attitudes toward assertiveness just noted (Taylor, 1995).

In August 1993, upon completing the training for maintenance management and achieving these improvements in attitude and safety, plans were laid to move the program into the ranks of mechanics. Other concerns interfered with the continued progress of MRM and eventually only a small proportion of mechanics were trained. By that time top management's concerns had turned from communication and safety to station closures and cost-cutting, and the excellent results of their MRM program began to reverse (Taylor & Christensen, 1998, pp. 128-129).

Case 3: Assertive aircraft mechanic communication skills and performance: Before the above mentioned reversal in the enthusiasm about their MRM program began in earnest, the MRM program was modified for mechanics by changing only the case-studies to maintenance-caused accidents or incidents and leaving the purpose, the timing, the major topics and the exercises in place.

Beginning in September 1993 about 450 participants (one-third new supervisors and two-thirds mechanics) from 28 work units attended that MRM training. By June 1994, after a period of just over six months, the pace for this training had declined to a trickle—mainly as a result of top management succession and changes in maintenance priorities.

Little, if any, of this type of intervention with mechanics (hereafter called Aviation Maintenance Technicians, or AMTs) and other operational hourly personnel had been previously attempted in North America. Common wisdom held that communication training for AMTs and other hourly workers was an unnecessary expense in a period of prolonged financial hardship—and, in any event, that this kind of interpersonal training would probably benefit management participants more than hourly employees. Recurrent training for AMTs was typically limited to passively viewing videos produced by the company's Technical Training Department, or to on-the-job training (OJT) by leads or senior mechanics. Given those assumptions, the results of this MRM training were surprising. Like the management results in Cases 1 and 2, the 300 AMTs showed clear enthusiasm. Eighty percent of them reported that they expected moderate to large changes in their behavior as a result of the MRM training (Taylor, et al., 1997). These AMTs were also asked to write their responses to the question: 'How will you use this training on your job?'. Content coding of those answers resulted in the bulk of the responses divided into five categories: 'Dealing better with others', 'Being more assertive', 'Being more aware of other's behavior', 'Being a better listener', and 'Fighting complacency/being more careful at work'. The first two categories were classified as 'active communication' intentions—to be carried out with coworkers, while the latter three were consider to be more passive coping behaviors—and could be done alone. Forty percent of the AMTs responses were coded in the first two (active) categories while some 45% were coded in one of the three passive categories. This proportional division would prove to be very high for active communication. The AMTs' positive experience with MRM training leads to enhanced performance as well. AMT attitudes immediately following the training reveal a marked change toward accepting command responsibility and an increased appreciation of stress management. In the main, these results obtained for technicians parallel those reported for maintenance managers and support professionals (Taylor, 1995; Taylor & Robertson, 1995). In part the AMT data proved even stronger than the management results in showing positive effects of collaboration and human factors training (Taylor et al., 1997). In particular, stronger relationships between AMT post-training attitudes and safety performance in the six months following training is evidence of the fact that because AMTs are the persons directly effecting performance, their attitudes should most quickly relate to their performance. That brief program proved to be a successful venture into MRM training for AMTs. It is unfortunate that it was halted so soon after it began.

Second Generation MRM Program

A single example of second generation program has been documented (cf. Taylor, 1994). It began in 1992 as a set of focus groups of foremen and mechanics and sought to directly address communicating and understanding maintenance errors. This approach led to on-shift meetings and mechanics' participation in planning technical changes that improved safety. This second generation program was also limited in scope.

Case 4: Using Focus Groups to Reduce Errors in Aviation Maintenance: During 1992-1994, the Quality Assurance (QA) department in another large airline (employing nearly 2,000 AMTs and foremen in 37 line stations) began an informal cooperative arrangement with the trade union (International Association of Machinists and Aerospace Workers—IAMAW) representing its AMTs, and with its FAA Flight Standards District Office (FSDO). This cooperation was intended to reduce a high incidence of errors in maintenance documentation by opening communication channels among the company, the union, and the regulator.

The program lasted two years and covered three phases. It began with 30 group interviews, involving over 150 AMTs and foremen in eight line maintenance stations. These interviews focused on maintenance paperwork errors, their causes, and their solutions. In the second phase of the project, the results from the interviews in the first phase were fed back to all parties and management took action based on the proposed solutions. In some cases the solutions/changes affected all of the company's line stations, and in other cases the changes were tried in one station (a "natural experiment") and reviewed against suitable comparisons. In the third phase, the changes were given time (up to 28 months after the onset of the MRM program) to affect measured error rates in maintenance documentation, and the results were distributed to all parties.

One of the solutions recommended and implemented involved passive engagement (e.g., formal training in paperwork for all line AMTs). The effects of that paperwork training on error rates was immediate, but short-lived (Taylor, 1995, Taylor & Christensen, 1998).

Two other solutions required active involvement and communication (e.g., pre-shift team meetings in order to open communication channels, and AMT group participation in re-designing the aircraft logbook form).

The two active communication solutions were implemented in one line maintenance station – one that had previously participated in the focus group interviews. Four months after their initial MRM focus group session, the station's employees were invited to join in a new activity. First, that station's foremen received training in communication and leading meetings, and they began holding daily crew briefings. Second, the AMTs had the opportunity to attend occasional, informal sessions to discuss ways to improve the aircraft logbook document layout. The logbook improvement sessions were led by a manager from the company's Quality Assurance department. The total paperwork error rates for this experimental station were matched with those of another line station of similar size and location that did not participate in the focus group interviews or in the crew meetings or logbook improvement effort. The main differences between the experimental and comparison stations were their reputations for morale and their relations with flight crews. During 1992-93, the morale and service reputation of the experimental station was considered poor, while the comparison station enjoyed a better image.

In May 1993, two months after the focus group interviews in the experimental station (but before any feedback to that station), its logbook errors were higher than either the comparison station or all stations combined. When the experiment began in August 1993, the experimental station subsequently experienced rapid and visible improvements attributed to the enhanced communication while the comparison station's error performance more closely matched the system overall (Taylor, 1995). For March through August 1994, nine to twelve months following the onset of the study, the experimental station continued to show a lower error rate than the comparison station and/or all stations combined. Thus, after the MRM interventions began there, the experimental station displayed a lower logbook error rate in both comparisons for every subsequent month available thereafter (Taylor, 1994; Taylor, 1995).

By 1995 the experiment concluded, not by plan, but by lack of momentum—the local managers and supervisors who supported the shift briefings and AMT participation in decision-making left the station and/or the company. Their successors were encouraged to support another (and department-wide) program in non-safety related employee communication and participation. The QA, IAMAW, and FSDO partners to this company's cooperative MRM relationship continued their efforts to reduce errors. In 1993, these three partners created an on-going human-centered error investigation process which was designed to analyze specific cases of maintainer mistakes using a participative process and to apply what is learned to system-wide solutions (Marx, 1998).

In general, such second-generation programs, although participative, are reactive to past problems. Thus they are, at least in part, focused on the past.

Third Generation MRM Programs

The third generations of MRM programs essentially consisted of training programs to increase individual mechanic's safety awareness and to improve individual coping skills in dealing with safety issues. Research shows that in programs with two days of training, increased awareness results in trends toward fewer injury and ground damage incidents. Significant increase in the quality or quantity of communication does not typically occur as a result of this third MRM generation. It is usually a one-shot program, without follow-up. That (together with its emphasis on individual coping skills) seems to place participants in the position of not knowing whether or how much the MRM program is working, or whether other people value the lessons of the training like they themselves do. As such, these third generation programs have been observed to exhaust their inertial influence within a limited time (Taylor, 1998b).

In 1994 the curriculum for a different kind of maintenance training program was developed and distributed through Transport Canada. The program, called Human Performance in Maintenance (HPIM) is based on a two-day training course designed specifically for AMTs. It soon became widely known because of the maintenance-oriented nature of its training materials and its ready availability. Among HPIM's most popular innovations is a set of safety posters—the 'Dirty Dozen' posters—one for each of twelve major causes of maintenance errors (Taylor & Christensen, 1998, pp. 145-6). As evidence for the strength of HPIM influence, all reported MRM programs implemented in North America since 1994 have included the 'dirty dozen'" as a core set of concepts. The purpose of HPIM training as described in the prototype participants' workbook is "to create an awareness of the human aspect of aircraft maintenance and develop safeguards to lessen the "human cause" factors in maintenance'.

In several ways HPIM has had a direct impact on the development of the third generation of MRM programs. First is the emphasis on 'awareness'. The HPIM purpose differs from the purpose of the CRM-based maintenance training in Cases 1 through 3 above. HPIM focuses on awareness and coping mechanisms or safeguards, while the MRM of Cases 1 through 3 focuses on skills such as assertiveness. Second is the emphasis on the individual. The objectives of the initial 1994 HPIM course emphasizes three of the dirty dozen—lack of communication, stress, and fatigue—two of which are primarily personal issues that can be best managed by the individual. Third is the emphasis on internal and passive change rather than interpersonal and active change. In HPIM both its curriculum and workbook illustrate this emphasis. The workbook includes a section on communication that emphasizes listening (passive rather than active communication) as the major technique. This trend that MRM was taking on an "awareness training" orientation has been noted by others (Kanki, et al., 1997).

One adaptation to the third generation of MRM has been to divide two days of training over several months. This may offer several advantages over the one-shot training model. First, it provides the opportunity for program facilitators to follow-up and elaborate on the lessons from the first session. Second, the subsequent session begins to demonstrate management's commitment to an ongoing MRM program. Third, it may satisfy participants' desire for recurrent training. Initial evaluation results presented below appear to show that safety trends improve as a result of the MRM program and these trends continue after the second training day.

Although the several cases of third generation MRM described below differ in significant detail from one another they all share a training purpose focused on awareness as well as resulting overwhelmingly in intended and reported changes which are passive and individual-level coping adaptations rather than active changes in communication.

Case 5: AMT awareness leads to improved performance: In 1996 a large airline undertook to provide MRM training for all of its AMTs. The purpose of the program, stated in participant's workbook is to create an awareness of the impact of human performance on maintenance-related errors and personal safety. The learning objectives for the course were as follows: relate how AMT characteristics and personal behavior can impact the maintenance process; identify 12 performance factors ('dirty dozen'") and their role in the chain of events leading to maintenance-related errors; develop personal techniques to minimize risk and maximize performance; and give and receive feedback with coworkers related to personal safety.

The company trained over six thousand employees during a two and a half year period. It addressed its MRM training exclusively to AMTs (supervisors and managers account for less than 1% of the total trained in that company). The AMT's union and the company's management cooperated to initiate the training. Training materials were adapted from the HPIM package and the company standardized them for its own use— including the use of local case illustrations. In addition to the three of the dirty dozen items emphasized in the HPIM syllabus a fourth 'dirty' item, 'complacency', was added to the core curriculum. Training then continued at the local level with facilitators coming from the ranks of both AMTs and their first-line supervisors. This group of facilitators represented excellent use of local operational experience and leadership abilities. The training was coordinated and supported by the company's training and education department. Enthusiasm was positive immediately following the training even if some participants hedged a little on their interpretation of substantial change. Over 60% of the participants said there would be a moderate or large change in their on-the-job behavior (Taylor & Christensen, 1998). Although a clear majority believed that the training will affect their actual behavior, this level of enthusiasm did not approach the high ratings—between 80% and 90%—reported for the earlier three MRM cases. These AMTs also responded to the question: 'How will you use this training on your job?'. Content coding of those answers resulted in the bulk of the responses divided into several categories including 'Interacting with others', 'Being more assertive', 'Being more aware of other's behavior', 'Being a better listener,' and 'Fighting complacency/being more careful at work'. The first two categories—'active communication' intentions—can be compared with the more passive coping behaviors that can be done alone. Twenty-seven percent of the AMTs' responses were coded in the active category while nearly 46% were coded in the passive category. This result is substantially lower for active communication than the AMT sample described in Case 3. This tendency toward passive coping behaviors is consistent with the purpose and objectives of the program.   Statistically significant improvements were found in attitudes about sharing responsibility, communication, and stress management immediately following the training sessions. The change in the value of stress management was particularly striking.   Furthermore, those same three attitudes remained stable for months after the training.   Attitudes toward assertiveness did not improve as a result of the training (Taylor & Christensen, 1998, pp. 154-155). The AMTs' positive attitudes following MRM training leads to enhanced performance as well. In particular, the marked increase in appreciation of stress management two months after training showed the strongest correlations with low rates of injury and aircraft damage (Taylor, 1998a). Stress management is primarily a passive coping activity and its improvement following the training and its relationship to safety performance improvements is entirely consistent with this company's MRM purpose. In 1998, the performance trends for 1995 through 1997 for this case were promising (Taylor, 1998b), but at least for base maintenance AMTs who had not completed their MRM training, more time would be necessary to observe performance over a longer period (Taylor, 1998a).

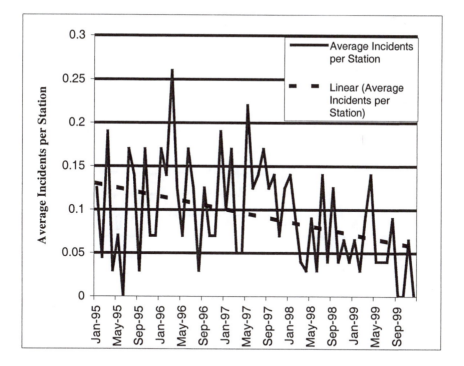

Figure 3-1: **Ground damage across 42 line maintenance stations over 5 years**

Note: January 1996 through May 1996: Before MRM Training
         June 1996 through December 1997: During MRM Training
         January 1997 through December 1998: After MRM Training

Figures 3-1, 3-2, and 3-3 show performance data for the expanded five-year period 1995-1999. All figures show linear trend lines (obtained using the method of Least Squares) for the 'before', 'during' and 'after-training' periods superimposed over the actual monthly data points.

Figures 3-1 and 3-2 show the trends before, during, and after MRM training for occupational injuries and aircraft ground damage for line maintenance performance.   Figure 3-3 shows similar trends for occupational injuries for base maintenance.

It is clear from the trends in Figures 3-1 and 3-2 that a dramatic improvement took place for the line stations taken together. Furthermore, this improvement directly after the onset of the MRM program and its rate of change continues in the two years *following* the completion of the MRM training. This strongly suggests that the 'awareness' program worked through its effect on stress management and situational awareness—at least in this company's line maintenance organization.

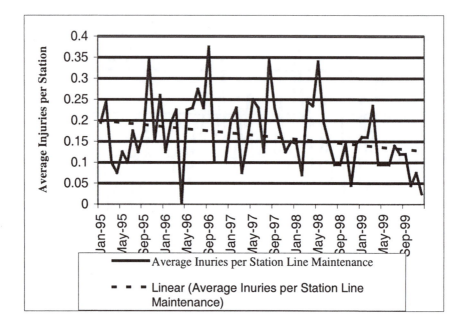

Figure 3-2:   Lost time injuries across 42 line-maintenance stations over 5 years

Note: January 1996 through May 1996: Before MRM Training
        June 1996 through December 1997: During MRM Training
        January 1997 through December 1998: After MRM Training

For the Base Maintenance organization the effects were also encouraging. Figure 3-3 shows that the trend for lost time injuries remains low during the period of MRM training and that it rises and falls only gradually in the 15 months after the training was concluded. However, because of the sharply downward trend before the training began we must question whether the lower rates during training and after the training, are a continuation of some previous program to lessen injuries in the hangars or they are the result of the MRM training.

It is ironic—given the apparent success of this MRM program as expressed in long-term safety outcomes—that AMTs' enthusiasm for the program turned from positive to negative. Earlier reports examining the attitudes and opinions of line maintenance employees in the months following their MRM training have described the apparent frustration and anger these individuals voiced (Taylor, 1998a). They expected more support by their managers and co-workers in fulfilling the promise of the MRM program to improve communication and collaboration (Taylor, 1998b). Subsequent interviews and observations in the company's repair hangars confirm this 'backlash' exists in heavy maintenance as well. AMTs and inspectors reported discouragement waiting for some management safety initiative that was based on the content of the MRM course.

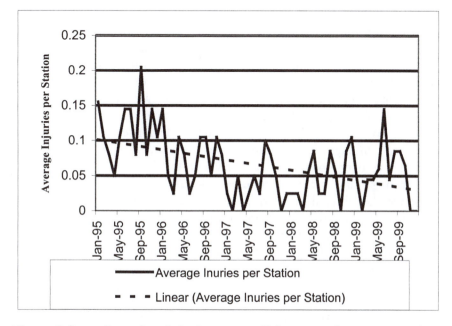

Figure 3-3: **Lost time injuries across 40 heavy-maintenance stations over 5 years**

Note: January 1996 through May 1996: Before MRM Training
        June 1996 through December 1997: During MRM Training
        January 1997 through December 1998: After MRM Training

This individual-based awareness training, with its emphasis on building individual's coping skills, appears to give AMTs little subsequent information about whether or how much the MRM program is working, or whether other people value the lessons of the training like they themselves do. Months after the training many AMTs reported still being careful, fighting complacency, and managing their own stress levels. But many also did not think the MRM program would be very useful in the future

(Taylor & Christensen, 1998, pp. 152-160). Many said they did not know or could not tell if others were using the lessons learned from the training—they rarely talked about MRM informally and were never encouraged to do so by their leaders.

Case 6: Distributing third generation MRM training: One adaptation of the third generation MRM has been to divide two days of training over several months. A large U.S. airline created its own MRM training after reviewing the HPIM training model. The AMT's union and the company's management cooperated to initiate and design the training. Training materials were inspired by the HPIM package, but most of the exercises and cases were created specifically for this application. This material provided participants with specific human factors principles and techniques to help them work more safely. The definition of MRM, stated in the participant's workbook, '...is the process where we work together, using available resources, to reduce errors and to promote safety'. The statement goes on to say, 'MRM addresses human factor errors and problem resolution through open and honest communication between all maintenance operations personnel, and with the FAA'. The training topics for the first day were as follows: identify human factors elements; recognize the 'dirty dozen' error causes; identify the chain of events in accidents; effective written communication; identify norms; establish safety nets; recognize safety mechanisms

Although the MRM definition quoted above is more active and interpersonal than is typical for the HPIM (third generation) model, the supporting topics are largely 'awareness' or conceptual issues—with 'written communication' as the 'active skill' exception. At the beginning of the second (Phase-2) training day the definition of MRM is reiterated. The training topics in the participants' workbook for the second day are as follows: recognize the nature of errors and how the affect participants; focus on how to manage errors; 'dirty dozen' topics; 'lack of assertiveness' and 'lack of awareness' are emphasized; introduce tools to use in error reduction; emphasis on situational awareness

Likewise these topic labels for Phase-2 training seem more conceptual than behavioral. The module on lack of assertiveness is, however, focusing on active communication. On the other hand, the main 'tool' in the final Phase-2 topic list, situational awareness, is an individual, passive mechanism. This MRM program appears to be bridging between the third generation model of individual AMTs coping with safety hazards and issues and the interpersonal communication techniques of the original maintenance safety training.

By design, Phase-2 (the second day of training) is conducted about two months after the first one. The course is designed for all maintenance employees and each session is expected to include management and hourly employees from a variety of functions within maintenance. Initially, the training took place in a large line station and both Phases 1 and 2 were completed there before the program was moved to two cities containing both base and line maintenance stations. Eventually all 8,000 maintenance employees throughout the system were expected to attend the training.

Phase-1 training for the first city (line maintenance station 'A') was 85% completed between January and March 1998 and the remainder (for a total of some 500 maintenance employees) was finished in July. Phase- 2 was completed during August and September 1998. The second city ('B') to begin the MRM training included both a large line station and a major heavy maintenance base. City B began Phase-1 training in September 1998 and completed it with about 1,000 maintenance personnel in April 1999. Phase-2 began in city B during June 1999 and was about 50% completed by December 1999. A third city (also both a large line station and a major heavy maintenance base) began Phase-1 training in July 1999 and, with over 900 employees remaining to be trained at the end of December 1999. Results from cities A and B will be used below to illustrate the effects of distributed training and the modified course purpose and topics.

Enthusiasm for city A is moderate when compared with past MRM experience described for the cases above. Slightly over 60% of the participants following Phase-1 said there would be a moderate-to-large change in their on-the-job behavior. Following Phase-2, 65% city A participants said there would at least a moderate increase in their at-work activities. This modest increase is encouraging, but statistical tests of this result, or that between the associated Phase-1 and -2 mean scores, do not show significant differences. For city B the enthusiasm following Phase-1 is also moderate with some 69% saying there would at least a moderate change in their behavior. Following Phase-2, 85% in city B say they expect moderate to large change in their at-work activities.

Figure 3-4 shows the mean scores for attitudes and opinions for city 'A', the first station to complete the two-phase MRM program. Immediately following the Phase-1 training, participants revealed significant improvement in attitudes toward communication, stress management, and assertiveness. Following Phase-2 training all three attitudes increased again significantly. Although attitudes toward sharing command responsibility increased slightly over this time, the differences are not statistically significant.

Figure 3-4 also shows city A participants' evaluation of their station's goal setting and sharing remained unchanged between Phases 1 and 2. However their evaluations of the station's safety climate decreased significantly ($F=8.29$, $p<.001$) between Phases 1 and 2. Field observation at city A about 60 days after Phase-1 training and again four months after Phase-2 training confirm these survey results. AMTs, leads, and foremen reported that safety standards and program seemed to be deteriorating. Apart from their own individual care and awareness, they said, little was being done to support maintenance safety at their station.

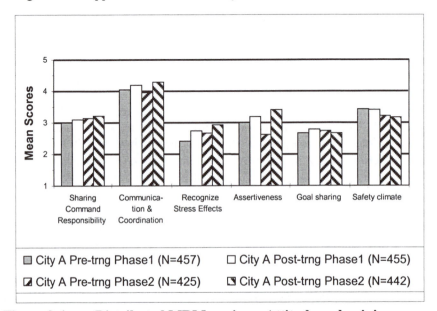

Figure 3-4:   Distributed MRM sessions: Attitude and opinion changes

The question, 'how will you use this training on the job?' was included in the surveys that followed both Phase-1 and Phase-2 training. City A participants' answers to that question were coded for intentions to begin active communication with management and coworkers, as well as for intentions to apply more individual, passive, coping behaviors. If respondents said they were not intending to change at all, that was coded separately. Those answers that did not fit any of the categories were coded 'other'. Answers to the same question from city B's MRM participants were similarly coded and can be compared with city A's results.

The post-Phase-2 survey asked the question, 'how have you used the MRM training on your job?'. The answers received were coded the same as those for the question of intention. Thus, both intention to change and the subsequent changes can be compared over time. These data are presently available for city A in its entirety as well as for first half of the city B participants who have completed Phase-2 training.

Figure 3-5 presents the expected behaviors at the end of both Phase-1 and -2 training. The figure also shows the actual behaviors reported by participants at the time of the Phase- 2 training. Although 11% in city A said they intended to communicate actively following Phase-1, only 8% reported having done so when they returned for Phase-2 training.

Fifteen percent expected to actively communicate after attending the second day. For city B a larger percentage (nearly twice as large as city A) reported having been more active communicators when they returned for Phase-2, and that proportion again, further expected to actively communicate with others about safety. These results, even though they shift slightly more toward active intentions following Phase- 2 training they do not favorably compare with the proportions of active-to-passive intentions found in cases in the first generation of MRM training. This ratio in Figure 3-5 (generally about 15% active to over 45% passive) is much less than the 40% active to 45% passive intentions in the earlier programs (Taylor & Robertson, 1995; Taylor, et al., 1997).

Four years (1996-99) of aircraft damage incidents charged to city A maintenance are compared with all line stations in Figure 3-6. The overall pattern of ground damage incidents for all (n=45) line stations in the system remains steady with a flat trend line during this four-year period. The results for city A, however, show an increasing incident rate before the MRM training began. That trend reverses following the Phase- 1 training and it continues downward for 16 months after the second training phase concluded. The initial ground damage results for city B are not portrayed here, but they track a similar pattern.

This improvement in safety results is further evidence for the effect that MRM awareness instruction can have on maintenance performance. This, coupled with sustained enthusiasm following more than a year from the completion of the training suggests that the distributed, two-phase training program may avoid some of the frustration and anger caused by a perceived lack of support by their managers and co-workers to improve the safety climate (Taylor, 1998b).

This two-phase MRM training appears to provide several additional advantages over the one-shot training model. First, it provides the opportunity for program facilitators to follow-up and elaborate the lessons from the first session. For example, some changes to the Phase-2 curriculum for city B were made after the program had been used at city A.

Second, the subsequent session begins to demonstrate management's commitment to an ongoing MRM program. Unlike the experience in Case 5 above, where interest in changing behavior declines steadily in the months after training, some enthusiasm for the program in the present case continues months after the initial training. Third, it should satisfy those participants who want recurrent training on these topics. Typically about 10 to 12% of participants in previous MRM programs have said that recurrent MRM training would make an improvement to the one-shot model. In this case, the expectation for further MRM training may be higher with a two-phase program. In this regard nearly 20% of the participants' following the second phase of training said even further recurrent training would improve this model. Another 20% are eager to see more management and employees from other maintenance groups experience this MRM training.

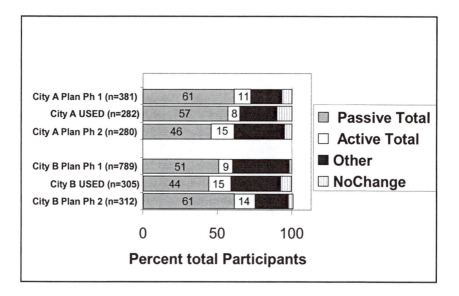

Figure 3-5:   Planning for, and using, the MRM training

Despite the successes reported for Cases 5 and 6, together with the added advantages of the distributed awareness training, they remain as programs that influence the values and awareness of individuals. Most third generation MRM programs have limited success in the following areas: (a) structure and the process for improving safety at a systemic, interpersonal level, (b) a clear safety goals, (c) rapid feedback of results, and (d) appropriate reinforcement for those who are behaving more safely.

Without these systemic, organizational features, MRM programs like those illustrated in Cases 5 and 6 seem destined to suffer the irony of increased long term improvement coupled with participants' ignorance about that gain and greater pessimism about the quality of maintenance safety programs. The sheer professionalism of the AMTs themselves makes these present programs work. AMTs are reminded of the dangers of the 'dirty dozen' causes of errors and accidents and they respond appropriately—on their own and apparently for a period of months or years, not weeks.

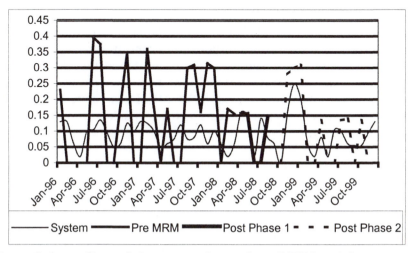

Figure 3-6:   Ground damage and two-phase MRM training

Fourth Generation MRM Programs

A fourth generation of MRM programs is now taking hold. It is characterized by a commitment to long-term communication and behavioral change in maintenance (Patankar & Taylor, 1999b; 2000a). Now, at the beginning of the 21st Century, the emergence of MRM should be seen as more than mere 'awareness training', or coping skills for individual mechanics—it is the conscious process of increasing trust among maintainers, their managers, and their regulators that enable them to learn from present behaviors in order to improve future quality and efficiency. It is a process of cultural change.

The fourth generation MRM programs are using the knowledge gained from the experience of the past three generations and from recent innovative processes to standardize communication and tactical decision-making. For the first time, these programs are being designed and implemented from a systemic perspective. Data from the past three generations of MRM programs show that different MRM programs usually achieve different results. Therefore, airlines are now adding a skills development module to their classroom instruction and making it a true "training" program that is more likely to result in more open communication (Patankar & Taylor, 2000a). These airlines are also aware of the interpersonal trust issues that impede self-disclosure, and they are striving to incorporate a maintenance error investigation (MEI) module in their training, and in their larger program, so that the participants understand the goal and the procedure of such investigation. In the skills training module, at least some corporate aviation departments in the U.S. have started to train their maintenance personnel to use simple, standard processes to detect and resolve differences in information through third-party validation. The airlines, on the other had, are now better informed about the capabilities and limitations of MRM programs, and they are embarking on a new result-oriented approach to safety through strategic, system-wide changes.

Understanding the human factor in unanticipated events: Real time knowledge of what human factors lie behind classes of maintenance errors is important to obtain, and central to the long-range and comprehensive success of MRM.   Processes for a human-centered maintenance error investigation (MEI) are becoming objects of serious interests in aviation maintenance organization (Allen & Marx, 1994; FAA, 1999).   However, full-blown maintenance experience with such programs is limited. A recent expert assessment of MEI in the U.S. shows that there has been little commitment yet by either the air carriers or repair stations to see such error investigation and analysis become a new way of doing business (Marx, 1998).

Trust within the maintenance system: Informal reports from users suggest that AMTs' limited trust of the MEI process creates an obstacle to its widespread diffusion. Why should an AMT cooperate with management in investigating his/her own mistakes?   Unless a strong culture for open communication and assertiveness already exists in their organization, relatively few AMTs will voluntarily or willingly disclose what they believe to be the 'real story'.   AMTs' individualism (Taylor, 1999; Taylor & Patankar, 1999) and self-reliance (Taylor & Christensen, 1998) can limit their trust in others.

In order to develop a strong safety culture, a maintenance organization must first recognize its own organizational and occupational culture, and it must appreciate the interplay between these two with the effects of national origins and cultures of its individual members (Taylor, 1999; Patankar & Taylor, 1999a).

Now, at the beginning of the 21st Century, MRM is being seen as more than mere 'awareness training', or coping skills for individual AMTs – it is the conscious process of increasing trust among maintainers, their managers, and their regulators that enable them to learn from present behaviors in order to improve future quality and efficiency. MRM is now a process of cultural change.

Direct focus on behavior change: The focus of contemporary MRM programs is now moving toward active error reduction through structured communication. Patankar and Taylor (1999b) describe a case from the corporate aviation environment that uses a 'behavior-change first' approach instead of the prevalent 'attitude-change first' of awareness-based MRM. In the earlier MRM generations (1 and 3), companies simply provided classroom instruction and hoped that the desired change in attitudes and behavior would take place automatically. This strategy focused on changing the participants' attitude toward safety through education and persuasion, and sometimes skill-training. Its developers hoped that participants' behavior would change as a consequence of the classroom experience alone. Unfortunately, the evaluations of such programs for improving communication revealed that the subsequent behavior change is limited— either in scope or duration.

At the same time there were companies that began to provide a simple structure and process for communication among all departments associated with aviation operations: flight crew, maintenance, and administration. These companies assumed that if they provided a simple, consistent communication and decision-making process, and the outcome of this process was promptly acted upon and continuously supported, their employees would continue to use it and could eventually change their attitudes. The immediate interest of these companies was in changing their employees' work-related communication behavior, they did not use the better known 'attitude change' approach taken in the first two generations of MRM.

The structured communication process: Basically, there are two aspects to achieving new communication behavior: first, a structure which requires connected parties to communicate, and second, a process that is followed consistently by all members of the system.

An example of structure might be an organizational policy for line maintenance which requires that for each flight an AMT act (either by direction or discretion) as its liaison AMT. This person is expected to meet with the flight crew and discuss the maintenance issues with them. The pilots are expected to wait after arrival to discuss maintenance discrepancies with the AMT. During such discussions, both the flight crew and the AMT(s) are required to follow the pre-agreed communication process described below.   Another example of structure is a policy requiring that maintenance shift turnovers take place face-to-face and that among other standing agenda items is the expectation that AMTs, leads, and foremen briefly review the outgoing shift's use of the pre-agreed decision-making process.

The process for enhanced aviation communication has been observed and documented (Lynch, 1996; Patankar & Taylor, 1999b). Its originators have titled it the Concept Alignment Process, or 'CAP'. According to this process, a 'concept' is an idea or a piece of information presented by an observer of, or a party to, a technical decision. All members are expected to present their concepts. If the members present differing concepts, they must validate their concepts from a third-party source such as a flight manual, air traffic controller, maintenance manual, company policy, etc. If only one concept can be validated, it is executed; if none of the concepts can be validated, the most conservative concept is executed; and if multiple concepts can be validated, the senior ranking person has the authority to choose any one of the valid concepts. Additionally, when multiple concepts are stated, whether valid or not, the members are required to investigate the reasons for the existence of multiple concepts. Such an investigation is aimed at providing systemic feedback to minimize the occurrence of multiple concepts, at least the non-validated ones. Also, once one concept is selected as the course of action, the CAP enters a "judgment phase" wherein the strengths and weaknesses in that course of action are monitored by the team. Such monitoring that may necessitate a change in course, encourages the team members to be assertive if any new information becomes available.

The Concept Alignment Process addresses the following causes of human error accidents (Lynch, 1996): non-adherence to procedure, incorrect tactical decisions, inattention or complacency, and failure to challenge another member's error.

The CAP provides objective procedures, thus making the use of the process observable to all. It provides team members with decision-making and conflict-resolution methodology. It reduces chances of acting on incorrect concepts that may force collaborative task completion and decision-making. It reduces interpersonal conflict and defensiveness through the understanding that what is challenged is the concept and not the individual. All of these benefits have been observed in the use of CAP in the maintenance environment. The following description of Case 7 highlights those benefits.

Case 7: Concept Alignment Process to facilitate crew communication and consistent decision-making among all members of a corporate aviation department: The aviation department of a large U.S. corporation trained all of its flight crew and maintenance members to use this system and the management used it as well. The CAP, a communication and decision-making protocol, was implemented to enhance systemic safety through early identification and management of risk. With this approach, management intended to impact behavior and did not aim to directly or immediately change attitudes toward interpersonal relations at work.

The management required that all aviation employees use CAP actively and held them accountable for it. Therefore, the use of the system was not voluntary. This is consistent with the behavior-first strategy discussed earlier. However, Patankar and Taylor (1999b) observed that once the employees (both flight and maintenance crew members) experienced successful implementation of the process and consistent support from the management, even if it meant making policy changes or confronting the local FAA, their belief in the process grew and their attitude toward safety and toward the use of this process changed over time. Most maintenance employees agreed that it took some time for them to really understand the process and be able to apply it consistently. The flight operations personnel had been using CAP for almost three years before the maintenance manager began learning the process. He customized the original flight-oriented program to a maintenance-oriented program and called it 'Error Reduction and Decision Making Process'.

A year after the Maintenance Error Reduction Program began, AMTs were surveyed for their attitudes and opinions about it. Only 40% of the AMTs said the program had at least moderate effect on their behavior, but nearly three-quarters of them reported that the program had been useful to others. Regardless of how they may discount the program's effects on themselves, these AMTs could see the effects on the others around them.

Compared with our standard dataset (Taylor, 2000), the survey for this aviation department showed favorable attitudes toward sharing command responsibility and for assertiveness. These people do value speaking-up and making decisions. Their attitudes toward communication however, were substantially below our standard benchmark. That is, they appear not to value or enjoy communication for its own sake. Their assessment of goal setting and sharing is at the benchmark norm, while their evaluation of the department's safety climate was higher than the norm.

The behavior changes were almost immediate. Because the change was mandatory and the employees were evaluated based on their ability to use the process, everyone tried to use it. Although some did not believe in it as much as others did, they all used it. There were a few product champions who consistently used the CAP process and more assertively addressed the concepts of others. Self-reports of how the process was used and the stated intentions to continue using it are encouraging. Two-thirds of the AMTs reported that the program caused them to communicate actively while only one member described behaving passively as a result of the CAP process. Reported intentions to further use the process were weighted toward active communication vs. passive reaction in a ratio of two-to-one.

As the AMTs observed that the management supported the process, regardless of the outcome, they started to trust this new communication protocol and continued to use it. There were times when the flight crew and the maintenance crew had disagreements and each party was able to validate its concept (Patankar & Taylor, 1999b). Under such circumstances, the department manager was able to step-in, validate the application of the process, and determine an outcome that was consistent with the CAP protocol. Consequently, all parties emerged with an increased trust in the process.

As a result of the CAP process, the maintenance personnel, the flight crew, and the management were more actively engaging external vendors, aircraft manufacturers, and their local FAA for more accurate and acceptable solutions to problems. Additionally, the maintenance manager was able to follow-up on several information discrepancies, determine their root cause, and make the necessary structural or procedural changes so that the same discrepancy would not arise in the future.

Processes such as CAP focus on behavioral outcomes rather than attitudinal change by providing a simple structure and process for communication among all parties involved in aircraft operations. The consistent use of this pre-agreed process, regardless of the outcome, in genuine pursuit of systemic improvements toward safety builds trust among all parties. Through consistent use of this process, the corporate aviation department was able to raise the performance standards at an individual as well as organizational level. Such an approach shows strong potential for long-term changes in the aviation safety culture.

Organizational safety culture and management support: One might assume that organizational culture has the potential for the greatest impact on safety because it is expected to 'channel the effects of national and professional cultures toward standard practices, and it is the organizational culture which shapes members' attitudes toward safety and productivity' (Helmreich & Merritt, 1998, p.110). Management needs to present strategies to unify and strengthen the organizational culture and aim to introduce safety as a shared value. Management's commitment, Helmreich and Merritt suggest, is prerequisite to successful implementation of new process or protocol because although an organizational culture is shaped by all of the employees, an organizational change is defined by the upper management. The change has to be top-down, through concrete and consistent examples.

In Case 7, the CAP communication protocol worked as an outstanding strategy to unify and strengthen the organizational culture because the top management agreed to manage risk through team decision-making. On the flight side, the pilots were required to conduct preflight briefings and post-flight debriefings for every flight. Similarly, in the maintenance department, the AMTs were required to conduct regular briefings with the flight crew and follow the approved protocol. In addition maintenance personnel agreed to discuss the recent use of CAP during their daily shift-turnover meetings. The management fully supported these briefings and meetings by agreeing to act on the subsequent recommendations in a timely manner.

By visibly supporting these activities, the management created an environment that expected everyone to follow the CAP protocol in making decisions and to base these decisions on safety concerns as well as on scheduling. Every employee does not need to believe in this communication process, but he/she is required to practice it. Awards and penalties are based on the employee's ability to follow the process. With a demonstrated consistent support to the process, regardless of the resulting recommendations, the employees gain confidence and build safety as a shared value.

The Next Generation of MRM Programs

After understanding the evolution of MRM programs in the United States, it is now timely to think about the future of such programs. Where do we go from here? Remember, in Chapter 1 we introduced the multi-faceted interpretation of the term *safety*. There, we discussed how safety means different things to different people. As we look forward, it is important to think about those differences and create a bold new generation of programs that go beyond regulatory compliance, are built upon the foundation of open communication and high interpersonal trust, and are designed to create and sustain a high-reliability organization.

The first step in creating such programs would be to open communication channels, both vertical—within the organizational hierarchy—as well as horizontal—across the traditional professional boundaries. Past successes with Round Tables and Focus Groups suggest that involving mechanics in solving problems has been very effective in reducing errors (Taylor & Christensen, 1998, pp.108-111, pp.117-118). Also, such programs have increased the mechanics' expectation for continued communication. Therefore, it will be imperative that mechanisms such as telephone hotlines and other anonymous reporting systems have a feedback loop announcing the results on a regular basis. If such feedback is not provided, the mechanics tend to lose trust in solicitation for open communication.

The next element of next generation MRM programs is interpersonal trust. Practitioners in the preceding generations of MRM programs have learned not only that interpersonal trust is essential, but also that it is very fragile. The programs such as Round Tables and Focus Groups were developed because of a high level of interpersonal trust between the people involved in those programs. Each member of those teams trusted that the others would act in the interest of safety. Now, as we consider the Maintenance-Aviation Safety Action Programs, interpersonal trust will have to be applied on a larger scale—across organizations and throughout the nation.

Finally, a high-reliability organization cannot coexist with blame culture. Everyone within the organization, as well as the associated regulatory surveyors, needs to work actively toward resolving systemic problems and steer clear of individual blame. At the individual level, it is essential for every maintenance professional to actively strive toward elevating his/her professionalism by continuing to steer clear of reckless behavior and by striving for systemic improvements through assertiveness and open communication.

MRM Implementation

MRM is basically a change program. As such, it can be implemented 'top-down' or 'bottom-up'. The specific choice of strategy will depend on the organizational culture. However, commitment from both the management as well as the workers is essential to the success of this program. Typically, it is a program that should be supported by management via resource allocation, willingness to make organizational changes to improve safety, and consistently choosing safety over performance. Such programs are supported by the workers by using their training to affect active, positive changes in the workplace. Ultimately, if the workplace safety-level has to change, both organizations as well as individuals must change. These changes are not intended to be *quid pro quo* trades made by the two groups, but as collaborative actions that are necessary to achieve the team's goals.

MRM Master Plan

An MRM Master Plan is a document that should be developed during the design phase of an MRM program. This document is essential for several reasons. First, it encourages the designers to articulate the goals of their program. The question to ask is, 'What do you expect this program to achieve?'. Several research studies described in this chapter illustrate that an MRM program can achieve a variety of goals that range from awareness about safety to a complete transformation of the safety culture. Once the goal for an MRM program is identified, the resources (personnel as well as financial) must be allocated, timelines must be established, and measurement techniques must be agreed upon. All too often we have seen MRM programs fail because of lack of management follow-up. By developing a written document such as a master plan, the probability of success of MRM programs can be improved. The MRM Master Plan is expected to protect against one key obstacle: revolving door management.

Revolving Door Management: Research (Patankar & Taylor, 2000b) indicates that the managers in the U.S. airline industry tend to change assignments every three to five years. So, it is quite likely that by the time an MRM program is implemented, at least one of the ardent champions of the MRM program will move to another assignment. If that happens, will the MRM program be affected? If the MRM program is strongly dependent on a particular manager's support, it is quite likely to fade away after that manager leaves. In some cases, mechanics and mid-level managers have been able to hold-up some of the initial enthusiasm with the hope that when another suitable manager comes in, the rest of the crew will be ready to continue with the MRM implementation. In most cases, however, employee morale as well as reputation of the MRM program suffers—the MRM program is quite likely to be tagged as 'flavor of the month'.

Targeted MRM Programs

Since MRM programs can be designed to achieve a variety of goals, it is advisable to consider the specific short-term and long-term goals that the designers want to achieve. For example, these goals could be as varied as follows: raising the awareness regarding effects of human performance on safety; reducing documentation errors; improving shift-turnovers; or minimizing ground damage. Depending on the goals of the program, the specific treatment will differ. Also, the return on investment will defer (see Chapter 8).

MRM Evaluation

With the visible success of Cockpit Resource Management (CRM) in flight operations during the 1980s, the first two airlines intentionally improving communication in maintenance (Taggart, 1990; Fotos, 1991) each modeled their maintenance efforts after CRM programs within their company's flight operations. Naturally the creators of these pioneering maintenance programs drew heavily on the available research and hands-on experience from CRM. That included proven evaluation tools (Gregorich, et al., 1990) and successful training programs (Helmreich, et al., 1986) which were lightly modified and quickly applied to the initial maintenance communication program (Taylor, et al., 1993).

Development of MRM topics has continued and expanded to include attitudes and opinions about maintenance management and operations, of intentions to use knowledge obtained from MRM, as well as of self-reports of subsequent behaviors (Taggart, 1990; Taylor, 2000). A database of over 15,000 mechanics, maintenance managers, and other maintenance personnel from some dozen air carriers and repair stations is now available at Saint Louis University and is used to compare city and company results against standardized scores.

In addition to such standardized instruments, organizations may also want to use internal performance measures such as improvement is shift-turnover communication, reduction in logbook errors, reduction in rework, etc. Many organizations already collect this data, but only few analyze it, and even fewer are able to connect this data with the specific targets of their MRM program.

As the fourth generation programs continue to evolve, the idea of *maintenance debriefings* is gaining momentum. These debriefings are being used to identify not only the systemic errors, but also as means to identify the errors recovered. Such measurement represents a significant milestone in the pursuit of a safer culture because it (a) acknowledges that systemic errors are going to continue to exist, (b) provides a means for work-teams to proactively diffuse these systemic, error-inducing conditions, and (c) enables the work-teams to celebrate the number of errors recovered—a true measure of safety.

Chapter Summary

Ergonomics and Human Factors programs focus on the human-machine interface aspects; whereas, Maintenance Resource Management programs focus on the interaction among people, their maintenance environment, and their maintenance work processes. MRM programs have achieved several different types of changes in the quality and safety at the work site. However, in most cases, the effects of MRM programs have been short-lived. In order to implement a sustainable change through MRM programs, there needs to be a strong commitment from the company's management—now for a fourth generation MRM program—accompanied by a specific master plan.

Review Questions

1. Differentiate between *ergonomics, human factors,* and *maintenance resource management.*
2. Use the Ergonomic Audit Program to evaluate the operating instructions for a household appliance. (Ergonomic Audit Program is available at http://hfskyway.faa.gov)
3. Discuss the specific contributions of each generation of MRM programs.
4. What is the most significant advantage of a fourth generation MRM program over its predecessors?
5. What is an MRM Master Plan and why should one develop such a plan?
6. Why should MRM training programs be evaluated?
7. List some of the different changes that MRM programs have been able to accomplish.

Chapter 4

Maintenance Safety Culture and Sociotechnical Systems

Instructional Objectives

Upon completing this chapter, you should be able to:

1. Recognize that in order to effect a long-term organizational change, such as cultural change, both technical as well as social issues need to be addressed.
2. Discuss the obstacles in successful implementation of safety programs such as the Maintenance Resource Management program, from a sociotechnical perspective.
3. Describe how sociotechnical principles can be applied in the aviation industry to optimize both production as well as safety.

Introduction

International experts in the industry recognize that aviation maintenance is a "sociotechnical system" (McDonald, 1994a,b; Pidgeon & O'Leary, 1995; Drury, 1998). This recognition acknowledges that safe and successful maintenance and repairs are not achieved by technology alone, but require maintenance people guiding and working with technology. As aircraft and aviation become more complex and sophisticated, the sociotechnical bond becomes even more important. The technology and the people are each necessary for successful maintenance, but neither alone is sufficient. To work best they must be seen together and they must be designed together.

Sociotechnical systems are purposeful (Ackoff & Emery, 1972, Taylor & Felten, 1993). Effective sociotechnical systems occur when the people responsible for achieving the work *understand* the common ground between their goals and the goals of the enterprise and where those people also *know* how they specifically contribute to reach those common goals, and with whom they must collaborate to achieve them. The joint optimization between the technical and the social entities is only possible when the purpose and values of the enterprise are both shared among its people and served directly by its technology. Purpose and value comprise culture, and culture can effectively drive the simultaneous design of both the technology and the social system.

Sociotechnical systems (STS), in operation, are successful when they equip their members to "manage in the void" or to have the motives and the ability to make decisions and to act quickly and accurately in new or novel circumstances (Taylor & Felten; 1993, pp. 94-95). In order to do this, system members must be skilled in understanding the purpose and product of their system in order to have the confidence to make adjustment for events that have never (in their experience of knowledge at least) occurred before.

STS is a powerful organizational model describing purposeful work systems in complex environments (Emery & Trist, 1965). System thinking presumes that any system is a set of parts or pieces that are closely interrelated with reference to their shared environment. Systems are also seen to be parts of larger systems in turn. Organizations or work systems can thus be seen as part of larger system—for example, a line maintenance station is usually a part of a larger maintenance department, which is part of an aviation company, which is part of a national aviation industry, and so forth. That larger aviation industry in turn exists in a complex of environments such as the consumer market, government regulators, manufacturers, the economic climate, and international diplomatic relations; each of these subsystems also has unique connections.

STS is a specific kind of system thinking which helps to determine 'goodness of fit' among people and technology as they respond to their environments to achieve system success. This STS viewpoint contains three elements: (a) the technical subsystem or program, tools and processes designed to achieve system success; (b) the social subsystem or people and their roles which are expected to provide judgment and guidance for the technical subsystem; and (c) the enterprise system which defines purpose, values, objectives, boundaries and salient environment in which the technical and social subsystems exist. Organizational 'culture' is contained in the dominant purpose and values of the enterprise. That culture may be highly motivating to its members, and the degree that it is, will determine the long-term success of the enterprise.

Aviation maintenance organizations have been analyzed as sociotechnical systems and this has aided in understanding the wide range of effectiveness among companies and stations (Taylor, 1991; Drury, 1998). Effective sociotechnical systems are characterized by a specific organizational *structure* and *process*. The structure requires people to work with each other to attain collective goals (those of the enterprise) and the *process* provides both essential business of the enterprise as well as permits the benefits of human adaptability, flexibility, and cooperation in managing variances in day-to-day operations (Taylor & Felten, 1993).

Managing in the Void

Although aviation maintenance is a highly technical field it is not strictly 'black and white'. There are usually instances during any mechanic's normal day in which ambiguity or uncertainty will occur. Vague elements in work or work context are not something mechanics want or seek, but such elements occur regardless – they remain shades of gray in a black and white world. These shades of gray can result from many causes or sources.

Shades of gray comprise a void—they are cases that initially seem neither right nor wrong. A void is the absence of substance—in this case the absence of substance for the mechanic. For instance, there may be a right way to do a job, but it is in a "void" if unavailable to the mechanic. How such "void" experiences are managed is of prime importance in the prevention of errors, and thus the prevention of subsequent incidents and accidents. An effective sociotechnical system is one in which management in the void is not only possible, but planned for—the so called 'performance by design' (Taylor & Felten, 1993).

Maintenance Culture

Occupational culture, company culture and national cultures all shape the culture in any particular maintenance station. In Chapter 2, we discussed the individualistic occupational culture of aviation maintenance technicians (AMTs). Those in the AMT occupation are, on average, even more individualistic than those in individualistic occupations of airline pilots and surgeons. Likewise we have reported that AMTs from the national cultures in North America, Western Europe and Australia are more individualistic than their counterparts in Latin America and Asia. Similar differences among company cultures emphasizing teamwork and participation have also been noted (Taylor, 1996; Freiberg & Freiberg, 1996). Effective sociotechnical systems require teamwork and collaboration, as well as candor and assertiveness among employees. Modern sociotechnical systems need teamwork, collaboration, candor and assertiveness much more than do the traditional, hierarchical, individualistic organizations of the past. Changing traditional cultures in aviation maintenance organizations is bound to be difficult because it means challenging national and occupational cultures and probably changing the company's culture as well. Individualism and collaboration are pitted against one another in a struggle for change.

Changing Maintenance Safety Culture

Perhaps the worst kept secret in the North American aviation maintenance industry over the past decade is that most Human Factors programs have been intending to change the safety culture. The casual observer does not need much to reveal this secret—that the industry's *ideal* safety practice is one in which mechanics will cease to be silent loners, and will openly communicate with one another. This communication would, ideally, be with management, and with other technicians, about their own human errors, about technological flaws, and about how to prevent them.

This revelation is clear because the content of *so many* Human Factor programs includes some aspect of open communication and discussion of human error mitigation. The secret is *not* revealed because much candor is actually seen or known of. Human Factors in Maintenance programs have rarely succeeded in improving open communication, but they emphasize the imperative to do it, or importance of it, the techniques for doing it, the opportunity to do it, or the reward for it. These programs 'talk the talk', but rarely 'walk the walk'. The ubiquitous presence of this *ideal* has not done much to change behavior. The safety culture of the individual professional mechanic has not changed much since 1988.

After a dozen years of experience, Maintenance Resource Management (MRM) programs are still a long way from delivering a safety culture of open communication and error reduction. There are some improvements at the individual level but they are, comparatively speaking, not very great. This is because three obstacles limit the change efforts themselves. *First*, these programs are limited by remaining focused on awareness of what's good, rather than on acting to do good; *second*, they are reactive and must wait for an incident or accident to occur before learning can take place; and *third*, they deal with the individual mechanic and ignore the fact that mechanics working together are an essential part of a sociotechnical system.

Obstacle One: Focus on Awareness Not Behavior

Most MRM programs have been limited to classroom instruction about effects of stress, importance of communication, and general awareness of safety issues. Awareness instruction was successful in raising the awareness of the individual mechanics—they made some internal changes in terms of their attitudes toward stress management, interpersonal communication, handling of complacency, etc. However, awareness instruction was not successful in engendering a lasting change in *behavior*.

Awareness of safety and the awareness of the consequences of stress can, and do, make a difference to mechanics who make genuine attempts to be more vigilant and try to monitor their own stress. Favorable attitudes toward stress management are directly related to improvement in safety performance (Taylor & Christensen, 1998; p. 157). On the other hand, the awareness of communication, conflict-management, good decision-making, or awareness of the importance of interpersonal trust does not often produce the desired change in behavior. More often such awareness programs backfire on their promoters because they create inflated mechanic expectations for management changes that never come, which in turn lead to frustration and discouragement (Taylor & Christensen, 1998; pp. 158-159).

Improving communication and trust: MRM is a multiparty cooperative program in maintenance that is designed to improve communication and reduce errors.   As originally conceived, the practice of MRM involved mechanics, leads, and foremen in a structured process of suggesting ways to reduce errors, and then involving them in implementing those suggestions. That direct approach, in those individual stations where it was applied, was shown to be successful (Taylor & Patankar, 2001).   As it became clear that a wider diffusion of change in the company's safety culture was necessary, the program evolved from continued (albeit diminished) use of the structured discussions and changes, to a training course with joint emphasis on concept awareness about clearer communication and on skills training in more effective communication (Taylor & Christensen, 1998, pp. 48, 118-119). The widespread use of that training program was begun and initial results showed that it produced a small, but immediate effect.   More detailed investigation indicated that a lack of local management support had a pronounced dampening effect on the diffusion of initial successes which had improved communication (Taylor & Thomas, In Press b).

Adding skill to awareness can lead to improved performance. Those Human Factors programs that have avoided the 'awareness-only trap', such as the MRM approach just described, include practical training in skills intended to support the awareness. Such programs have been more effective in effecting intended behavioral change and more comprehensive changes in safety culture.   Some essential ingredients for changing the culture are increased *trust in the program and in one another*, combined with *coaching and training* in improving *communication and decision-making skills*. The increased trust must start with conscious management decisions, and can only spread with sustained, consistent, and active management support for the program at all levels. The issue of interpersonal trust is discussed in great detail in Chapter 5.

To overcome management's reluctance to actively and consistently support the human factors programs they choose to implement, they must provide more than 'lip service'. Additionally, it is far better if managers begin by supporting a program that trains themselves in improving their own open communication skills as well as promoting open communication among their AMT subordinates.

Obstacle Two: Reactive vs. Proactive Programs

Learning from mistakes: Maintenance error investigation procedures are of growing interest in North America. In these programs it is intended that mechanics can go to specially trained safety counselors, or committees, with problems they observe, or errors they themselves commit. The aim is to increase the body of safety information to try to stop accidents from happening.   Among the best known of these programs are 'MEDA' (Maintenance Error Decision Aid), a program created and sponsored by the Boeing Aircraft Company (Allen & Marx, 1994), and 'ASAP' (Aviation Safety Action Programs), an approach created by American Airlines and endorsed by the FAA (FAA, 1997). A more local, but similar program, called 'Roundtables', is the product of US Airways (Marx, 1998; Taylor & Christensen, 1998). The success of these error investigation programs is harnessed to the twin achievements of learning from mistakes and learning to trust that organizational learning is more important than punishing the guilty. Both achievements are difficult, given present levels of distrust in the industry (Goglia, et al., 2002), and the programs' successes have so far been limited. Another drawback with these error investigation tools as a method of risk management is that they are 'after-the-fact'—they are reactive. They do not attempt to directly mitigate current errors. If they are not soon combined with some of the more effective MRM skill training—to increase good communication skills and to begin to develop trust among aircraft mechanics, and between themselves and management—these reactive error reduction programs do not stand much of a chance to succeed.

Obstacle Three: Addressing Mechanics as Individuals

As we discussed in Chapter 2, aircraft mechanics are more individualistic than pilots. So, human factors programs designed to enhance the extant feelings of individualism can only limit the success of attempts to reduce errors because they do not tend to foster team-development. If mechanics are allowed to ignore one another, or worse yet compete with each other across shifts or departments, trust will never develop among them and error reduction and risk management will remain forever bereft of the benefits of people working together.

Sociotechnical Systems (STS) Application

STS overcomes the above-listed obstacles by operating on designing organizational structures and processes to (a) promote actions as well as awareness, (b) provide the ability to prevent errors in the present as well as the future, and (c) treat the maintenance department social system as an essential ingredient—mechanics and managers are thus seen as system members collaborating for a shared purpose, rather than individuals laboring to external regulations.

Organizational Structure and Sociotechnical Systems

There are many ways that structure can work for, or against, the purpose of an enterprise. A few examples taken from actual cases in aviation maintenance can help us understand this concept.

Organization by physical location can work against goal attainment: An airline's line maintenance operation in a large hub city was structured into three shifts with the third shift having responsibility for repair and maintenance of aircraft remaining over night (RON). RON aircraft were repaired both at the terminal flight line as well as in a hangar reserved for that purpose, located a few hundred yards away. RON aircraft were expected to be ready for scheduled service for the first flights each morning. In fact, if delays were incurred with the first flights, then the airline's entire schedule for that day could be disrupted in a giant 'domino effect'. Having all RON aircraft ready for first flight was essential to the airline's operation and profitability—aircraft readiness for first flight was a *key variance* (a key variable in goal attainment) in the maintenance process. This company had structured its third shift line maintenance operations so that the flight line crew was managed separately from the 'hangar crew' (this distinction didn't occur on first or second shift since the line hangar wasn't used until aircraft arrived for the night). The effect of separately structuring line and hangar crews was an unfortunate one for first flight availability. If the flight line crew began to work on an aircraft and discovered that the job would (or might) take more time than the shift would allow, then it was taxied or towed to the hangar. Not only was the extra time to move the aircraft subtracted from the time available to fix it, the unanticipated workload on the hangar meant the redeployment of hangar crew mechanics from jobs they had been working. This shuffle resulted in interrupted tasks and extra pressure to work faster. If the hangar crew failed to finish all its RON aircraft for the shift it would not be rewarded or commended for absorbing extra work, while the flight line crew would not be punished for offloading work it could not finish. This inequity between the third shift crews developed into resentment by the hangar crew with a consequent loss of morale. Finally, it festered into conflict between the crews. Several months of this unfortunate choice of structure resulted in lowered production, more errors, and increased aircraft ground damage. The maintenance department's key variance of first flight's readiness suffered directly. One cure for this would be to combine the third shift flight line and hangar line personnel into one crew with one goal to have high-quality aircraft ready for their first flights. Rather than concealing poor work habits and interpersonal resentments, the combined personnel could rotate through both locations in order to understand the problems faced by the others and management could reward the combined shift on its goal attainment and its flexibility in meeting its challenges.

Structuring by department (or function) can work against goal attainment: In heavy-maintenance operations, there are usually occupational distinctions between mechanics, planners, inspectors, back-shop personnel. But when those distinctions are carried up to higher levels of management through 'silos' of departmental specialization they can create unanticipated consequences. In one heavy-maintenance hangar the work planners were not only separate from the mechanics, they were led and directed by several levels of planning department managers. The highest planning manager in the station exercised greater authority than either of his counterpart managers of maintenance operations or quality control. This planning-directed structure manifested itself in a planning cubicle on the hangar floor which was off-limits to mechanics and leads, and in which planners would arrange work packages for heavy maintenance with little input from either maintenance or inspection foremen. The planners' first response to 'surprises', or variances, discovered during maintenance (e.g., corrosion in belly skin, or fatigue cracking in a structural member) after initial inspection was completed, was an inflexible adherence to 'plan' without much discussion with operations foremen or lead mechanics. Inevitably, the plan would be changed to accommodate the 'surprise', but time would be lost while operations waited for planning to adapt to the new situation and morale would suffer because mechanics received little information or status updates during the wait. A cure for this inefficiency and distress would be to combine operations and planning under a lower level of management in order to promote collaboration between the two groups during all phases of the work—and especially to be prepared for unanticipated events (variances) that are bound to happen during the work process.

Structuring by combining departments or functions can benefit goal attainment: Senior managers in one regional carrier developed a maintenance structure which was efficient in its use of skilled manpower, more satisfying to those mechanics, and which proved more effective in reducing human error and promoting organizational learning. Management satisfied the aviation regulations for quality control in maintenance through the creation (in the usual way) of a Director of Quality Control (QC), but they also chose to populate their staff of QC inspectors from a multi-skilled mechanic workforce. QC Inspectors were identified from the ranks of the most experienced and senior mechanics. When inspection tasks were required these people immediately became responsible to the QC Department and acted as Inspectors. At all other times they acted as aircraft mechanics and reported to a Maintenance Supervisor. They were mechanics working beside and with other mechanics most of the time, but performed inspection tasks on others' work when it was required. As the most experienced mechanics, the 'inspectors' usually had comprehensive and unique knowledge of the work they were inspecting and were expected to provide some information and training for correcting defects to the people whose work they were inspecting. These mechanic/inspectors were aware of the disruption caused by this dual responsibility and had developed techniques for reducing its effects.

This maintenance department proved effective on a number of criteria. Among these improvements, the skill-level of the organization was raised through this focused application of on-the-job training. Likewise, the level of defects found diminished over time as the skill level increased. More efficient use of skilled labor raised the productivity of the department. Further, the inspector/mechanics experienced a high level of satisfaction from the greater contribution they were making to maintenance excellence, and the entire department displayed good morale that was fostered by the collaborative and cooperative nature of the relationship between inspectors and mechanics (Taylor, 1991).

Structuring overlap between work shifts can benefit goal attainment: The maintenance department in a corporate carrier (operating under 14CFR § 91) structured the work hours of its mechanics so that they began to form a single sociotechnical system over a twenty-hour period. Night shift communicated status of their work to day shift in the usual way—via written log and voice mail. But a one-hour overlap each afternoon, between the day workers and oncoming night mechanics, was also structured into the work schedule. To complement this overlap a structured requirement for a daily face-to-face shift-turnover meeting was also initiated. These turnover meetings were used to review the operational and maintenance status of all aircraft in the hangar, but they were also used to review maintenance problems or issues experienced during the preceding 24 hours. The Concept Alignment Process (as discussed in Chapter 3 under *Fourth Generation MRM Programs*) was applied throughout the workday and the results and success of the decisions made were also 'debriefed' (discussed and evaluated) during the turnover meetings. The novel structure of work hours and meetings, combined with the CAP process, creates an effective sociotechnical work system that promotes active avoidance of human error, improves work-related communication, and heightenes mechanics' trust in management's safety practices. As we learn more about it, this CAP method and its supporting structures seem increasingly like a way to aid 'managing in the void' in aviation maintenance.

Structured communication as a risk-management tool: CAP is a new and proactive method of recognizing and trapping errors before they happen. The basic goal of CAP is to mitigate errors—minimize the effects of past errors, prevent present errors, and increase the body of safety information to stop future errors in the same system. This new process has been studied in field observations and interviews of aircraft mechanics, pilots, and managers in the corporate aviation department described above. Their specific *structure* and a *process* to facilitate team decision-making has been described in more detail in Chapter 3. The aviation department's *structure* in their approach was the required briefings among flight crews, among maintenance technicians (e.g., their shift turnover meetings), and between maintenance and the flight crews. Their *process*, called the Concept Alignment Process (CAP), is a way of ensuring that all parties act on the same concept. CAP provides a way of resolving ambiguous and/or conflicting viewpoints among the communicating parties in various briefings. In maintenance, this technique is used in decision-making on the hangar floor, in briefings between the flight crew and maintenance personnel at the end of each flight, and it is further reported and documented in maintenance shift-turnover briefings. CAP is a simple communication protocol that has been successfully used to identify and manage risks in aviation maintenance. Acknowledging one's uncertainty or lack of knowledge in a new situation requires a level of trust in the process and in one's coworkers and managers. Continued use of the CAP process also helps to reduce and manage conflict that might otherwise impede communication and risk management if mechanics feel they were being personally or individually criticized. Another most significant effect of CAP is that it has the potential to address both the active as well as latent failures described by Reason (1997).

The mission or purpose of this corporate aviation maintenance department is to have safe and attractive aircraft ready for flight when required by the company's employees and executives. Their key variances are the complexity of modern executive aircraft, the diversity of their fleet (aircraft from four manufacturers in three countries), and the ever-changing schedule for arrivals and departures. Their maintenance workforce is a mixture of age and experience levels. All mechanics are FAA-certificated (both A&P ratings), but not all have received manufacturers' type training on all aircraft in their fleet.

In order to adjust to their key variances, or to control them, the mechanics need to cope with many kinds of ambiguity and of uncertainty (need to 'manage in the void')—including, but not limited to, repair manuals translated into English, inspection programs out-of-date to present aircraft configuration, incomplete or unclear 'squawks' from flight crews, unclear or poorly communicated department policies, and discrepancies between flight crew and maintenance 'normal practice' regarding ground operations. All these 'ambiguous' situations, and more, can have safety implications and can also have more than one 'right' answer. The CAP process, duly practiced by the pilots, mechanics, and their managers, permit (and require) people within and between groups to challenge the 'concepts' of the other, to confirm differences between the concepts, to reconcile differences by seeking additional information (e.g., from documents and manuals, manufacturers, management, or from the FAA), and finally, to choose one concept based on its adherence to the highest safety standards. That choice is used to avoid committing an error in the present, and it is also used to modify policy or documentation to prevent future errors of the same type.

MRM, Sociotechnical Systems and Safety Culture

Over time, the definition of safety culture in maintenance has become clearer. At a most general level, it is open communication and self-disclosure. But maintenance safety culture is also more specific than that. MRM provides for some of those specifics. It is an approach to provide individuals and groups with the knowledge, skills, and processes (such as communication, decision-making, situational awareness, workload management, and team-building) to manage errors that are within their control. Part of MRM is training, but part of it must be the application and management of the attitude, skills, and knowledge that only training and behavior change—together—can provide. Further, MRM must include methods and processes to trap many errors before they happen, and to learn from those mistakes that do occur to prevent them in the future. Bound together with wise leadership, these elements form the cultural values of a safe and effective sociotechnical system.

Chapter Summary

In its simplest sense, the sociotechnical systems perspective tends to optimize the changes in technology and those in the society such that the people are able to achieve the most benefit from the technology, toward their collective goal. One of the greatest challenges to safety programs, particularly the human factors programs or the maintenance resource management programs, is to address ways in which a mechanic can manage decisions in the absence of specific instructions—management in the void.

Review Questions

1. List some examples of good applications of sociotechnical principles, include those from outside the aviation industry. Describe how they apply the sociotechnical principles.
2. List some examples of poor or inadequate application of sociotechnical principles, include those from outside the aviation industry. Describe how they could be improved.
3. Describe the concept of 'Management in the void' and explain at least one strategy that you would use in such a void.

Chapter 5

Virtual Airlines and Mutual Trust

Instructional Objectives

Upon completing this chapter, you should be able to:

1. Explain the significance of a virtual organization from a safety perspective.
2. Describe the forces affecting a repair station operation.
3. Explain the similarities/differences of the repair station challenges. discussed in this chapter with your understanding/experience of a virtual airline.
4. Describe the role of interpersonal trust in virtual organizations.

Introduction

By *Virtual Airlines*, we do not mean a virtual reality game. We mean workgroups that are geographically distributed, yet work for a common goal. By this definition, we would include multi-national conglomerates like the Airbus Industrie, or the multi-airline alliances based on code-sharing or a linked frequent flyer program. Therefore, we see virtual airlines as organizations that have the minimum core infrastructure, yet they are able to look and work like a conventional airline. Sometimes, new "low-cost" airlines start as a virtual organization—lease airplanes, outsource maintenance, contract employees, and use electronic ticketing—they do not own any airplanes or hangars, nor do they employ any flight, maintenance, or ground crew. The core management team simply manages the different functional groups of the company as interdependent profit centers. However, as the company builds revenue and market share, its organization tends to resemble a conventional airline—increased number of employees and decreased number of contractors.

Historically, airline personnel have demonstrated a great sense of solidarity and pride in working for their airline. Virtual airlines force the employees to re-examine their allegiance, their responsibility, and their mutual trust. This chapter is aimed at providing the aviation maintenance personnel with certain known aspects of virtual organizations from aerospace as well as other industries. Also, a common thread that emerges in the literature regarding virtual organizations is that of trust. Hence, this chapter presents an analysis of the current level of trust among maintenance personnel.

Virtual Organizations

What is a virtual organization and why is it 'virtual' as opposed to 'real'? Well, there are several definitions and characterizations of 'virtual organizations'. Consider the following quotes:

> A temporary network of independent companies linked by IT [Information Technology] to share skills, costs, and access to one another's markets (Business Week, cited by Skyrme, 2001).

> An organization distributed geographically and whose work is coordinated through electronic communications (Skyrme, 2001).

> Virtual teams and networks—effective, value-based, swiftly reconfiguring, high-performing, cost-sensitive, and decentralized —will profoundly reshape our shared world. As members of many virtual groups, we will all contribute to these ephemeral webs of relationships that together weave our future (Lipnack & Stamps, 2000).

Skyrme's (2001) two definitions suggest an underlying theme of a workgroup linked by a common purpose or goal, rather than a common building, and computer-based communication network, rather than face-to-face meetings. Lipnak and Stamps' characterization suggests that virtual teams are high-functioning and very efficient. But Lipnack and Stamps also acknowledge that virtual teams have a high failure rate.

What seems to separate virtual from real is that virtual is asynchronous in time and space; whereas, real is synchronous in time and space. That is to say, if a task gets done by people who work on it during the same time interval (could be an hour or a shift) and in the same place (either an office or a hangar), then, it is 'real'. On the other hand, if they work in different time intervals and in different places, it is 'virtual'. A virtual organization is much more fluid in terms of its labor force. Thereby, it is able to re-shape itself to meet the dynamic demands of the industry.

Let us take a moment to imagine what life would be like for an aircraft mechanic in the virtual world...

> The mechanic would be known for his/her knowledge and skills, and would be able to bid for work online. Managers would post the tasks that need to be done, the skill-set required and the compensation available. The mechanic would bid for the job based on his/her knowledge and skills. He/she would be responsible for his/her own training, days off, vacation planning, etc. He/she would be a free agent! The job security would be in the acquired knowledge and skills. As long as the individual has the knowledge and skills that are required, he/she will have a job. Hopefully, compensation will be based on the quality of the job: greater the skill-level, better the pay. Tremendous emphasis will be placed on self-responsibility, mutual trust, and competency-based selection.

How is the above scenario different from the "real organization" today? In the real organization, the job security is based on seniority and the workflow is managed by the supervisors. The interpersonal trust is developed within small teams over a long period of time, but not between the management and the workforce. Competency-based selection is subtle because we find that the supervisors know who the "performers" are and they distribute the jobs accordingly. In certain cases, we also know that supervisors abuse this knowledge in the interest of meeting the schedule and give the job to the person who is going to put speed before safety and release an airplane with questionable airworthiness. In such an environment, training is an organizational responsibility.

Virtuality in the Airline Business

The concept of virtual worlds and virtual teams is not as foreign to the airline business as it might sound. If we examine the characteristics of a virtual organization, we will discover that they have been creeping into the aviation industry gradually over the past few decades. For example, we now use video conferencing technology to communicate with original equipment manufacturers (OEMs) regarding maintenance issues on the floor, an entire airplane can be designed and built without a single paper drawing or a mock-up, airlines are both contracting-out as well as contracting-in maintenance activities, etc.

Multi-party Collaboration

Whether it is due to military base closures, airline mergers/acquisitions, or the emergence of startup airlines, the fact is that the amount of maintenance performed by FAA certificated repair stations for airlines increased during 1995-1996 and was projected to be on the rise for the following five years (Seidenman & Spanovich, 1995; 1996). Also, the competition in this market is such that many airlines look for the best cost-to-reliability ratio while selecting a particular vendor. Therefore, it is quite likely that the vendor for a particular maintenance action may be different every few years, depending on the existing competition. The 1997 annual report of the *Aviation System Indicators* by the FAA provides an excellent snap-shot of the dynamics in the outsourcing market. In the first quarter of 1997, there were fifty-four new 14CFR § 145 certificate holders (repair stations) compared to the previous quarter and in the very next quarter, fifty-four certificate holders lost their certificates. This could be a coincidence but in fact, the overall number of § 145 certificate holders by the end of 1997 was thirty-eight less than the previous year. It is probable that some repair stations have either been acquired by the larger, more established ones, or they have simply been forced out of the business.

In mid 1996, the industry trend seemed to indicate that outsourcing fell into three primary categories 'passenger to cargo conversions, fleet standardization, and life extension' (Seidenman & Spanovich, 1996). To deal with these fluctuating market conditions, many repair stations used contract labor so that they did not have to enter into any long-term commitments with new employees. Such an approach may be successful in keeping the company resilient enough to change its workforce and its skills to adapt to the existing market trends, but it does not help build an organizational safety culture. If there is no stable workforce, most likely, there is not going to be a stable organizational safety culture. As Pidgeon and O'Leary (1995,49) state, 'culture refers primarily to *shared* characteristics of a social group, organization or society'. They further define safety culture as a set of 'beliefs, norms, attitudes, roles, and social and technical practices within an organization which are concerned with minimizing the exposure of individuals, both within and outside an organization, to conditions considered to be dangerous'. Without a consistent workforce, it will be extremely difficult to develop a lasting organizational safety culture.

Fluctuating labor force represents a radical change because it is not just a change in the people, but also a change in the skill-set. Hayward (1995) presented a preferred organizational model for the development of safety culture as the one which promotes 'incremental change' rather than 'radical change'. But the aviation industry has a unique opportunity to be both resilient and adaptive: it can embrace the "genius of AND" and reject the 'tyranny of OR' (cf. Collins & Porras, 1997) by making an incremental *and* radical change in the aviation safety culture.

The following section uses the familiar lift-drag-weight-thrust (LDWT) model to present the "forces" affecting repair station operations. Particular emphasis is placed on the *thrust* force to illustrate how human factors knowledge could be used in maintenance and management *practices* to effect an incremental *and* radical change in the aviation safety culture.

The reasons for outsourcing: Outsourcing, third-party maintenance, multi-party maintenance, and subcontracting essentially represent the same organizational concept. Until the past couple of decades, most of the maintenance work was performed within the airline; however, several challenges of the prevailing market conditions have driven many airlines to out-source some of its maintenance (Seidenman & Spanovich, 1996). The reasons for outsourcing, from the perspective of the airlines, have been either one or more of the following: lower maintenance cost, greater technical expertise, better geographical location, or higher dispatch reliability (Seidenman & Spanovich, 1995; 1996).

But what is the purpose of the repair stations that perform the contract work? Whether the actual work performed is specialty work no longer not economical to an airline or routine heavy maintenance which may be beyond the technical capability of a startup airline, the fundamental purpose of the repair stations seems to be to efficiently facilitate aircraft maintenance, an operational necessity.

The 'Forces' affecting repair station operation: As illustrated in Figure 5-1, an introductory course in aerodynamics presents the fundamental forces acting on an aircraft as lift, drag, weight, and thrust.

This model is intimately familiar to all aircraft mechanics and pilots. If it is applied to the repair station operations, it could be said that *Lift* equates to increased professionalism among the technical personnel, better safety record for the organization, and improved business opportunities for the organization; *Drag* equates to increased number of different types of maintenance packages that the organization must provide to its customers, perhaps because of the increased *Lift*; *Weight* equates to the merger mania and rapid growth which may result in lack of attention to the culture change within organizations and differences in communication process among the constituent groups; and *Thrust* equates to human factors in maintenance and management *practices.*

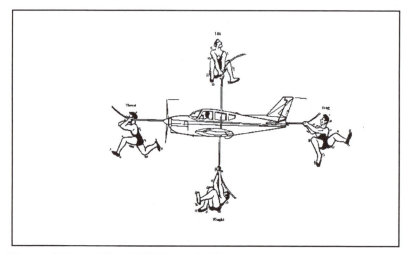

Figure 5-1:   The LDWT model for repair station operations
Source: FAA AC 65-12A

Lift: Professionalism, safety and business success: *Lift* is a positive and desired force. It is equated with attributes such as professionalism, safety, and business success. Professionalism is a core value which maintenance organizations and FAA certificated personnel should have. From a more tangible perspective, professionalism represents the manner in which knowledge is applied and the standard to which work is performed.   The knowledge, however, is often limited to technical information about the specific aircraft, system, or part and general information about the acceptable maintenance practices as required to obtain the FAA aircraft mechanic or repairman certificate. With a smaller number of certificated personnel employed by repair stations compared to airlines (Goldsby, 1996), these handful of individuals hold the responsibility to observe safe maintenance practices. It is not a collective responsibility because each individual has the authority to grant his/her own airworthiness approvals. The performance standard includes technical accuracy and the operational safety to which work is actually performed may be a function of personal and organizational safety cultures. If professional people perform in a professional manner consistently, safety will be enhanced.   If they coordinate their efforts with each other, they could be even safer.

Increase in business opportunities is certainly another positive attribute. But as illustrated by Collins and Porras (1997), most visionary companies stress the importance only of a *reasonable* profit. Profit is essential for a business to succeed and progress, but it should not be the sole purpose of the business. From a repair station's perspective, intense competition exists to deliver a service with high reliability-to-cost ratio. Therefore, the repair stations may tend to employ low-cost labor, relocate to a location with lower overhead costs, and may even compromise safety standards while rushing to acquire market share. If professionalism and safety are maintained at the core and business growth is considered as an essential positive attribute, a more successful maintenance organization is likely to prevail.

Drag: Diverse maintenance packages: According to the principles of aerodynamics, as the angle of attack increases, so do the lift and drag forces, and then comes a point where suddenly lift is no longer produced– the airfoil stalls! Same could be said about the forces on repair stations. With aggressive marketing efforts and sales techniques (angle of attack), the business opportunities could be improved (lift could be increased); however, there is also an associated increase in the number of different types of maintenance packages that the organization has to deliver (the drag). Most airlines, when contracting-out certain type of maintenance actions, send their own maintenance personnel to supervise the work performed by the contractor. This supervision is maintained to ensure that the airline's maintenance standards are upheld and that all the paperwork is completed correctly (Chandler, 1996). With increased business, there is a likelihood of increased number of clients, not just more business from the same clients. This presents the potential for diversity in documentation requirements and thereby resulting in an increase in the potential for paperwork errors and communication errors.

To put this potential in context, consider the case of documentation errors in a major U.S. airline (cf. Taylor, 1994). The major airline had recently merged with two other carriers and many of its mechanics had moved around the system from station to station. Consequently, the workforce at line stations consisted of several discrete cultures instead of one homogenous culture. During 1991-1992, the paperwork and documentation errors had increased drastically and so the local FAA Flight Standards District Office, airline management, and the Union (International Association of Machinists and Aerospace Workers) joined forces to develop appropriate training. The training was successful in reducing the paperwork errors. But within a year after the training, the paperwork errors started to rise (though not as high as they were before the training).

The point is that when a systemic or organizational attention is not focused on the differences in documentation practices and procedures among customer organizations, documentation errors are likely to increase.

Weight: *Merger mania*: The term *merger* is used in a broader sense because we are more interested in the migration of the mechanics rather than the corporate umbrella under which they happen to be. We define *merger mania* as a phenomenon associated with a forced change in the values, vision, and communication practices of personnel following their entry into another company. This would happen when two or more organizations merge in a more traditional sense or when one organization goes out of business and its workforce joins another organization in the same industry. In either case, a merger necessitates attention to the cultural change and communication process in order to retain professionalism. Note that repair stations are susceptible to merger mania just as much as airlines. As with aerodynamics, the lift force must be equal to the weight for level flight; so in our analogy, professionalism must be able to effect positive cultural change and appropriate alignment of the communication processes.

Thrust: Human factors in maintenance and management practices: No doubt, it is possible to have lift without a propulsion device, but such a flight will be considered a glide and will not be practical for commercial transportation purposes. From a repair station or a maintenance organization's perspective, the propulsion device would need to be a reliable mechanism that continuously drives the organization forward. Implementation of Human Factors principles in maintenance and management practices is required to provide the *thrust*.

Considering the analogy of 'time tellers' versus 'clock makers' presented by Collins and Porras (1997), *time tellers* would be those leaders in aviation organizations who, through their charismatic leadership style, launch the organization on short, soaring flights of success. Such successes are short-term because they lack the underlying structure of 'visionary companies' which are successful over a very long period of time, under a number of chief executive officers. The systemic management perspective referred to here will provide a propulsion system for the company and generate thrust: it will create *clock makers*.

It will be valuable to take this analogy one step further and connect it with the work done by Westrum (1995). Westrum compared aviation fuel to information and claimed that a free flow of information is just as essential to an aviation organization as fuel to an aircraft. The *propulsion system* presented earlier can hardly work without fuel!

To understand the role of Human Factors education in the creation of a *propulsion system* for our organization, it will first be essential to note the success of past Human Factors training programs. These training programs in maintenance have been successful largely in creating an awareness of the safety implications of maintenance actions; but, as we have discussed in Chapter 3, the applications of Human Factors in enhancing safety have not proved to be as long lasting. Therefore, one could conclude that the recent efforts in effecting safety improvements through training alone are comparable to the glider launches (flights are achieved but are not sustained due to the lack of a propulsion mechanism).

The organizational engine: The organizational engine is comparable to the operating cycle for a gas turbine engine, with information as its fuel. During the intake stage, new ideas are welcome and creative problem-solving is encouraged. Best people are hired and they are given the responsibility and the authority. During the compression stage, adequate training is provided, responsibility is shared and everyone is held accountable. Actions that are inconsistent with the company's core values are not tolerated. During the combustion stage, it is emphasized that power lies in the ownership of the organization. Whether the employees are the stock holders or not is not as important as the feeling of ownership or 'attachment with the organization' (cf. Beaumont, 1995). When the employees take pride in their work and feel a sense of 'belonging to the company', the company's business will automatically grow and the safety record will improve (cf. Bethune & Huler, 1998). During the exhaust stage, out-dated practices and procedures, and bad norms are discarded. Mechanisms such as required briefings and de-briefings have proved to be successful for flight crews (cf. Bovier, 1998; Dismukes, et al., 1997) in proactively identifying and addressing risk factors. Such techniques are also being used in maintenance applications (Taylor, 1994; Taylor & Christensen 1998; Patankar & Taylor, 1999b).

Note that the operational engine above is compared with a gas turbine engine to emphasize that all the four events are taking place simultaneously within the engine. These are not events which simply pop-up at certain times; they are a set of events that are sustained on a continuous basis.

The role of human factors: Human Factors generally refer to the human element in a system. Researchers on the flight side have presented it as Crew Resource Management (CRM), those on the maintenance side have presented it as Maintenance Resource Management (MRM), and from the business perspective, it has been presented as a set of successful business practices. The crux of the matter is that because the human element has been studied from a systemic perspective in the past few decades, considerable evidence is now available to make scientific decisions for the future.

Dynamics of the current repair station business present a unique opportunity for the aviation industry to adopt sound business practices as documented by Collins and Porras (1997) and create a visionary industry. There are a few ideas to be adopted by the MRM practitioners from the CRM practices. For example, the Cockpit Resource Management (CRM) was introduced in the late 1970s (Wiener et al., 1993) and nearly twenty years later the CRM principles have been incorporated in the knowledge requirements for the Airline Transport Pilot Certificate (14CFR § 61.156c) (cf. Maurino, 1996). The European Joint Airworthiness Requirements (JARs) have recognized the need for such requirement in maintenance and proposed that 'maintenance engineers...have a basic grounding in human factors pertinent to their job' (Havard, 1996, 396). Human Factors knowledge is needed at the aircraft mechanic level because this is the core quality control point and also the primary building block of the larger, systemic aircraft maintenance culture. Some mechanic training programs have shown signs of incorporating human factors elements in their curriculum, but these attempts seem to be limited to the level of awareness (cf. Lopp, 1997; Thom, 1997).

Recent attempts in the industry to change the safety culture through human factors training of the mechanics have attained limited success because they represent pleasure flights of a *glider launch* and not a *sustained flight* resulting from a systemic *engine*. Such systemic design takes time and begins early. Appropriate use of Human Factors training in the maintenance curriculum could help build the systemic *engine*.

Responsibility, Blame, and Liability

Aircraft mechanics are responsible for the airworthiness of an aircraft. When a mechanic returns an aircraft to service, he/she is taking responsibility for the technical integrity of that aircraft. The mechanic is so confident about its safety that he/she is willing to fly in that aircraft, he/she is willing to have his/her family fly in that aircraft, and he/she is willing to have hundreds of passengers fly in that aircraft. Such confidence is not based on chance, but it is based on design. The mechanic actually vows, with his signature, that he has followed all the latest approved procedures, used only the approved parts, and that the aircraft meets the airworthiness standards prescribed by the regulator.

Therefore, it is the mechanic's responsibility to do the following: (a) have the requisite knowledge and skills, (b) use the appropriate tools, approved parts, and approved information resources, (c) be a conscientious judge of quality. In a recent case against mechanics in the United States, "the government made it clear that when mechanics become licensed, they are taking on the responsibility for the lives of the flying public and also the risk of criminal prosecution for making a mistake" (Thurber, 1999). Such responsibility and the society's thirst to associate an individual with the extant problem leads to blame and the associated development of blame culture. In order to move away from blame culture without losing sight of professional responsibility, some organizations have committed themselves to the development of a just culture.

Blame culture: Historically, high risk—high consequence industries such as aviation, medicine, and nuclear power have all suffered from blame culture. When a mishap occurs, the general tendency in many national and organizational cultures has been to blame the individual responsible for the last action prior to the mishap. In some countries, as described in Chapter 2, this practice is so prevalent that the licensed AMEs/A&Ps have accepted the blame culture as a professional risk—they get significantly higher wages for holding the license and so they are expected to take the blame if one needs to be assigned.

Just culture: A just culture differentiates between *carte blanche* forgiveness of the guilty party and the blame culture. It is based on the premise that as responsible professionals, aircraft mechanic/engineers are expected to perform to certain basic professional and ethical standards. If they perform within those standards and commit an error, the error is forgivable. On the other hand if the performance is in violation of those standards, the error is classified as 'reckless', hence unforgivable.

Professional liability: In maintenance, professional liability is long-term. The mechanic or the AME is liable for his/her actions until either the aircraft is retired or until the maintenance action is superceded by a subsequent action. Consequently, the emphasis on quality of work and the need to err on the more conservative side of the tolerance should be higher in maintenance.

Building Trust

Trust influences the behavior of aviation maintenance personnel in a variety of ways. First, there is interpersonal trust among peers; then, there is trust between management and workers; and lastly, there is trust between the regulators and the certificate holders. Each of these categories of trust is a function of certain trust-building factors and certain trust-destroying factors. Typically, words such as *trustworthiness, honesty, reliability,* and *integrity* are associated with trust among people; while words such as *lie, misleading, cruel,* and *false* are associated with distrust among people (Jian et al., 2000).

As maintenance professionals, aircraft mechanics and aircraft maintenance engineers are responsible for evaluating the safety of an aircraft. Their primary job is to determine whether a particular aircraft is fit to fly, whether it is airworthy. In order to make this determination, they must rely on approved technical data and used approved parts and techniques while performing repairs. The acceptable standards of repair are established by the regulator. Because this information is documented and is traceable, maintenance personnel often tend to trust the 'written word' more than the spoken words. Unfortunately, many-a-time, the written documentation is ambiguous or erroneous. When mechanics are subjected to ambiguity or errors in documentation, their trust in the documentation is violated.

From the perspective of interpersonal trust, one of the norms in the industry is to have one person do the work and have another person sign for it. This practice is documented through ASRS reports as well as FAA enforcement actions against aircraft mechanics. The fact is that managers have used their power to bring-in another mechanic to sign-off work that a particular mechanic refused to release.

There are several obstacles in building trust in virtual airlines: lack of face-to-face contact, lack of consistency in work standards—different customers, different requirements, and ambiguous accountability.

Whose tail is it? Irrespective of who performed maintenance, especially when the work was performed by a third party, it is the operating organization whose reputation is at stake. The contract maintenance organization can certainly be connected with the organization and is also very likely to suffer in its reputation; however, the operating airline suffers the most immediate effects. So, in terms of trust, many airlines that outsource some or part of their maintenance, often station their own people to ensure that the maintenance work meets their quality standards. When airlines perform maintenance work for other airlines, lack of trust is less of an issue.

The AC 120-66, the next challenge in building trust: In the interest of safety, several attempts have been made to share error data among the operators; however, these efforts have been handicapped by possible abuse of the data. The FAA Advisory Circular 120-66 provides information regarding self-disclosure programs. Such programs can be established at any maintenance organization, in consultation with the local FAA Principal Maintenance Inspector. There are some success stories of such implementation and there are some failures. The failures have occurred because the information provided by the mechanic was used against the individual—the level of immunity was apparently misunderstood. The success stories, however, have occurred when such arrangements were made informally or at the most by a simple memorandum of understanding (MOU) between the management, labor union, and the FSDO. Through such cooperative MOUs, one team has been very successful in identifying systemic issues and solving them without penalizing the person who disclosed the problem. Through repeated and consistent application of this process, the team has been able to build a high level of mutual trust among all the parties.

The Concepts of Professionalism and Trust Among Maintainers

Professionals are characterized as persons with a high degree of (a) competence in their field, (b) control (both in authority and ability) to make decisions based on their competence, (c) commitment to the greater public good, and (d) being central to the operation of the larger enterprise (Taylor & Christensen, 1998, p.83). Two factors, assertiveness and stress management, have emerged as most effective in supporting such professionalism among aircraft mechanics. In previous research, competence, control, commitment, and centrality of the professional are seen to be supported by the ability and willingness to speak up, even in the face of adversity and social pressure (Taylor & Christensen, 1998, pp. 134-135; Patankar & Taylor, 1999b). Likewise the documented willingness of professional aviation mechanics to actively mitigate the effects of stresses and strains on their decision-making abilities supports and enhances their professionalism and their safety performance (Taylor & Christensen, 1998, pp. 135, 157).

Elements of professionalism among maintainers have been reported in terms of responses to the MRM/TOQ surveys (Taylor, 2000). The aviation industry is quite heavily regulated to establish the minimum standards in all aspects of the aircraft operation, with the ultimate goal of providing safety of flight. The maintainers are subject to such regulations because those who hold the FAA Aircraft Mechanic certificate, are individually certificated by the federal government to perform maintenance on aircraft. As such, each *individual* is held accountable for his/her behavior.

Such responsibility and the personal risks of violating rules covered by the professional certificate influence the trust that mechanics hold for their coworkers and their management. For example, maintenance managers who, in the US at least, encourage or advocate faster work can engender a speed-accuracy dilemma for mechanics—a kind of role conflict that causes mechanics to suspect that their management will not make the most safety-conscious decisions. Trust of coworkers is also affected by the individualism engendered by the mechanic's certificate. A protectiveness of one's certificated authority and a respect for a colleague's individual authority leads to little willingness to share work with others (especially between shifts). If one does not share or cooperate much, there is less reason for or need to seriously trust coworkers. Finally, the industry's recent move to encourage mechanics to participate in the investigation of incidents in which they played a part (cf. Marx & Graeber, 1994) depends heavily on mutual trust between mechanics and those managing that investigative process. Such trust is hard to gain when there is already some distrust of management and little impulse to trust one's colleagues.

Analysis of Mutual Trust Among Maintainers

During 1999-2000, 3,150 employees in five aviation organizations completed MRM/TOQ questionnaires. They came from five airline maintenance samples that bracket the range of organizations and job types in the commercial aviation industry. The group includes maintenance departments in major airlines, maintenance departments in small airlines as well as commercial aviation repair stations. Each sample represents a US-based air transport company or a separate sample within an airline company. Participants include mechanics, maintenance managers, and maintenance support personnel. All can be considered naïve subjects in so far as they completed their survey before they were exposed to organizational change programs intended to influence their attitudes or opinions. All surveys were collected in the years 1999 and 2000. A summary of the differences between the five samples is presented below.

Sample A: It is a 10% stratified random sample of the maintenance department of a large passenger airline operating under 14CFR §121. The participation (75% return rate) was quite high for this type of mail survey.

Sample B: It consists entirely of respondents from the maintenance department of a large airline (also operating under 14CFR §121) who volunteered to attend a Human Factors and Safety Training program. Sample B's surveys were administered before the training began. This sample contains a larger number of college-educated and female respondents, and is heavily weighted toward management respondents.

Sample C: Its respondents are maintenance department participants in a mandatory Human Factors and Safety training program in another airline (also operating under 14CFR §121). Sample C's surveys were also administered before the training began. The distribution of job titles is closer to the typical for its proportion of hourly workers in the line and base maintenance operations and its proportion of middle management.

Sample D: These respondents are all maintenance employees in a smaller regional airline (operating under 14CFR §121 and 135).

Sample E: This sample is from a large US-based aircraft repair station (operating under 14CFR §145). Sample E's responses are all from the same survey form but were obtained from two data collection efforts. Over forty percent (42.5%) of dataset E is comprised of a 10% random sample of mechanics who participated in a mail survey. The other 57.5% of the company E dataset is the entire population of maintenance managers in the company. The managers completed the same surveys as the mechanics, but did so immediately prior to receiving Human Factors and Safety training.

Taylor and Thomas (In Press b) conducted factor analysis using these five samples. They reported the presence of two trust factors and two professionalism factors that were consistent across samples. These factors became the basis of four scales. The two trust scales were titled 'Supervisor's Safety Practices are Trustworthy' and the 'Importance of Coworker Trust and Communication'. The two professionalism scales were titled 'Importance of Stress on Decision Making' and 'Importance of Assertiveness'. That study demonstrated a high reliability and validity of these scales across the five samples and their ability of differentiate among different organizations, occupations, gender, and age.

In this chapter, data from the above five samples were used to illustrate the degree of trust mechanics and managers have in their superiors' safety practices, as well as the importance they place on trusting coworkers and communicating with them.

Multivariate Analyses of Variance (MANOVA) were used to test trust scale differences among the five companies, among occupational categories, between gender, and among age categories.

Implications of Individual Professionalism and Mutual Trust

Individual professionalism encompasses all aspects that are more likely to be within an individual's span of control. For example, assertiveness, complacency avoidance, situational awareness, distraction avoidance, etc are matters of individual professionalism. Mutual trust, on the other hand, includes aspects that depend on interpersonal communication, the perceptions of a supervisor's or the company's safety priorities based on past experiences, and also on the camaraderie that may exist among coworkers. Therefore, elements such as poor procedures, lack of training, and management support are considered to be part of mutual trust.

The results of the MRM/TOQ survey obtained in this study are discussed from the context of posterior probability results obtained by Patankar and Taylor (In Press).

MRM/TOQ Results

Survey data from the five samples were analyzed to determine the influence of various indices/scales on individual professionalism and mutual trust. Results for the entire dataset of five samples as well as individual samples are presented here.

Inter-company differences: Significant differences were found for 'supervisor trust & safety', but not for 'value of trusting coworkers'. Figure 5-2 shows mean scores for the two trust scales among the five companies. A statistically significant MANOVA 'F' score was found for the Supervisor Trust and Safety scale ($F=7.69$, $p<.000$). The mean differences among companies for the Value Coworker trust scale were not large and thus the MANOVA result was not significant.

Across the five companies, we find a high of 68% and low of 31% of all respondents say they agree or strongly agree that their supervisor is trustworthy regarding safety issues—stated as the converse, 6% to 26% respondents either say they disagree or strongly disagree with this (see Figure 5-3).

Occupational Differences: In general there is a perceived difference between mechanics and managers in their interpretation of safety. As a probable consequence, mechanics tend not to trust their managers as much as one might want in this high-risk industry.

Figure 5-4 shows the mean scores among occupations for all five companies combined for the scale 'Supervisor's Safety Practices are Trustworthy'. The MANOVA 'F' score of 8.55 is significant $p<.00$).

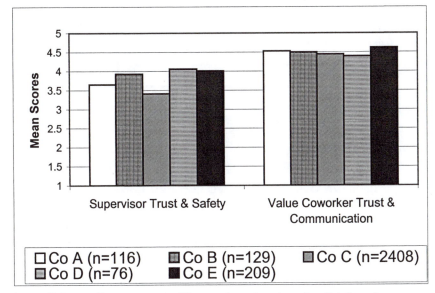

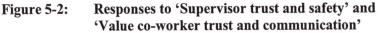

Figure 5-2: **Responses to 'Supervisor trust and safety' and 'Value co-worker trust and communication'**

Figure 5-5 shows that across the five companies, a high of 63% and low of 24% mechanics say they agree or strongly agree that their supervisor is trustworthy regarding safety issues—stated as the converse, 7% to 31% mechanics say they disagree or strongly disagree with this.

Figure 5-6 displays means among occupations for the scale 'Importance of Co-worker Trust and Communication'. Substantially more respondents from all companies 'value open, trustworthy communication with coworkers', but managers are still higher than mechanics. The 'F' score for these results is 3.25, p<.00.

Professionalism

The Taylor and Thomas study (In Press b) found two other scales dealing with professional issues: 'Importance of Stress on Decision Making' and Importance of Assertiveness'. Like the two trust scales, these professionalism scales revealed a high reliability and validity across the five samples and showed an ability to differentiate among different organizations, occupations, gender, and age.

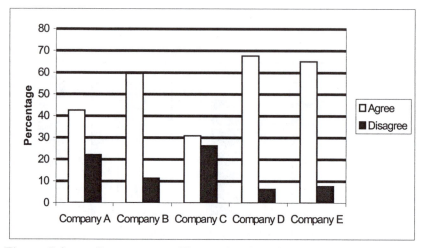

Figure 5-3:   **Responses to 'Supervisor's safety practices are trustworthy', across five companies**

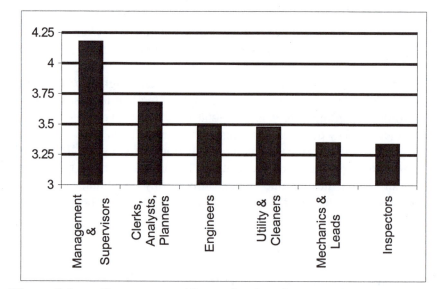

Figure 5-4:   **Responses to 'Supervisor's safety practices are trustworthy', across six job categories**

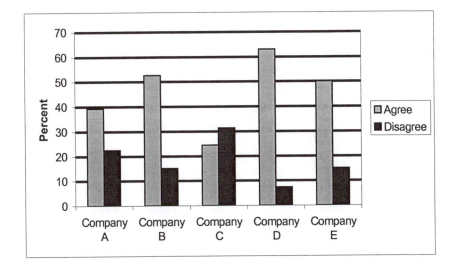

Figure 5-5: **Responses to 'Supervisor's safety practices are trustworthy' by mechanics, inspectors and leads only**

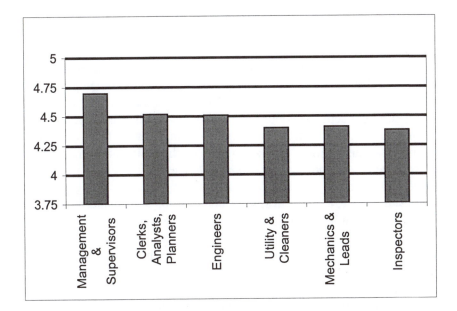

Figure 5-6: **Responses to 'Importance of co-worker trust and communication'**

Significant differences among companies and among occupations were found for 'stress management', but not for 'value assertiveness'. Significant differences for 'value assertiveness' were found both for respondent gender (greater for men) and age (increasing from 20 to 45 years, and decreasing thereafter). A significant and linear relationship was found between 'stress management' and age, where this appreciation increased from the youngest to the oldest category. Historically these two professionalism scales have shown sensitivity to MRM training—they both increase after training (Taylor & Patankar, 2001).

The scale 'Supervisor trust and safety' incorporates a trust of one's supervisor in regard to ethical behavior and safety practices involving their superior-subordinate relationship. Agreement with the five items identifying this factor implies a favorable opinion toward a superior's trustworthiness in support of safety. The scale 'Value coworker trust & communication' expresses a high value for trusting one's co-workers' communication in meetings and discussions. These two scales do support the expectation that aviation maintenance people find interpersonal trust to be a central concept in human factors.

The scale 'Effects of my stress' emphasizes the consideration of stressors at work and the possibility of compensating for them. Though not related to the theme of human communication or interpersonal relations this factor proves to be an important concept for maintenance personnel. The scale 'Value Assertiveness' emphasizes the goal of candor and openness in maintenance and safety-related communication. It is apparent from the present data that valuing assertiveness is independent of trusting others or their trustworthiness. Despite such independence, candor and honesty is also a central concept to maintenance personnel and it is also an important part of many human factors programs. Both stress effects as well as assertiveness scales reflect professionalism of the maintenance occupation. Stress management shows professional awareness by granting importance to conditions that may degrade decision-making. Likewise being willing to speak candidly shows a professional concern for safety and quality that perhaps should not be suppressed by social convention.

A review of the posterior analysis study reported by Patankar and Taylor (In Press) indicates that causal factors such as lack of awareness (13%) and complacency (8.4%) are responsible for unairworthy dispatch of a revenue flight. Both these factors are within an individual's span of control. On the other hand, causal factors such as poor procedures (11%), lack of training (1.3%), and maintenance management (3.5%), which are also responsible for unairworthy dispatches, are outside the individual's span of control. They are organizational issues that may contribute toward reduction of mutual trust. For example, we have noted during our field observations that some companies have established a specific protocol for the communication of safety information; however, the effectiveness of that protocol is unclear. Consequently, continued use of such means is affected because the users do not receive a meaningful feedback. Over a period of time, such degradation of communication channels have led to lack of trust for the management's safety priorities. Similarly, if the mechanic uses out-dated procedures because the incorrect procedures were not updated, that mechanic is likely to not believe that the management values quality and safety. Also, the ASRS data indicate that there have been cases where the management personnel have signed-off work that was not performed. After such instances, the mechanics are not likely to trust the managers. As far as training is concerned, there are many ASRS reports that indicate that mechanics are forced into working on tasks that they are not trained to accomplish. Again, after such instances, the mechanics are not likely to trust their managers or the organization. Therefore, it is not surprising that the MRM/TOQ data indicate that, for some companies, as few as a third (31%) of all maintenance employees trust their superiors—for mechanics alone, that trust sinks to less than a quarter (24%).

Development and sustenance of a safety culture in the aviation maintenance environment depends on individual professionalism and mutual trust. This chapter illustrates that both mechanics as well as managers value open communication and trust their coworkers; however, 7-31% of the mechanics do not think that their supervisors are trustworthy regarding safety issues. Furthermore, a review of the ASRS data and the causal factors for maintenance errors indicates that both individual professionalism issues (21.4%) as well as mutual trust issues (15.5%) contribute toward unairworthy dispatch of a revenue flight.

As more self-disclosure safety processes are introduced into aviation maintenance operations, the importance of interpersonal trust will increase because individuals are being encouraged to be assertive. Continued use of the MRM/TOQ to explore linkages to safety performance should benefit from the use of the two new trust measures presented in this chapter. Also, continued analysis of ASRS data will help stabilize the posterior probabilities of causes of maintenance errors.

Chapter Summary

In this chapter, we reviewed some of the characteristics of a virtual organization and how those would apply to the aviation industry. One key issue that emerged in this discussion was that of mutual trust. Already, in traditional airlines, we see that about a third of the mechanics do not trust that their managers will make decisions in the interest of safety. As or if we move toward a more virtual organization, the need for mutual trust will be heightened. Also, mechanisms to build trust, question unconventional decisions, and build reliable decision-making strategies will be required.

Review Questions

1. Based on your experience, discuss the concepts of *virtual organization* and *mutual trust*.
2. Discuss the impacts of outsourcing and in-house third-party maintenance, from the perspectives of mutual trust and safety.

Chapter 6

Professional Habits for Aviation Maintenance Professionals

Instructional Objectives

Upon completion of this chapter, you should be able to:

1. Identify elements of professionalism in the aviation maintenance environment.
2. Describe the role of professional behavior in influencing the safety culture within a maintenance organization.

Introduction

In the United States, an aircraft mechanic has been perceived as a semi-skilled individual, sometimes even less skilled than maintenance professionals in other industries such as automotive and computer technology. Somehow, people outside the aviation industry tend to view an aircraft mechanic as a person who is dirty, lacks social skills, and is uneducated. Perhaps, the most discouraging part of this unwarranted image is that being unkempt is equated with being risky and unsafe. Obviously, the certificated aircraft mechanics are furious about such an image and are trying very hard to change it. They are trying to educate not only the general public, but also the new mechanics joining their profession.

This chapter presents the core concept of this text: risk, in the maintenance environment, can be managed through consistent practice of professionalism. The elements of professionalism in the maintenance environment are further defined and explored to discuss the implications of specific actions as well as inactions.

Types of Risks Taken by Aviation Maintenance Professionals

In this section, we present our classification of four different levels of risks taken by aviation maintenance professionals. This classification is based on our review of 939 mechanic reports received by the Aviation Safety Reporting System (ASRS), thirty regulatory violation cases, and ten fatal accident cases.

Level 1: Good Samaritan Risk

In order to ensure continued airworthiness of an aircraft, several maintenance actions such as repair, overhaul, process treatment, inspection, etc. are introduced in the maintenance process. Every time one of these actions is executed, the aircraft may need a certain level of disassembly. Every such disassembly, or intrusion, carries the basic risk of incorrect re-assembly. For the most part, maintenance professionals are very good about exercising due diligence in ensuring that the re-assembly is correct; however, once in a while a person gets distracted during a seemingly routine and simple task, consequently forgetting to perform a vital task such as securing the inspection panel, cowling, or the oil cap. Consider the following ASRS report which illustrates this point.

We call such risk 'Good Samaritan Risk' because this is an inherent risk, present in every maintenance action. Of course, the person performing maintenance may not realize that the very reason that a maintenance action is being performed increases the likelihood of error.

Level 2: Normalized Risk

When a maintenance task is envisioned by the technical writer or by the design engineer, it is impossible to consider all possible permutations of operating conditions under which that task is likely to be performed. In order to accommodate for the differences between the manufacturer's vision of operating conditions and the actual conditions that are more likely to exist in a particular airline, the airline customizes the maintenance instructions. When the maintenance professionals are actually faced with the maintenance instructions under actual working conditions, the true validity and usability of those instructions is tested. Sometimes, the steps in a maintenance process may be so far out of sequence that it would be impossible to carry them out in the recommended sequence. Consequently, they are carried out in a sequence that is practical and presumed to be reasonably safe. Every time a person deviates from the prescribed course of action and no adverse event occurs, there is a subtle reinforcement that perhaps the deviation was okay. Diane Vaughan (1996) calls such phenomenon 'normalization of deviance'. We would like to extend that concept further by saying that normalization of deviance leads to normalization of risk or increase in norm-based risk. The following ASRS report gives an example of a systemic problem wherein it is normal to inspect the blade dampers at a time in the installation process when it is impossible to detect whether they are correctly installed. Normally, the inspector may be assuming that the mechanic has installed them correctly— every time such installation is correct, the inspector's risk and the mechanic's risk are normalized!

Box 6-1: ASRS report number 425875 (unabridged copy of a public document)

Flight ABC left YYY to XXX on Jan/XX/99. While enroute to XXX, the flight engineer on B727 noticed #1 engine oil quantity to go from 3 gallons to 1 gallon. The captain pulled #1 engine throttle to idle and continued to XXX. Logbook write-up was as follows: '#1 engine oil quantity decreased from 3 gallons to 1 gallon and stabilized. Oil temperature and pressure remained normal'. Corrective action was as follows: 'Found oil cap off the oil tank, put in 12 quarts of oil'. The B727 ship #XYZ had a scheduled service check the night before on Jan/XZ/99.
At XA03, the B727 arrived at YYY. Myself and two other maintenance technicians were assigned to work on the aircraft. I did the engine items for the #1 engine which were replace engine oil filter, hydraulic filter, service CSD wet spline, service engine oil to full, check chip detector. After all those above items had been accomplished, I had the other technician run #1 engine for leak check. No leaks were found. I closed the engine cowling and decided I should check the oil quantity one more time. I opened the oil access door removed oil cap and put in 2 quarts of oil. I remember putting the oil tank cap back on. When the other technician yelled something to me from the ground about he was going to start on the double brake change and that he was only able to find one brake. I turned my attention to him and called the lead technician on the radio to inform him of the situation. After that, I looked back at the engine and closed the oil service door. I don't recall if I secured the oil cap lock lever. I then lowered the lift truck down and went to help the other technician with the double brake change. With so many things going on, at one time it's not hard to get distracted.

Box 6-2:   ASRS report number 421402 (unabridged copy of public document)

Aircraft XYZ. I worked on a job/job card to install fan blades on #2 engine of this aircraft XYZ. My part of the job was to check that the fan blade dampers, spacers, retainers, and blades were installed correctly. I also installed the rear and front spinner cone. On Nov/XA/98, this aircraft developed an engine vibration. The blades were removed and upon removal found all 38 aircraft XYZ blade dampers incorrectly installed. My signoff on the job only permitted me to see the front of the blades and dampers as they were all installed with retainers and spacers. I believe to the best of my knowledge that the dampers were installed per the job card in question.

Callback conversation [conversation between the reporter and one of the ASRS representatives] with the reporter revealed the following information: the reporter states that the engine fan retention installation was checked by the reporter after the installation was accomplished by another mechanic. The reporter said the check is made looking at the face of the fan disk and only look at the end of the parts which would not reveal any incorrect damper installation. The reporter stated the job card to install the dampers has no drawings or visual aids to prevent the incorrect installation but the maintenance manual has clear instructions and good visual aids. The maintenance manual was not used in this case.

Level 3: Stymie Risk

The word 'stymie' is a golf term describing a situation wherein one player's ball obstructs another player's stroke. We are using this term to describe situations wherein a mechanic needs to remove a part or disable a system in order to gain access to his/her specific task. Every time a person "disturbs" the original installation or configuration of the *interfering* part, that person takes the risk of not returning *that interfering part* to its original configuration. As illustrated by the following ASRS report, such risks are more likely in line maintenance environment, especially with instruments and avionics issues.

Level 4: Blatant Risk

Blatant risks are clearly under the individual's span of control and include the following issues: performing maintenance without proper training, poor tool control, sign-off of work not performed, and use of old parts as reference to obtain replacement parts. Accidents have occurred due to all three of the above issues. The issue of using old parts as reference to obtain replacement parts, however, is of more serious concern because it is such a prevalent practice—it is an extreme case of normalized risk. The following ASRS report is an example of how easy it is to encounter blatant risk.

Box 6-3:   ASRS report number 394560 (unabridged copy of public document)

At approximately XA30 Feb/XA/98, I was assigned aircraft YYY (a commercial passenger B737-300 turbojet) turning over from prior shift maintenance. The pilot write-up was that they were getting an 'ATT' flag in the captain's Altitude Director Indicator (ADI) during climbout. The prior shift A&P mechanic replaced the left Inertial Reference Unit but did not fix the problem. On my shift, I troubleshot the problem to the Left Digital Analog Adapter (DAA) unit, but our station did not have one in stock. I swapped the right DAA unit with the left DAA to verify that the left DAA was in fact faulty. It was. While swapping the left DAA unit with the right DAA unit I accidentally must have disconnected the flex line to the air data computer. Before I closed the electrical bay door, I looked around the areas that I was working and everything appeared to be in place. I was done with my shift at XI00. At approximately XJ40, aircraft YYY was on takeoff roll, the captain noticed he had no airspeed indication and aborted takeoff and returned to gate. The mechanics on the day shift fixed the problem and the aircraft departed with no further incident.

Defining Professionalism

When people receive their mechanic certificate or their maintenance engineer's license, they become part of a unique profession. They receive certain very important privileges and carry a tremendous amount of responsibility. Their privilege is that they are authorized by their country's regulatory agency to return an aircraft to service and their responsibility is that they are expected to uphold the legal expectations of safety. In this sense, they become the marshals of airworthiness of an aircraft. As professionals, they are expected to have the adequate level of technical knowledge and the ability to apply that knowledge to be the marshals of airworthiness.

Box 6-4:   ASRS report number 403262 (unabridged copy of public document)

I work line maintenance for an air carrier. On May/XA/98, I was told that aircraft XYZ had caution light panel problems. Maintenance control gave me a class control number for a new caution panel in parts room I was told to got to the gate at XX35 and remove and replace it. The aircraft had a down time of only 20 minutes, so I had to work fast. When the plane arrived, I looked at the logbook and there was no open write-up, so I made the write-up that the caution panel needed to be replaced. Once I installed the new caution panel, I started to remove the old caution panel modules one by one and install them on the new panel. When I got to module #9, I noticed the pins that hold it in place were broke. So instead of ignoring the problem like the mechanics before me by duct taping it in, I looked at the part number on it and called maintenance control to order me a new module. When I received the new part, I looked at the rotatable tag to make sure that part numbers matched, installed the module on the caution panel and made sure the lights worked. I finished the job, signed off the jobs: (1) installing the panel and (2) installing the module. On May/XB/98, it was brought to my attention by quality control that I installed the wrong module. The one I installed had a blank filter, but should have had a caution light for the #2 hydraulic isolation valve. I found the old part and rotatable tag and showed them to my chief inspector. The part I removed had the pre-mod part number, but should have had the post-mod number. I felt I did my job correctly. On the line, you don't have time to go to the shop and look up part numbers. I relied on the part number that came off the old caution light module, and it fit correctly. If I had any reason that I was doing something wrong, I would have stopped what I was doing. The company has to disclose to the FAA the situation.

Once employed to exercise the privileges of their authority, these maintenance professionals are subjected to various influences of organizational as well as national cultures (as described in Chapter 2), which in turn, tend to affect the practice of their responsibility. For example, they learn about the organizational norms (sometimes, bad norms such as using belt-loaders as stands while working on aircraft or pushing back an aircraft without the use of wing-walkers). Thus, throughout their career in aviation maintenance, the mechanics receive cultural training as well as technical training. The technical training is through formal classroom and on-the-job training sessions wherein they learn how to perform certain maintenance action. The cultural training is much more subtle and it tends to take place by the virtue of being immersed in the environment—new professionals observe what their peers do and do not do; they observe what the management's expectations are regarding technical as well as safety issues; and they observe the effects of non-compliance with management's expectations. Overall, through such immersion in the maintenance environment, they acquire technical as well as cultural knowledge that enables them to better align themselves with their peers. In this sense, we are saying that the type of professionalism developed by an individual is highly dependent on the organizational and national cultures surrounding that individual.

Now, the question is, 'Does an organization shape an individual or does an individual shape an organization?'. We would answer this question as, 'It depends!' We believe that each individual should have a certain threshold of professionalism. It is that individual's responsibility to raise the individual professionalism of his/her subordinates—in this sense, the individual is shaping the organization by shaping the people within his/her span of control. If the organization's expectations are higher than the individual's threshold, the individual should improve his/her practices to meet the organization's expectations. The organization, on the other hand, should have (a) structured on-the-job training to help the individuals improve themselves and (b) a periodic evaluation system to assess the individual's performance. If the organization's expectations are lower than the individual's threshold, the individual has three choices: acquiesce to the organization's expectations, seek proper channels to improve the organization, or leave the organization.

We define professionalism as follows: Professionalism is the ability to refuse to take Blatant Risks and persistence to minimize Stymie Risk, Normalized Risk, and Good Samaritan Risk. Therefore, professionalism is a work in progress, a journey not a destination!

Elements of Professionalism

We present six elements of professionalism that are specifically applicable to the aviation maintenance environment. We also explain the implications and rationale behind these six elements. These six elements can be remembered using the acronym CAPWIT: Communication, Assertiveness, Preparation, Work Management, Integrity, and Teamwork.

Communication: Practice closed-loop communication with your team-members as well as family members. The more you practice this technique, the less misunderstandings you or your teammate are likely to have.

Remember, each communication is successful when both the transmitter and the receiver have the same understanding of the message. Therefore, there must be some means of informing the transmitter exactly what the receiver has understood—there must be a feedback loop.

Communication problems are not limited to face-to-face communication. For maintenance personnel, one of the most significant communication problems is that of shift-turnover, including written and secondhand verbal turnovers. Although some companies have acknowledged this problem, their efforts in minimizing such communication problems have been limited. For example, one company has a limited space in its parking facility. It will be impractical for that company to require face-to-face turnovers between mechanics as well as supervisors because these two groups from both shifts will have to be present at the same time—the parking facility cannot accommodate two shifts!

We already know from Chapter 2 that maintenance professionals are more individualistic than pilots. Therefore, it is going to be quite challenging for them to implement this element of professionalism. Special training and feedback may be necessary to effect long-term changes in the communication practices among maintenance professionals.

Assertiveness: Speak-up when you do not know how to do a particular job, you think that one of your team-members is doing it incorrectly, or when you discover your own or systemic errors. Assertiveness includes filling out an ASRS form and reporting the problem to NASA.

Assertiveness involves verbal alerting of a discrepancy as well as constructive analysis of one's own judgment. In essence, we are talking about assertiveness toward others as well as assertiveness toward oneself. When the inner voice tries to raise concerns, it is time to consider that concern—that is assertiveness toward oneself.

Assertiveness is not only 'speaking-up', but also attending to others when they are speaking-up.

Typically, inspectors and AMEs are very good at speaking-up because their professional responsibility is to identify discrepancies. Mechanics tend to not speak-up because they either do not know that they have committed an error or they are afraid of the consequences of disclosing their error (Remember the trust issues discussed in Chapter 5?).

Preparation: Your education is a lifelong process that is facilitated everyday. Learn from experienced peers as well as technical literature. Be prepared, with knowledge, skills, and tools to perform your job.

Legally, a mechanic is not supposed to accept a job that he/she has no experience or training in. Unfortunately, mechanics are placed in compromising situations where if they refuse the work, they may be terminated for insubordination or incompetence.

Consider the following classic systemic problem: Due to decreased training budget, several companies have had to reduce classroom/laboratory instruction and depend heavily on on-the-job training. Some such companies have a bimodal distribution of their mechanics—many junior mechanics, few mid-level mechanics, and many senior mechanics. Since the shift bids are handled according to seniority, most of the senior mechanics are on the day shift and most of the junior mechanics are on the night shift. Now, a majority of heavy maintenance work is accomplished by the night shift—a team of inexperienced mechanics working against their circadian rhythm. The company may think that the reduced classroom training is being compensated by increased on-the-job training, but seniority-based shift system does not encourage the senior and junior mechanics to meet! In some instances, management and labor organizations may have been able to provide appropriate connections of mechanics across shifts so that the junior mechanics benefit from their seniors' experience, but such efforts are limited to specific individuals or specific locations.

Innovative means need to be developed such that interpersonal communication flows across organizational silos and systemic factors that inhibit the development of a safer culture are addressed regularly.

Work Management: Recognize that complicated jobs, lack of time, self-imposed stress, and lack of technical/human resources are all factors that multiply the probability of committing an error. Awareness regarding these factors and application of proper work management techniques will assist you in performing your work safely and accurately.

Good work management depends on good communication and preparation, with situational awareness being the prerequisite. Mechanics take pride in being able to 'figure it out'—it is a part of the learning process.

The reality in aviation maintenance is that we almost always have to work with inadequate human and technical resources—we are doing more with less. Every time we embark on a task with limited resources, we increase the risk of failure. Now, if we are addressing complex tasks or working under additional time constraints or battling against environmental limitations the cumulative risk increases exponentially.

Basically, the work management element of professionalism addresses the ability of the individual mechanic or AME to recognize the risks associated with every task and incorporate appropriate mitigation techniques. For example, we now know that every maintenance task carries the *Good Samaritan* risk. How do you actually minimize it? Remember the Hawkins-Ashby model from Chapter 1? We suggest that before embarking on a maintenance task, you evaluate the situation according to the Hawkins-Ashby model, determine which SHELL component(s) is outside the system and then decide which other SHELL component(s) needs to change and to what extent.

Integrity: Do not sign-off any work that you have not actually performed and document all your work. Do not perform any work for which you either do not have the knowledge or the experience. If you are in a supervisory capacity, do not persuade your subordinates to perform or approve work for which they are not adequately qualified.

Remember our discussion about *defining moments* from Chapter 2? As a supervisor, you have the long-term responsibility of influencing a mechanic's character—you are the role model. Everything that you do, or do not do, will be observed by your subordinates. So, think about the long-term implications of your actions or inactions. Think about the phenomenal opportunity you have! Similarly, every mechanic has to face his/her own defining moments. Each time he/she is placed in a situation of undue risk, how does he/she manage that risk? Again, everything that he/she does, or does not do, is observed by his/her peers. Each defining moment shapes the individual as well as his/her image among his/her peers.

It seems like the technical writers expect mechanics to follow their procedures verbatim and sign-off each step as it is completed. In reality, the operating environment, the equipment configuration, and personal work habits make it very difficult to meet these expectations, especially signing-off items as they are accomplished. Consequently, mechanics tend to sign-off all the items on their task card in one sitting, after the work has been completed. Also, when bad work habits get positive reinforcement or do not get negative reinforcement, they result in normalization of deviance (cf. Vaughan, 1996). Therefore, after some time people tend to think that it is okay to sign-off all the items on their task cards in one sitting; it is okay to not tag circuit breakers that are pulled prior to a borescope inspection; it is okay to work around certain steps in the maintenance manual; etc.

Teamwork: Two minds are better than one, but both need to be active. As a team-member, your responsibility is to explicitly understand your role in the team, alert your team if there are any reasons to expect diminished performance, and execute your role to the best of your abilities, always bearing the team's success in mind.

In maintenance, the concept of team may be somewhat vague and fluid compared to the concept of team in the cockpit. In a cockpit, it is clear that the team includes the flight deck and the cabin crew; also, it is clear that the responsibility is for the duration of the flight. In maintenance, a job can continue across multiple shifts and within each shift, there may be a wide variety of people involved. Also, the effect of a maintenance error may not manifest itself for years after the task has been performed. Additionally, we have discussed in Chapter 2 that mechanics are more individualistic than pilots. Therefore, it is harder to practice teamwork in maintenance than it is in a cockpit.

Teamwork involves communication and collaboration among individuals toward a common goal, typically greater than what one is capable of accomplishing by oneself. Therefore, goal-sharing becomes an essential prerequisite to effective teamwork. If nobody knows what the collective goals are, or if the goals of the different professional groups conflict with each other, effective teamwork is impossible.

Perspectives on Professionalism Within the Maintenance Community

According to Mr. Allen Booher, FAA Airworthiness Inspector, aircraft mechanics are not recognized as professionals because "not enough of us have a professional attitude" (Source: http://www.amfanow.org/just_Mechanics.htm). He lists the following characteristics that would help us improve our professionalism:

a. A true aviation professional loves his/her work: This is his or her chosen profession. He or she wants to be the best that they can be Aviation professionals are always seeking to learn and grow in their chosen profession. They have an insatiable curiosity about everything related to their chosen field of endeavor.

b. An aviation professional takes the same amount of pride in a tire change as a turbine engine overhaul. To an aviation professional, there are no minor jobs. Each task deserves and gets the same effort and attention to detail. An aviation professional seeks, performs and maintains a high-quality standard in everything they do.

c. An aviation professional dresses the part. He or she is clean in appearance, exudes confidence, and speaks from knowledge. An aviation professional would never use language which is offensive, regardless of the place or situation. For these reasons, professionals are sought out by their customers, colleagues, and associates.

Mr. Mike Bland, Northwest Airlines, has a more practical perspective on professionalism. According to him, a professional is not "some stoic and cold individual" who never gets dirty. He sees professionalism as "responsibility to those who fly on the aircraft I fix: I do not lie, I do not hide, I have pride in my work, and even though I don't love to work on a clogged lav dump tube, I do it knowing that it is necessary" (Source: http://www.amfanow.org/just_Mechanics.htm).

The Pacific Aircraft Maintenance Engineers Association has formalized its beliefs regarding professionalism in the form of the following statement of creed. It is the only known code of conduct/ethics developed by maintainers. The six elements of professionalism discussed earlier in this chapter are articulated very well in this creed.

Box 6-5:   Aircraft Maintenance Engineers Creed

I swear that I shall hold in sacred trust the rights and privileges conferred upon me as a licensed Aircraft Maintenance Engineer, knowing full well that the safety of others is dependent upon my skills and judgment, I shall never knowingly subject others to risk which I would not be willing to assume for myself, or for those dear to me.

In DISCHARGING this trust, I pledge myself never to undertake work or approve work which I feel to be beyond the limits of my knowledge, nor shall I allow any non-certificated supervisor to persuade me to approve aircraft or equipment as airworthy against my better judgment, nor shall I permit my judgment to be influenced by money or other personal gain, nor shall I pass as airworthy aircraft or equipment about which I am in doubt, either as a result of direct inspection or uncertainty regarding the ability of others who have worked on it to accomplish their work satisfactorily.

I REALIZE the grave responsibility which is mine as a licensed Aircraft Maintenance Engineer, to exercise my judgment on the airworthiness of aircraft and equipment. I therefore, pledge unyielding adherence to these precepts for the advancement of aviation and of the dignity of my vocation.
(Source: http://www.pamea.com/about/creed.html, 2002)

How Do I Practice Professionalism?

In this section, we present two scorecards: one to be used before performing a task and the other to be used after performing that task. This concept of using scorecards was based on a set of before- and after-task personal minimums checklists developed by the FAA (for details, visit http://www.faa.gov/fsdo/awsp/p_min.html).

On a scale of 1-5 rate the following statements. After you have rated all the statements, calculate the average rating by adding the individual ratings and dividing the sum by 5. Enter this average score as your Pre-task Score. 1=Strongly Disagree, 2=Disagree, 3=Neutral, 4=Agree, 5=Strongly Agree.	Write your score (between 1 and 5) for each item.
I am *prepared* to do this task because I have the adequate knowledge, technical data, and tools/equipment to perform this task.	
I am mentally *prepared* to do this task (my stress, distractions, and time pressures are at a safe level).	
I am physically *prepared* to do this task (any physical discomforts such as aches and pains, fatigue, etc. are at a safe level).	
I have taken proper precautions to handle the *work-management* issues associated with this job: exercise tool control, make sure all the panels and access doors are securely fastened, and verify parts conformity with the IPC.	
I have practiced closed-loop *communication* to receive as well as give turnover about this task or to seek clarification about this task.	
Pre-task Score = Total/5 =?	

Figure 6-1:   Pre-task scorecard

The FAA uses a yes/no checklist rather than a scoring system suggested in our example. We believe that a scoring system will enable the users to acknowledge that there is a certain degree of risk in every task and find means to continually refine their work habits to minimize that risk. The pre-task scorecard is presented in Figure 6-1 and the post-task scorecard is presented in Figure 6-2.

Your goal should be to use the above listed six elements of professionalism to achieve a score of 5.0 on both scorecards, consistently.

If you notice that you are scoring less than the perfect five on any of these items, we hope that it will raise your awareness of that issue and you will seek guidance from your peers or supervisors to mitigate the risks and improve your comfort-level with the task at hand.

If these scorecards are used consistently by all mechanics/engineers in an organization, they could be analyzed to determine systemic areas of vulnerability as well as track organizational improvement. Notice, that there is no place for individual names. If the organization intends to resolve systemic problems, individual identity should be protected.

On a scale of 1-5 rate the following statements. After you have rated all the statements, calculate the average rating by adding the individual ratings and dividing the sum by 5. Enter this average score as your Pre-task Score. 1=Strongly Disagree, 2=Disagree, 3=Neutral, 4=Agree, 5=Strongly Agree.	Write your score (between 1 and 5) for each item.
I was *assertive* in identifying systemic deficiencies or errors as well as in acting on the deficiencies that were within my span of control	
I practiced good *teamwork* because I was able to seek or give assistance to others, detect and rectify someone else's error, or resolve information/interpersonal conflict without increasing risk.	
I did not compromise my professional *integrity* because I documented all the work that I did and I did not sign for any work that I did not do.	
I took appropriate safety precautions to prevent personal injury to myself as well as others	
I complied with all applicable regulations	
Post-task Score = Total/5 =?	

Figure 6-2: **Post-task scorecard**

Some Examples of Professionalism in Action

In the following paragraphs, we present some success stories to show you that some forward-thinking maintenance professionals have been successful at raising the professionalism at both individual as well as organizational levels. If they can do it, so can you!

Round Table Discussions

Taylor and Christensen (1998) describe the use of Round Table error-discussions as means to produce systemic and comprehensive changes and prevent the recurrence of similar errors. One maintenance organization developed this innovative approach using a team of four people: a maintenance manager, a union representative, an FAA inspector, and the person admitted to have committed the error. This team endeavored to steer clear of the prevalent blame culture (see Chapter 2) and seek a better understanding of the causal factors leading to the error. By adopting this approach, the team was successful in winning the labor force's trust and truly implementing comprehensive and systemic solutions.

Focus Groups

At a particular line maintenance station, an airline was experiencing significantly higher paperwork errors. This approach was presented in Chapter 3 under Case 4. A consultant was employed to hold discussions with foremen and mechanics, which were focused on the causal factors leading to the paperwork errors and their possible solutions. Through such focus groups, a joint labor-management team was able to redesign their logbooks, their maintenance manuals, and otherwise significantly decrease the paperwork errors.

ASAP in Maintenance

With the introduction of Advisory Circular 120-66A, the Federal Aviation Administration (FAA, 1997) is trying to encourage industry as well as their own inspectors to form collaborative teams under the Aviation Safety Action Plan (ASAP). This plan is similar to the Round Table discussions presented above. At least five airlines are in the process of implementing their ASAP. The effectiveness of such programs is not known.

MEDA-type Post-event Investigations

In 1996, Boeing released Maintenance Error Decision Aid (MEDA), a document that could be used during an event investigation to analyze the effect of an error, the type of error, and the factors contributing to the error (cf. Rankin & Allen, 1996). Some companies have recently started to track the error types and their causal factors using a computerized version of the MEDA form. Trends regarding effects of errors, types of errors, and contributing factors can be tracked. Whether it is a MEDA investigation, ASAP, Round Table, or any other investigation that is initiated after the accident/incident, it is a retrospective analysis of the causal factors. Such post-event investigations are intended to identify systemic problems; however, examples of such investigations for the implementation of comprehensive solutions or reduction of errors have not been documented or at least not published for a wider audience.

Concept Alignment Process: Team Decision-making

Not all improvement efforts need to be retroactive analysis of errors already committed. Examples of proactive programs to reduce errors in aviation maintenance also exist.

The Concept Alignment Process (CAP), a development of CMR, Inc., has been discussed in Chapters 3 and 4. From the perspective of professional habits presented in this chapter, one can note that the CAP integrates all these habits quite effectively. The fact that, under CAP, individual concepts need to validated by an external source necessitates the effective use of communication, assertiveness, preparation, work management, integrity, and teamwork.

From the perspective of the four levels of risks discussed in this chapter, one can note that the CAP process and the "judgment phase" (see Chapter 3) consider these risks throughout the maintenance process as well as after maintenance

In essence, the CAP process has been successful in stopping an ongoing error trajectory as well as to preventing future errors. Success in the use of this process has been documented by Patankar and Taylor (1999).

Chapter Summary

Professionalism, in aviation maintenance, is the process of managing risks. Certain habits such as being prepared for the task, practicing closed-loop communication, being assertive about systemic as well as individual deficiencies, practicing good teamwork, and above all, maintaining integrity, will help an individual achieve professionalism. Again, professionalism is a journey, not a destination.

Review Questions

1. Four different levels of risk were presented in this chapter. Use either your own experience or archival data such as the ASRS reports or NTSB accident reports to give additional examples of each level of risk.
2. Compare your views on professionalism with those expressed by the authors.
3. Pick five maintenance tasks. You can choose them in one, or all three, of the following categories: household maintenance, automotive maintenance, or aircraft maintenance. Then, use the pre- and post-task scorecards presented in this chapter to determine your scores. Discuss your scores. If you used all three categories, discuss the similarities and differences in your scores across the three categories.
4. Collect and summarize additional success stories that illustrate good professionalism.

Chapter 7

How Far Will Reliability Take You?

Instructional Objectives

Upon completing this chapter, you should be able to:

1. Explain the fundamental concepts of reliability theory, as they apply to the aviation maintenance environment.
2. Differentiate between the normal-accident theory and the high-reliability theory.
3. Describe the role of an individual in sustaining systemic reliability.

Introduction

Reliability, from a technical sense, is the measure of how often a system or a component meets its standards. In this chapter, we will review some of the basic concepts in the field of reliability. Then, we will consider humans—the mechanics or maintenance engineers—as one of the components of the overall reliability equation. Finally, we will describe how the overall reliability of a system such as aviation maintenance can be improved by better understanding the issues that influence its failures.

Fundamentals of Reliability

Like safety is often defined in terms of risk, reliability is often defined in terms of failure rates. Simplistically, the lower the failure rate, the higher the reliability. Then, what is failure? Failure is defined as 'non-conformance to some predefined performance criterion' (Smith, 2001, p. 13). This non-conformance can be defined in terms of simple binary options—the system either works or does not work—or it can be defined in terms of degradation of the performance. For our discussion, and for simplicity, let us limit the definition of non-conformance to simple binary options.

Consider the simple hydraulic system illustrated in Figure 7-1. We have a reservoir, a supply line, an electrically operated pump, a selector valve, a double-acting actuator, and a return line. In order to operate this system, we need to turn-on the electrically powered hydraulic pump, then move the selector valve to either position for an associated movement of the actuator.

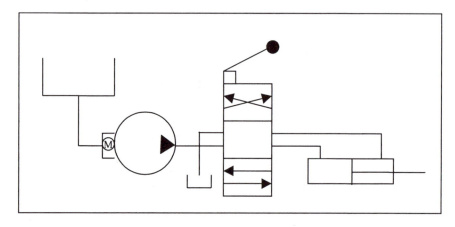

Figure 7-1:   A simple hydraulic system

Now, let us consider the failure scenarios. According to our simplified definition of failure, when we turn on the pump and move the selector valve, nothing happens—the system does not work, the actuator does not move. The failure could be either due to an electrical problem, a mechanical problem, or a simple loss/lack of fluid. Such classification of reasons for failure can be expressed in terms of a Fault Tree Analysis, presented in Figure 7-2.

As you review Figure 7-2, notice that any one of the three reasons could cause the system's failure. Therefore, if we know the probability level of each reason, we can determine the probability of failure for the system. In this case, the probability of failure due to mechanical problems has been assigned to be 1×10^{-5} (one failure in 100,000 operations); the probability of failure due to loss of fluid has been assigned to be 1×10^{-4} (one failure in 10,000 operations); and the probability of failure due to electrical problems has been assigned to be 1×10^{-6} (one failure in 1,000,000 operations). Therefore, we can say that the weakest link in this system is the probability of failure due to loss of fluid—1×10^{-4} (one failure in 10,000 operations). Remember, since the logic operator among these events is OR, failure of any one of the items will cause the system to fail—the probability of failure of the system as a whole is the same as that of its weakest link: in this case, 1×10^{-4}.

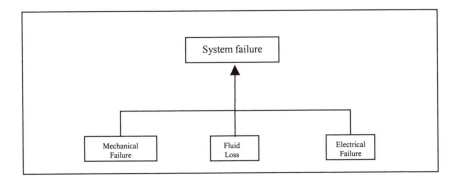

Figure 7-2:   A basic fault tree for the sample hydraulic system

Now, what can we do to increase this system's reliability? We can either increase the reliability of each link (mechanical, fluid, or electric) or we can provide redundancies. Let us see how this works.

Since we identified our weakest link to be failure due to loss of fluid, let us say that we added a backup reservoir to supply fluid to the pump, in the case of total loss of fluid in reservoir A. Assuming that the independent probability of failure of each fluid source is still 1×10^{-4}, the combined probability of failure is their product—1×10^{-8}. Now, the weakest link is mechanical failure!

We can improve mechanical reliability by using better quality parts. So, again, we can improve systemic reliability by either improving the quality of the individual components or by providing adequate redundancy.

Reliability in Maintenance Actions

To apply the concepts of product or systemic reliability in maintenance actions, we will have to first redefine failure or non-conformance. Since we are still using humans to perform maintenance actions, we are concerned with failure of a human, somewhere in the maintenance process. Therefore, we define failure in a maintenance process as an event, caused by a human, that increases the probability of a systemic failure or regulatory non-compliance. That is how we move from technical reliability to human reliability—what is the probability that a human will perform a given maintenance action to the established standards, consistently?

Unlike machines or physical components, humans tend to degrade in their performance more often than simply fail. Such degradation is not absolute, and certainly not irreversible; hence, it is difficult to detect, even by the individual who is affected. Some such degrading factors include stress and fatigue levels; limitations in technical knowledge or skill; ambiguity in, or lack of, correct and current technical literature; lack of appropriate equipment/resources; unreasonable environmental conditions and corporate culture; and also the lack of regulatory authority to perform maintenance actions. If we connect these factors to the elements of professionalism that were discussed in the previous chapter, we can revise the definition of professionalism as the ability of an individual to maintain high individual- as well as systemic-reliability under varying levels of degrading factors. The bottom line is that degrading factors are always present. Since nobody can predict the levels of such factors and their effects on a particular individual's performance, each individual needs to be aware of these factors and develop their own coping strategies. Again, remember our discussion about the next generation of MRM programs (in Chapter 3). We are striving to build programs that go beyond compliance.

As we saw in the hydraulic system example regarding technical reliability of a system, we can increase human reliability at the individual level—by better managing our individual degrading factors—or at the systemic level—by building appropriate redundancies—or by employing a combination of both strategies.

In a system consisting of human activities, such as maintenance, redundancy can be provided either in number or in function. Let us say we need one mechanic to perform a particular task, we can provide redundancy in number by having two mechanics work on that job, with the understanding that one would act as a back-up for the other. If, on the other hand, we have two mechanics working on two different and independent tasks, we can provide redundancy in function by training the two mechanics to do both tasks. The understanding here would be that if one person does not report to work, the other person would be able to take-on the additional task and the pair would still achieve its target (of completing both tasks).

All this sounds fine in theory and works well with machines; however, in the case of humans, the actual level of redundancy is likely to be different from the intended level due to differences in individual personalities. Also, this level is very likely to change over a period of time.

Posterior Probabilities, an Alternative to HRA in Aviation Maintenance

Gertman and Blackman (1994) present several models and data tables that have been used in Human Reliability Analysis (HRA), but all of them have been outside the aviation industry. Although some data such as the probability of installing a hydraulic valve correctly are comparable to the probability of installing a fluid control valve in a nuclear powerplant, the validity of such cross-industry comparison is unknown. In reality, we will have to do our own data collection, analysis, and modeling if we want to understand the human reliability aspects in aviation maintenance. In the meantime, we present an alternative.

The Aviation Safety Reporting System (ASRS) dataset provides an exhaustive, albeit skewed, data regarding maintenance errors. These data provide a means of understanding the relationship between certain causal factors that contribute to maintenance errors. We can use Bayes theorem to quantify the probabilistic relationship between the maintenance errors and their consequences: such applications in medical diagnostic systems are common (Durkin, 1994).

Bayes Theorem

The Bayes Theorem is a specialized application of conditional probability to determine the probability of a specific event being caused by a certain causal factor. Since such a probability value is obtained by analyzing past data, it is called posterior probability. As additional data becomes available, the posterior probability of the event due to a certain causal factor is likely to change (Resnik, 1997).

In calculating posterior probabilities, a certain prior probability is assumed based on all possible causal factors being equally likely. Then, the historical data are analyzed to determine the frequency of various causal factors. If all the causal factors were equally likely, their probability would be unbiased. Therefore, their frequencies (and consequently their probabilities) would be equal. On the other hand, if certain causal factors had a higher frequency than others, these causal factors would be considered biased. The amount of bias would be equal to the percentage of times that causal factor was true.

Theoretically, as the number of cases increases, the posterior probability will stabilize. Once this value has stabilized, it could be considered as the true bias of that particular causal factor.

Application of Bayes Theorem

Patankar and Taylor's (2001) composite causal factor matrix enables maintenance error investigators to analyze events such as flight delay, air turnback, aircraft damage, unairworthy dispatch, etc. in terms of causal factors. Patankar and Taylor mapped eleven such events (see Table 7-1), and each event may be caused by any one of 11 types of maintenance errors (see Table 7-2). Each maintenance error, in turn, could be attributed to any one of 25 causal factors (see Table 7-3). Tables 7-1 and 7-2 were derived from the MEDA form (Rankin & Allen, 1996).

Table 7-1:   Maintenance-related events

Number	Event	Number	Event
1	Flight Delay	6	Diversion
2	Flight Cancellation	7	Aircraft Damage
3	Gate Return	8	Personnel Injury
4	Inflight Engine Shut Down	9	Rework
5	Air Turnback	10	Unairworthy Dispatch
		11	None

Table 7-2:   Maintenance error types

Number	Maintenance Error Type	Number	Maintenance Error Type
1	Improper Installation	7	Personal Injury
2	Improper Service	8	Sign-off of Work Not Performed
3	Improper Repair	9	Improper Documentation
4	Improper Fault Isolation/Inspection	10	None
5	Actions Causing Foreign Object Damage	11	Other
6	Actions Causing Equipment Damage		

A set of prior probabilities could be assigned to each of the causal factors and the ASRS data could then be analyzed to determine the posterior probabilities. In order to successively refine the posterior probabilities, the ASRS data need to be grouped into cumulative batches, in this case by years. Such successive analysis should continue until the posterior probabilities stabilize. If the difference between these probabilities, through the years, seems to be approaching a negligible value, one can conclude that the causal factors are biased according to those posterior probability values. The significance of such analysis is that corrective interventions can be targeted toward areas that are likely to provide the greatest improvements in safety outcomes.

Data Classification: Patankar and Taylor (2001) analyzed 937 ASRS maintenance reports submitted between 1996 and 2000 and determined that the most frequent effect of a maintenance error was unairworthy dispatch of a revenue flight (40% probability) due to improper documentation (34% probability). Theoretically, any one of 25 factors, listed in Table 7-3 could have caused improper documentation. Therefore, we can assign these events a *prior probability* of 1/25 = 4%.

Conditional probability of the existence of a particular hypothesis, P(H/E), can be calculated using the following formula:

$$P(H/E) = \frac{P(H) \times P(E/H)}{P(E)}$$

Where P(H) is the probability that a hypothesis (H) is true, P(E) is the probability that an event (E) is true, P(E/H) is the probability of an event (E) being true when the hypothesis (H) is true, and P(H/E) is the probability of the hypothesis being true when the event (E) is true.

All the above probabilities, except the P(H/E), were assigned based on the frequency distribution within a particular dataset. The P(H/E) was calculated using the above formula for Bayes theorem.

Once the posterior probability values for 1996 data were known, the same process was used to calculate the posterior probabilities of 1996-1997, 1996-1998, 1996-1999, and 1996-2000 data sets.

It was assumed that there was no external treatment influencing the value of posterior probability other than the volume of data. Table 7-4 presents the prior and posterior probabilities of unairworthy dispatch due to improper documentation. There were eleven possible maintenance-error induced events. If all these events were equally likely, each would have a probability of 1/11 (9%). Similarly, there were eleven equally likely maintenance errors. Hence each of them had a probability of 1/11 (9%).

Table 7-3: Patankar and Taylor's composite causal factors leading to maintenance errors

Number	Causal Factor	Number	Causal Factor
1	Physical Health	13	Hardware/Equipment/Tools/ Lack of Resources/Not enough staff
2	Fatigue	14	Aircraft Design/System Configuration/Parts Quality
3	Time Constraints	15	Maintenance Management/Leadership/ Supervision
4	Pressure from Management	16	Work Processes/Procedures/Qualit y of Information
5	Complacency	17	Error-enforcing Conditions/Norms/Peer Pressure
6	Body Size/Strength	18	Housekeeping
7	Personal Event/Stress	19	Incompatible Goals
8	Workplace Distractions	20	Communication Processes
9	Lack of Awareness	21	Organizational Structures/Corporate Change/Union Action
10	Lack of Knowledge	22	Training/Technical Knowledge/Skills
11	Lack of Communication Skills	23	Lack/Failure of Defenses
12	Lack of Assertiveness	24	Environmental Factors/ Facilities
		25	Lack of Teamwork

When the data were sorted to select only those cases wherein the maintenance error type 'Improper Documentation' was true, nine different events were possible. If these events were equally likely, each of them would have a probability of 1/9 (11%). When the data were sorted to select cases wherein the event 'Unairworthy Dispatch' was true, there were seven different maintenance error types possible. Assuming that they were equally likely, the probability of each of those errors was 1/7 (14%). All these probability values were designated as prior probabilities because they were calculated prior to analyzing the data and it was assumed that they were equally likely.

Posterior probabilities were assigned based on the percentage distribution of improper documentation [P(H)], unairworthy dispatch [P(E)], and unairworthy dispatch when improper documentation was known to be true [P(E/H)]. The posterior probability of improper documentation when unairworthy dispatch was known to be true [P(H/E)] was calculated using the Bayes theorem. Such analysis was performed on five datasets: 1996, 1996-1997, 1996-1998, 1996-1997, and 1996-2000. The results of the associated probability assignments are shown in Table 7-4.

Table 7-4:   Prior and posterior probabilities that an unairworthy dispatch was due to improper documentation

	Unbiased Prior (%)	Posterior Probabilities (%)				
		1996	1996-1997	1996-1998	1996-1999	1996-2000
P(H)	9	12.8 (n=109)	12.0 (n=241)	15.8 (n=374)	16.7 (n=600)	19.7 (n=934)
P(E)	9	22.0 (n=109)	30.2 (n=242)	30.9 (n=376)	39.5 (n=603)	40.3 (n=937)
P(E/H)	11	50.0 (n=14)	58.6 (n=29)	66.1 (n=59)	75.0 (n=100)	69.0 (n=184)
P(H/E)	14	29.1	23.3	33.8	31.7	33.7

P(H) = Probability that the condition 'Improper Documentation' is true
P(E) = Probability that the event 'Unairworthy Dispatch' is true
P(E/H) = Probability that the event E is true given that condition H is true
P(H/E) = Probability that condition H is true given that event E has
occurred

$$= \frac{P(H) \times P(E/H)}{P(E)}$$

Thus, the results in Table 7-4 indicate that the causal probability of improper documentation contributing toward unairworthy dispatch is about 33%.

The Aviation Maintenance Industry: "High Reliability" by Design, but "Normal Accident" by Circumstance

In safety theory, there are at least two distinct schools of thought: The normal-accident theory and the high-reliability theory. The normal accident theory was developed by Charles Perrow (1984). According to this theory, in its most simplistic form, in complex, tightly-coupled systems such as aviation, nuclear industry, or healthcare, it is normal for accidents to occur. In other words, we can never, realistically, get the accident rate to zero. On the other hand, the high-reliability theorists such as Karl Weick (1987) and Karlene Roberts (1990) argue that some organizations, despite the complex interaction among variables and tight coupling, have managed to avoid accidents. Scott Sagan (1993) presents a very interesting discussion of these two theories. Based on his examples that support both theories, one could conclude that some organizations are more reliable than others or the same organization could go through cycles of heightened reliability, due to a recent accident, and relaxed complacency due to the absence of an accident. Reason (1997, p.11) uses a "safety space" model to illustrate how different organizations could be distributed across the safety space—from increasing resistance to increasing vulnerability to hazards.

So how do these theories apply to aviation maintenance? The entire aviation industry is designed around high-reliability. The FAA, the U.K. CAA, and the respective regulatory agencies from other countries provide specific guidance on almost all the aspects of the industry—from design to accident investigation. The multi-person flight crew, the required inspection items, and the technical redundancies aboard aircraft are all designed to provide a high-reliability system. Then, why do we have accidents? The answer lies in understanding the degradation of the system.

By design, the aviation maintenance system has both the advantages as well as the disadvantages of a high-reliability organization. The advantages are that there are multiple checks-and-balances built in the system so that failures could be trapped in time and catastrophic effects of failures could be prevented. For example, the parts-numbering system is designed to provide traceability to the raw material level. Every component on the aircraft is accounted for in the Type Certificate Data Sheet. Yet, it is possible to find engines that are treated with special performance-enhancing coatings that are neither approved under a Supplemental Type Certificate nor under an FAA Form 337. Consequently, such aircraft are, technically, unairworthy. Similarly, the parts-numbering system is standardized to ensure standard hardware such as nuts and bolts meet stringent quality standards; yet, there is no way to guarantee that a specific bolt pulled out of a bin actually meets the design/approval standards—the approval system is based on a statistical sampling from a batch of newly manufactured bolts, not a 100-percent testing (see MIL-STD-1916 for details).

Another interesting example of differences in intent and reality is in the area of technical training. In accordance with Federal Aviation Regulations §65.81 (a), an aircraft mechanic is not authorized to perform maintenance actions that he/she has not performed before under another mechanic's supervision. Yet, perhaps due to financial constraints, mechanics are being asked to perform maintenance actions for which they are neither trained nor experienced.

The next generation aircraft such as the Boeing 777 and 737-800 and Airbus 320 and 340 are equipped with maintenance computers. These computers are designed to help the mechanic troubleshoot the aircraft and identify the faulty part. As these airplanes age—according to the normal accident theory—complications resulting from unforeseen combinations of complex technology, under-trained and under-experienced workforce, and over-dependence on computer-mediated troubleshooting are likely to face a normal accident, induced by a highly reliable technology. At that point, the humans in the system will have to implement equally innovative recovery strategy or we might just replace this technology with newer, more reliable technology! Remember the Hawkins-Ashby model discussed in Chapter 1? As the hardware changes, appropriate changes must be made to the liveware, software, or the environment, or a combination of these elements to minimize risks.

Chapter Summary

Reliability theory, as applied to maintenance professionals, can be used to understand the causal relationships among the various contributory factors and the ultimate failure or event. The reliability in maintenance actions can be increased by either increasing the individual human's reliability or by providing appropriate and effective back-up humans. When humans are used to provide back-up to each other, factors that may degrade such relationship should be addressed regularly.

In the absence of good quality data on human reliability in aviation maintenance, archival data such as ASRS reports or internal investigation reports could be used to apply the Bayes theorem for conditional probabilities. Repeated application of Bayes theorem will yield stable quantitative relationships among causal factors and failures.

The aviation industry is designed to be a high-reliability system, but due to extraneous conditions such as economic pressures, the barriers and defenses that are placed in the system are likely to be rendered ineffective. Moreover, the more sophisticated aircraft and powerplants that are introduced in the system require a lot less maintenance; consequently, mechanics are likely to be less skilled at troubleshooting sophisticated. Hence they are likely to depend more heavily on computer-assisted diagnosis and engage in more frequent removal-and-replacement actions than repair actions. According to the normal accident theory, it is likely that due to some unforeseen combination of events, the computer-driven technology will fail and challenge the human mechanics to maintain systemic safety.

Review Questions

1. Select a specific maintenance task such as a brake change on a Boeing 737-200 or a nose tire change on a Fokker 100. Review the work history for a specific aircraft to determine how often your selected task was performed and how often it was performed incorrectly. Use this information to calculate the probability of failure for this task.
2. For the same task as in the above question, apply the Bayes theorem to determine the causal probabilities for the factors contributing toward your selected maintenance failure.
3. Discuss the application or relevance of the normal accident theory and the high-reliability theory from the perspective of the maintenance failure that you analyzed in the previous two questions.
4. As a mechanic or engineer, what would you do to prevent recurrence of a similar failure as that presented by you in the previous question?

Chapter 8

Return on Investment

Instructional Objectives

Upon completing this chapter, you should be able to:

1. Understand the terms 'net benefit', 'variance explained', 'causal operator', and 'MRM costs'.
2. Use the above concepts to calculate the ROI of an MRM program.

Introduction

It is obvious that aircraft accidents represent substantial financial loss. As we discussed in Chapter 1, the indirect costs associated with an airliner accident could be as high as four times the direct costs. Therefore, from a purely financial perspective, accidents can force an airline into bankruptcy. But before we get to accidents, there are several other significant losses due to lost-time-injuries, ground damage, flight delays and cancellations, air turn-backs, etc. Such losses drain the vital financial resources on a daily basis. The National Business Aircraft Association (2002) estimates that the annual ground damage direct costs to be $100 million. In another study by Paul Clark (2002), the damages for one major international airline are reported to be about $11.5 million in the year 2000. As such, any money saved by minimizing these losses could be made available to other areas such as training, equipment, and bottom-line survival of the company. Intuitively, one would agree that safety programs can reduce loss and thereby improve productivity/quality; however, it is not always easy to support such intuition with data. In this chapter, we present methods for calculating the return on investment (ROI) for Maintenance Resource Management (MRM) programs.

Although some MRM programs have had immediate 'successes', their long-term success and survival depends on continuous support from top management and trade union leadership. For company management (and increasingly for union leaders) to provide the needed support, they require measures which establish that MRM programs are financially sound investments—and that 'safety pays'.

MRM as Instruction

Most MRM programs have started and finished as awareness instruction courses. Even this modest 'awareness instruction' can succeed in at least two ways. First, MRM awareness instruction can alert participants to new ideas, or remind them of what they have known or forgotten with time. Second, it can also provide participants with a common language in preparation for a system-wide change in values and culture. We have documented the success of MRM instruction over the past decade (Taylor, et al., 1997; Taylor, 1998a; Taylor & Patankar, 2001) but that success has been limited to the first outcome—an increase in individual enthusiasm for safety and individual responsibility. Such success has also been transitory and in 18 months, performance (and sometimes attitudes) has returned to earlier levels.

Instruction usually includes topics such as open communication, assertiveness, interpersonal differences, stress-management, and group decision-making. Documented evaluation seeks association between these factors with some aspects of safety—errors in repair or in maintenance documentation, damage to aircraft during servicing or repair, and/or industrial injuries. These correlations show persuasively that MRM instruction does influence positive attitudes toward the human role in safety improvement and increased passive awareness and individual responsibility.

This awareness of MRM ideas and their importance is largely an individual act and does not require the active support or subsequent communication with others. As time passes, those individual efforts to change show diminished returns and respondents complain that they see little support for the MRM safety initiatives from their management or from coworkers (Taylor, 1998a).

The effect of those safety initiatives will disappear over a relatively short period unless both management and organized labor actively and visibly support them. They are good as far as they go, but only with this sustained support do MRM programs survive past the initial enthusiasm of its participants (Taylor & Robertson, 1994).

Continuous and visible support by leaders is one very important avenue to continued program success. Measuring the ROI of MRM programs in standard and comparable terms is essential to obtaining this support. Very little ROI, or other financial evaluation of awareness programs has yet been attempted or reported.

MRM as Structure & Process

Another way of enhancing the success of MRM awareness training is to initiate and reinforce collaborative and cooperative behaviors among members of a company's maintenance department to continually improve safety performance. This may require training to improve active skills in communication, team membership, joint problem solving, and safety recognition. For example, all shift foremen in one line maintenance station in an airline were trained in conducting shift meetings (Taylor & Christensen, pp. 112-113). In the months following the training, foremen proceeded to conduct shift-meetings on a regular basis. Data showing improved mechanic attitudes as well as reports of improved relations with aircrews on the flight line, at that one station, confirmed the value of the regular maintenance shift briefings to exchange safety and operations information among employees.

Consistent with improved MRM skills-development and application to safety improvements are changes in work structure and process. The skills training in conducting shift meetings, just described, were combined with the process requirement that such briefings be held on each shift. Other examples of changes in work process in aviation maintenance are rare but a few have been documented. For example Hutchinson (1997) reports changes in the process of maintenance error data collection and display. Wulle & Lapacek (1997) describe the effects of experimental changes in media for the process of information transfer between flight crews and maintenance. Reports of planned change in both structure and process are rarer yet, but results are encouraging. Scoble (1994) reports improvements in quality of repair following structural changes in inspector work unit size and assignment, together with changes in the process of identifying significant defects earlier in the inspection process. We have also reported efforts to sustain maintenance performance and safety through the coordinated changes in both structure and process (Patankar & Taylor, 1999b). In Chapters 3 and 4, we discussed the use of Concept Alignment Process in aviation maintenance which was combined with a new structure of overlapping work shifts where the two shifts' joint meeting is used to report and discuss each day's results of using the new process.

Until recently little was done to evaluate such changes in structure and process and no serious effort was made to calculate their ROI. How then can such measurement be accomplished?

Return on Investment

Profits are derived from earnings. 'Earnings' are income minus investment. The rate at which earnings grow is a function of the company's return on investment (ROI). ROI is the ratio of net income to investment costs. Although ROI competes with other financial indicators (e.g., return on equity, return on assets) for an executive's attention, it is the longest-lived and most robust of the evaluation tools for management decisions (Phillips, 1997).

Evaluating the benefits of training has been long admired, but little practiced (Kirkpatrick, 1975). Evaluating the effects of organizational effectiveness (OE) interventions, such as those described in the previous section is likewise underdeveloped. Training and other OE interventions, especially for safety improvement, are rarely treated as investments and are usually just considered necessary costs of doing business.

Little wonder then that converting MRM benefits into a standardized and comparable format, such as ROI, is so little in evidence and has only recently become an idea in good currency within the training and organizational effectiveness community (Phillips, 1997).

Cost and Benefit

Assessment of costs and earnings are an essential first step in measuring ROI. Calculating the cash benefits resulting from an OE intervention is important. Likewise, it is important that true and accurate costs of any OE intervention (whether training, or structure/process, or a combination) be specified and calculated. Rules for listing, collecting and calculating those costs and benefits are beyond the scope of this chapter but can be found elsewhere (cf. Phillips, 1997).

Where either cost or benefit data are available alone, they are mistakenly presented as evidence that an intervention was a success—'it came in below budget' (low cost) or 'it saved (or produced) a substantial amount of cash' (high cash benefit). Most managers and executives familiar with financial analysis would consider such direct statements to be without reference and therefore without much meaningful information for decision-making.

When both cost *and* benefit data are available they are also, and all too frequently, combined by placing them in direct comparison with one another—in the familiar 'cost-benefit differences' or 'cost-benefit ratios'. These combinations cannot correspond with other efforts to justify the financial success of an intervention, nor are they a standardized measure to be understood in implied comparison with other results. These benefits minus (-) cost 'differences', or benefit divided by (÷) cost 'ratios', cannot be considered effective outcome measures by themselves because the actual practical effect may be magnified or otherwise skewed by the absolute size of the effort and its budget.

Standardized Format

ROI is traditionally reported as 'earnings', divided by 'investment'. In conventional terms, a company's 'earnings' are its 'income' minus its 'expenses' for some fixed period of time. Equation 1 shows this basic ROI.

$$ROI = [\text{INCOME} - \text{INVESTMENT}] \div \text{INVESTMENT}$$

Figure 8-1:   Equation 1, standard ROI equation

Given that definition of 'earnings', we can simplify the expression 'Income–Investment' in equation 1 by calling it 'Earnings'. Additionally, we can standardize the ROI expression, by multiplying the resulting quotient by 100 to convert it into a percent expression. That simplification and standardization is shown in equation 2.

$$ROI = \left(\frac{Earnings}{Investment} \right) \times 100$$

Figure 8-2:   Equation 2, ROI in terms of earnings and investment

Interpretation of ROI

As an illustration, an ROI of '25%' means that the investment costs are recovered—and an *additional* 25% of the cost amount is reported as earnings. ROI for a given program result, in a given period, can also be expressed as '$1.25 is returned for every dollar invested during this year'. This definition of ROI is in contrast to the direct cost-benefit ratio, since 'earnings' are not a direct equivalent to 'benefits'. The concept 'benefits' is more similar to the 'income' term in traditional ROI calculations.

Net MRM Benefits: In light of this, the MRM equivalent to earnings would be benefits minus costs, or 'net program benefits' (cf. Phillips, 1997). Thus for the calculation of MRM ROI, the numerator of the equation is the net program benefits, or 'Net MRM Benefits'. The denominator, 'MRM program costs', likewise compares to 'investment' in traditional ROI.

$$MRM \ \ ROI \ = \left(\frac{Net \ \ MRM \ \ Benefits}{MRM \ \ Costs} \right) \times 100$$

Figure 8-3:   Equation 3, calculation of MRM ROI

Using this formula, ROI calculations for MRM are thus commensurate with ROI calculations for more typical applications of the concept (i.e., efforts to increase productivity) because they are calculated to the same basic formula. Because ROI calculations are expressed as percentages they are standardized to the same scale. Executives and other policy makers who are used to thinking about ROI for earnings are likely to dismiss cost and/or benefit statements, but will accept the same data transformed through the ROI formula. This is because the comparable advantage of ROI for an MRM intervention is more apparent, so that the result will be less likely to be disregarded or overlooked.

Accounting for MRM contribution

Competing for credit: MRM programs are imperfect tools and cannot cause a perfect and total effect on intended outcomes. But in pursuit of this ideal of maximum effect, such programs typically undergo constant development and improvement. This motivation to pursue an ideal is especially true when dealing with certain core organizational outcomes, such as safety to an airline, which have central value to all members. In a complex organization, it follows that many different initiatives will simultaneously be in play to improve those core behaviors and outcomes. Passions can run high and the pursuit of total success can bias the champions of the competing programs toward attributing more effect to their own efforts than might be realistic. Post-hoc allocation of resulting improvements in those outcomes can therefore become the subject of debate among the organization's program champions, or change agents.

Obtaining estimates of cause-effect relationships: These estimates are often in the form of correlation coefficients between two variables (bivariate correlation)—one from measures of what employees learned from the

MRM program, and one from subsequent measures of safety outcomes for employee groups.

Correlation coefficients are expressed as a number ranging between minus one and plus one. A perfect positive coefficient (+1.00) would represent a perfect correspondence between two variables and a perfect negative coefficient (-1.00) would represent a perfect inverse relationship between two variables. A coefficient of zero (0) indicates the total absence of relationship between two variables. Given the complex nature of cause-effect relationships in human behavior, combined with the imperfect state of social science measurement, perfect correlations (+1.00, or –1.00) are rare. Coefficients larger than zero and smaller than one are more likely. Any correlation coefficient should be tested for statistical significance to determine the likelihood that its value is not a chance occurrence.

Cause-effect estimates in MRM research: Reasonable estimates of the causal relationships between an MRM program and later safety results have been obtained through the longitudinal collection of quantitative data in several samples and analyzed with fairly simple statistical tests. Taylor & Robertson (1995) report the new knowledge and attitudes from MRM instruction for maintenance managers and support professionals correlated with 30 months of subsequent lost-time-injuries (LTI) data. Taylor, et al. (1997), reporting the knowledge and attitude of MRM instruction for the same company's mechanics two years later, found significant correlations between stress-management and assertiveness attitudes and reduction in maintenance-related ground damage incidents. Taylor (1998a) and Taylor & Patankar (2001) report the results of other studies in which mechanics' attitudes toward stress management were also found to be significantly correlated with reductions in subsequent ground damage incidents. Correlations reported in all these studies were in the expected direction— i.e., attitudes improved, then behaviors changed, and safety increased.

Variance Explained: Correlation coefficients provide a convenient way to define the overall strength of linear relationship in terms of a proportional reduction in variation. Simply put, the square of a given correlation coefficient is equal to the proportion of variance in one of the two measures, which is explained by the other variable. Statisticians refer to this statistic (ρ^2) as 'the coefficient of determination' (Hays, 1963). Thus, if the correlation, ρ, equals -.50 between two variables, then the coefficient of determination, ρ^2, equals .25. In other words, a correlation of .50 (or -.50) explains 25% of the variability in one result by the other. These easily calculated 'coefficients of determination' provide us with conservative, quantitative estimates of 'credit' to be allocated to organizational effectiveness (e.g., MRM) interventions that we can now use in a new and *even more powerful variant* of the MRM ROI equation.

Obstacles to use of ROI in MRM

There are three major obstacles to overcome in developing a realistic and appropriate model of MRM ROI for safety. The first obstacle is lack of experience. The second obstacle is difficulty in assessing causality. Our new ROI model addresses both these factors. The third factor, however, deals with the fundamental issue of how funds are directed toward or away from safety-related expenses.

Lack of experience: The industry's use of broader organizational effectiveness tools for safety improvement—which include training, among others—is just beginning. The application of appropriate ROI models to this larger class of organizational intervention has only recently been attempted. Our model is tested using data collected from several real MRM interventions. These illustrations of our ROI model for MRM provides evidence, as well as instruction, for any aviation maintenance company wishing to assess the ROI as part of a planned intervention to improve 'and prove' organizational effectiveness.

Assessing causality: In most airline companies, everyone is focused on safety. This means that there are usually many initiatives to improve a particular safety outcome and if improvement is achieved many will want to take credit for it. The use of bivariate correlations between MRM outcomes (new knowledge, attitudes and behaviors) and safety results provides a way to conservatively estimate the degree of impact MRM has on safety, as well as providing a numerical value ('coefficient of determination') to use as a 'causal operator' term in the new ROI equation.

No line-item in the budget: In aviation, safety does not have a specific line-item in the budget. Funds are often used from other line-items such as training, parts and tools, personnel, workers' compensation, etc. So, how do we show a reduction in safety-related costs? Funds left over from one line item are typically used for another. Additionally, during rough economic times, personnel, training, and compensation budgets are shrinking as well. Consequently, there are even lesser funds for safety-specific programs. If managers 'borrow' funds from other line items, they will need to justify the return on their investment within the same fiscal year. Senior management is not likely to be impressed by a long-term ROI because the company may not even be in business by then. Such prophetic mindset came closer to reality in the year 2002 when both U.S. Airways as well as United Airlines filed for bankruptcy.

A New Model of ROI in MRM

Our model of ROI for aviation safety interventions builds upon the traditional model (Equations 1 & 2, above) and its variant developed for organizational effectiveness (Equation 3). Not only does this new model accept training interventions, but it also uses measures of changes in organization structure and work process as causes for behavioral improvements. This MRM ROI model's features build on the annualized percentage ratio of net program benefits to program costs—the ROI formula familiar to operating managers and their financial counterparts— and it also includes a novel component designed to account for the *degree of effect* the targeted MRM intervention has had on net program benefits (the ROI formula's numerator).

$$MRM\ ROI = \left(\frac{[Net\ MRM\ Benefits\ ] \times Causal\ Operator}{MRM\ Costs} \right) \times 100$$

Figure 8-4: **Equation 4, equation for net MRM ROI**

This equation (4) is similar to equation 3 above, with the addition of the 'causal operator' term as a multiplier on the net program benefits in the numerator. This 'causal operator' term is represented by the 'coefficient of determination' (the square of the correlation between the human MRM results and subsequent safety outcomes). In the earlier discussion of estimating cause-effect relations between two variables separated in time, the square of a correlation coefficient between them (known as the 'coefficient of determination'), was defined as measuring the variability in the later variable that is accounted for by the prior one. Thus the coefficient of determination can act as the 'causal operator', a quantitative measure for the contribution of MRM to safety in a given period of time.

The effect of this modification to the traditional ROI equation is to reduce the size of net program benefit by a positive factor between zero and one and thus change the benefit outcome downward to a level that acknowledges the residual as potential effects *on that benefit* belonging to background effects and to other interventions.

Two Example/Illustrations

This new ROI model has been tested using the results from several MRM training interventions and their effect on improving safety outcomes. Two examples will be presented to illustrate the model. One deals with instructing managers in MRM concepts and reducing personal injuries, and the other with instructing mechanics in similar programs and the associated effect on reduced ground damage incidents. Both examples are drawn from documented cases. The MRM cost data used in Example 1 is calculated from the design and implementation of a two-day MRM instructional program created at another airline.

Example 1: MRM Instruction for Managers and Impact on a High Cost Factor

An airline company presented a two-day MRM training program for all 190 of its maintenance management. The course covered a number of factors, including assertiveness, individual responsibility and leadership, behavior norms and safety, interpersonal behavior, problem-solving, and stress management.

For the purpose of this illustration, the amount of $251,660 was obtained by calculating the development of an actual two-day MRM training program for 1,600 airline maintenance employees and managers (not the actual program described above). These costs include training materials, and the hourly salary/wages of instructors and course participants. Development is calculated as $102,700, and the delivery to 190 management employees is calculated as $148,960, for a total of $251,660.

Surveys taken before and after the training showed significant improvements in attitudes toward participative leadership and assertiveness. In the two years following the MRM training, lost-time-injuries (LTI) decreased by 80%. Significant correlations in the expected direction ($-.26 < \rho < -.22$) were found between improved attitudes in the later surveys and the incidence of LTI up to 30 months later (Taylor & Robertson, 1995).

The value of $\rho = -.24$ is assigned as a midpoint of the range of correlation coefficients, $-.26<\rho<-.22$. The coefficient of determination for that value is $(-.24)^2$, or 0.0576.

For an airline with 1,600 maintenance employees and an average of 61 injuries per year, and an individual injury cost per incident of $13,465, an 80% reduction in injury incidents over two years represents a savings of $1,314,150.

The two-year benefit of $1,314,150 minus the MRM costs of $251,660 results in a net benefit of $1,062,490.

With the above cost and correlation figures, the MRM ROI (see Equation 4) can be calculated as follows:

Box 8-1:   MRM ROI, example 1

$$MRM\ ROI = \left(\frac{[\$1,062,490] \times .0576}{\$251,660} \right) \times 100 = +24\%$$

The resulting MRM ROI value for this management MRM training impact on reduced LTI is 24.3%. This means that even using the conservative estimate of 5.76%, LTI benefits accounted for by MRM, the program paid for itself in two years plus an additional 24% return.

Example 2: MRM Instruction for Mechanics and Impact on a Low Cost Factor

An airline company invited its mechanics to attend a one-day course based on that described in Example 1. Twelve-hundred mechanics completed the course in two years. The surveyed improvements in attitudes after the training were similar to the management group above. Over a two-year period, ground damage incidents decreased by 50%. The correlations between improved attitudes toward stress-management and assertiveness in the post-training survey and subsequent reduction in ground damage incidents were quite high, ranging from -.75 to -.71 (Taylor, et al., 1997).

Although several airline companies developed their own MRM training programs (at considerable expense), it is no longer necessary to do so because of the availability of high quality third-party training vendors, and of ready-to-use ('turnkey') MRM training curricula available free of charge through the FAA in the United States (FAA, 2002).

Without undertaking development activities, training costs are easier to calculate. For example, when employing one of the third-party vendors their development costs will be included in the delivery of the training, which is usually billed as a flat contracted fee, or a fee for each person trained. Alternatively, an airline company's use of a publicly available turnkey training program will also simplify cost calculation and reduce overall training costs. Indeed, using a free, turnkey curriculum entails little or no cost to customize it for local in-house administration, so the training costs are simply the sum of those costs of the training facilities, training materials, and salaries of the training staff and the trainees.

For the present example, of MRM instruction for mechanics we will calculate the training costs based on the use of one of the publicly available curricula for a one-day program. The costs are nil for developing the course, and $205,400 to deliver it to about 1,200 mechanics over a two-year period. That sum is derived from materials and facilities costs of $3,500, trainer salary (20% time) of $24,000, and $177,900 for eight hours apiece for 1,200 mechanics (average $18.50/hr).

The value of .73 is assigned as a midpoint in the range of correlation coefficients reported in Taylor, et al., (1997). The coefficient of determination for that value is $(.73)^2$, or 0.533.

For an airline company of 1,600 maintenance employees with an average of 12 damage incidents per year, and an average cost per incident of $5,479, a 50% reduction in incidents over two years represents a savings of $65,748.00.

The two-year benefit of $65,748 minus the MRM costs of $205,400, results in a net benefit of negative <$139,652>.

With the above cost and correlation figures, the MRM ROI (see Equation 4) can be calculated as follows:

Box 8-2:   MRM ROI, example 2

$$MRM\ ROI = \left(\frac{[-\$139{,}652] \times .533}{\$205{,}400} \right) \times 100 = -36\%$$

The resulting MRM ROI value for this mechanic MRM training impact on reduced ground damage is negative (-) 36%. This means that despite reduced MRM program costs and the dollar value of ground damage benefit accounted for by MRM, the program failed to pay for itself in two years. If success in reducing ground damage at 50% each year continues for 10 years (not assuming changes in the size of fleet operations or personnel—an unlikely assumption, but one useful to make this point), the total net benefit would still be negative <$81,095> and the MRM ROI would continue to be negative—in this case, –21%.

Discussion

These two illustrations help establish several points. First, substantial positive ROI is possible from expensive MRM programs that affect 'high value' outcomes (such as lost time injuries in Example 1). Second, even MRM programs 'on-a-budget', and which strongly impact safety outcomes do not always result in a positive ROI. In the case of Example 2, the safety outcome, ground damage, had a lower realized value than LTI in the first case, and that will have a persistent negative effect on ROI even over the long term.

From these two cases we can derive a third conclusion, namely that it is wise to plan and design one's MRM program to impact what one intends. If a 'low-value' outcome is desired then an ROI calculation may not do much to convince policy makers of the larger effectiveness of the program. A corollary is to seek other positive outcomes (such as MRM program's positive impact on employee morale) to supplement the weak financial results. Often improved morale can help to sustain a positive change beyond its expected duration and provide lasting benefits to a company that cannot be directly assessed in financial terms.

Chapter Summary

ROI can be assessed for organizational change programs as easily as for more traditional kinds of capital investments. Furthermore, ROI for MRM programs can be enhanced, using available program evaluation statistics, in order to favorably compete for available funds and appropriate recognition of the program's contribution.

The techniques and methodology for MRM ROI have been tested and are available for use by MRM program champions.

ROI and other financial results are helpful in obtaining the support for MRM by upper management and other policy makers and 'gate keepers', but there remain intangible benefits of MRM that financial indicators cannot represent. These 'softer' outcomes are also important in system success and program champions must seek ways of acknowledging them as well.

Review Question

1. Consult with your company's financial analysts regarding the desired return on investment for safety programs. Then, calculate your anticipated, or real, ROI using the equations presented in this chapter.

Chapter 9

Case Studies

Instructional Objectives

Upon completing this chapter, you should be able to:

1. Critically examine the causal factors associated with each accident case.
2. Describe how maintenance professionals, in the course of their routine activities, take different types of risk.

Introduction

In this chapter, we discuss eight cases (introduced in Chapter 1) wherein poor maintenance has been cited as one of the causal factors. The original accident reports were obtained either from the National Transportation Safety Board (www.ntsb.gov) or Air Accidents Investigation Branch of the U.K. Civil Aviation Administration (www.aaib.dtlr.gov.uk). Each case is analyzed to illustrate the causal chain that led to the particular accident, and specific risks involved in each accident are discussed.

The NTSB reports identify a single probable cause of the accident and multiple factors that may have contributed to the probable cause. The UK-AAIB reports, on the other hand, simply identify the multiple factors that may have contributed to the accident.

Case Number 1: Single-engine Airplane (NTSB Report Number SEA95FA213)

On September 10, 1995, a Cessna P210N was destroyed when it collided with terrain during an emergency descent after the loss of engine power. The commercial pilot, who was the sole occupant of the aircraft, was fatally injured. The aircraft had departed Eugene, Oregon, at about 0930, with a company flight plan, and was expected to return to Harrisburg, Oregon, at the end of the aerial photography flight.

Probable Cause

The pilot was unable to maintain glide speed and land the airplane safely. Contributing factors to this accident were the loss of engine power due to oil starvation at the crankcase main bearings and crankshaft main journals, resulting in the separation of four connecting rods due to thermal stretching and breaking of their rod bolts.

Aircraft Information

The aircraft had undergone an annual inspection on March 1, 1995. Since that date, it had accumulated approximately 290 hours of flight time. A factory-remanufactured engine had been installed in about January-February 1993 and had approximately 900 hours since then. In July 1995, six overhauled cylinders were installed. These cylinders had accumulated approximately 120 hours at the time of the accident. Pilots had observed that the oil pressure had dropped on at least three occasions prior to the accident, but that it had remained in the green oil pressure range. Each time, oil screens were checked and no metal was found. The aircraft was not consuming oil. During the 30 days preceding the accident, the oil relief check valve had been checked for condition, the oil cooler thermal control valve had been replaced, and at least two oil filters had been opened and checked for contamination. On September 9, one day before the accident, the oil pressure was reported to have been back up to the expected range.

Engine Analysis

Teledyne Continental factory in Mobile, AL noted, during the course of the disassembly, that the crankcase main bearings and crankshaft main journal exhibited oil starvation. Four connecting rods (cylinders 1, 2, 3, 4) were separated with thermal stretching and breaking of their rod bolts. The two remaining rods (cylinders 5 and 6) were removed. Their rod bearings were partially melted and extruded. Internal damage consistent with oil starvation was noted. One B- nut, which was tagged as loose by the salvage organization that shipped the engine to Mobile, was found to be 11/2 flats (of the hex nut) loose. The B-nut and the end of the oil inlet supply line were analyzed by the NTSB materials laboratory.

The NTSB Materials lab's examination revealed that, 'approximately three threads in the area where the oil line end is assembled were truncated, apparently during the manufacturing process. Major portions of the threads were covered by what appeared to be a deposit of aluminum, with some bright droplets'.

The Chain of Events

Figure 9-1 illustrates the chain of events, as described in the previous paragraphs. The dotted lines indicate that the causal relationship between the preceding events and the subsequent results is probabilistic (there is a good chance, but not certain that the events are related). As you can see, the B-nut could have been left loose either during one of maintenance checks that subsequent to the pilots' complaints regarding a drop in the oil pressure or during one of the maintenance actions in the 30 days preceding the accident. This chain of events indicates that *Good Samaritan Risk* and *Complacency* may have been the key factors contributing to this accident. It is clear, from the report, that the oil pressure problem was chronic. It is also clear that the maintenance personnel were trying a variety of solutions to address this issue. However, in the process of trying a variety of solutions unsuccessfully, they seem to have engaged in excessive maintenance actions, increasing their complacency in the tasks.

Causal Analysis

Based on the information contained in the NTSB report and Marx's (2000) causal analysis technique, a causal analysis of the above accident case is presented.

The final outcome of this case was that aircraft crashed and the pilot suffered fatal injuries. Working our way backward, to identify the specific causal links in this case, we find the following: (1) the aircraft crashed because the pilot was unable to maintain glide speed and land safely; (2) the pilot had to establish glide speed [no indication in the report whether the pilot was successful in establishing this speed] because of a total power loss/engine failure; (3) the engine failed because there was a total loss of oil pressure; (4) the engine lost oil pressure because a B-nut on the oil line of the turbocharger was loose and the oil leaked; (5) the B-nut was loose because of failure to fully tighten the B-nut.

Figure 9.2 presents the results of Marx's causal analysis method, in terms of three types of causes: mechanical failure (loss of engine power), rule violation (failure to establish/maintain glide speed and assumption that the oil pressure problem had been adequately addressed because there was no apparent pressure drop during the last engine run-up), and human error (failure to fully tighten the B-nut).

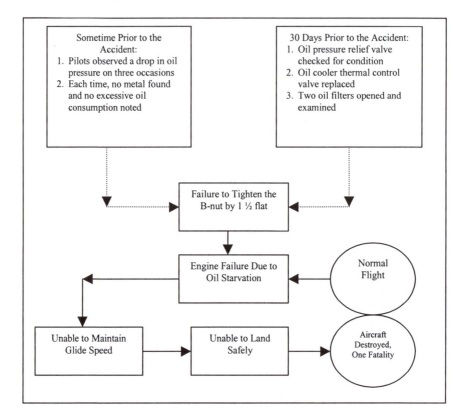

Figure 9-1:   The chain of events in the Cessna 210N accident

In order to minimize the probability of such an accident in the future, Marx (2000) suggests that the comprehensive solution should be such that 80% of the changes are at the systemic level and 20% of the changes should be at the individual level. Therefore, in this case, we would recommend that a dual inspection be carried out whenever maintenance is performed on a critical system such as engine lubricating system, engine fuel system, flight control system, etc. In recommending this solution, we are applying the reliability concepts learned in Chapter 7 and recognizing that humans are not reliable: they cannot be expected to perform a particular task repeatedly without making an error. Such lack of reliability from one individual can be improved by having an additional individual inspect the work. The probability of both individuals missing the same fault is very low.

From an individual perspective, we would recommend that pilots review their ability to establish glide speed upon engine failure and land the aircraft safely. Also, for mechanics, we would recommend that they exercise heightened attention to detail when working with safety critical systems.

Needless to say that pilots are supposed to be trained to handle in-flight engine failures. If the pilot had been able to establish glide speed, he could have landed the aircraft safely, in spite of the engine failure.

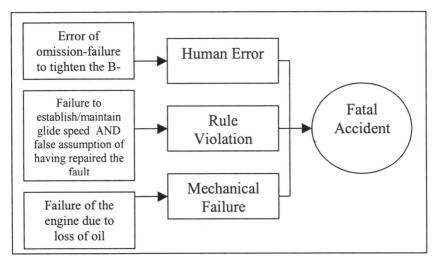

Figure 9-2:   **Causal diagram of the Cessna 210N accident**

Case Number 2: Twin-engine Helicopter (U.K. AAIB Aircraft Incident Report No: 2/08 (EW/C95/9/4), Aerospatiale AS332L Super Puma)

On September 27, 1995, an Aerospatiale AS332L Super Puma helicopter made an emergency landing at Longside Airfield after experiencing a sudden onset of severe airframe vibration. The passengers were evacuated without injury. Subsequent examination of the helicopter revealed that a tail rotor blade flapping hinge retainer had fractured on one side.

Causal Factors

The AAIB investigation concluded that the following causal factors led to this incident: (1) maintenance inspections conducted over a period prior to the incident flight did not detect a developing surface crack in the Blue tail rotor blade flapping hinge retainer, despite additional work on the associated tail rotor drive shaft assembly to rectify a tail rotor vibration problem, which was *detectable as a trend recording* [emphasis added] within the Integrated Health and Usage Monitoring System (IHUMS) about 50 flying hours previously and *was the subject of an associated alert 5 hours before the incident* [emphasis added]; (2) the undetected fatigue crack extended during the flight, fracturing one side of the flapping hinge retainer and causing excessive and potentially critical tail rotor vibration; (3) the fatigue crack had been initiated by fretting and corrosion of the flapping hinge retainer bore induced by abnormal cyclic loading of the retainer which was attributed to the effects of a defective flap needle-roller bearing during some previous period of the tail rotor drive shaft's life; and (4) the inspection provisions within the aircraft Maintenance Manual and associated Maintenance Requirements *did not specify periodic visual inspections of such retainers* [emphasis added], since they had been designed and certificated on a 'safe-life' basis.

The Chain of Events

Basically, this case is about how the issue of airframe vibrations kept resurfacing over at least 14 days and ultimately led to the failure of the tail rotor. Figure 9.3 illustrates the chain of events leading-up to the emergency landing of this helicopter.

Under Minimum Pitch On Ground (MPOG) conditions, two airframe accelerometers picked up a difference between the tail rotor lateral and vertical vibrations. Since there was no reason to suspect that the Integrated Health and Usage Monitoring System (IHUMS) may have been cross-wired, the engineer trusted the accelerometer indications and rebalanced the tail rotor. It is not clear from the incident report whether the engineer would have chosen a different option if the IHUMS unit was wired correctly. Nonetheless, the AAIB investigators discovered that it would have been unlikely for the engineer to visually detect the crack, while rebalancing the rotor, even though it may have been approximately 54 mm (just over 2 inches) long at that time.

Eight days, and 39 flight hours, later, the IHUMS log report showed five data integrity warnings associated with the tail rotor vertical vibration sensor. Since such warnings are typically associated with instrumentation problems, engineers were able to detect and correct the cross-wired accelerometers. At this point, we assume that the data integrity warnings did not re-appear and also that there were no unusual accelerometer readings after correcting the wiring problem in the accelerometers. The aircraft continued to be in operation.

The following day, five days before the incident, a work requirement was issued for a 3,000-hour 'on-condition' check of the tail rotor gearbox, as detailed in the Maintenance Manual. At that time the IHUMS log report showed a suspected shaft imbalance defect associated with the tail rotor gearbox output shaft. The 3,000-hour work requirement called for a visual inspection of the tail rotor gearbox to determine the probable causes of the shaft imbalance. In accordance with the approved inspection procedures, the engineer noted that there was vertical 'play' in the tail rotor shaft assembly, which he determined was within the gearbox itself. As he considered this to be *abnormal*, he advised the shift supervisor that the gearbox was unserviceable and *discontinued* any further work. The engineer documented his decision using the appropriate protocol.

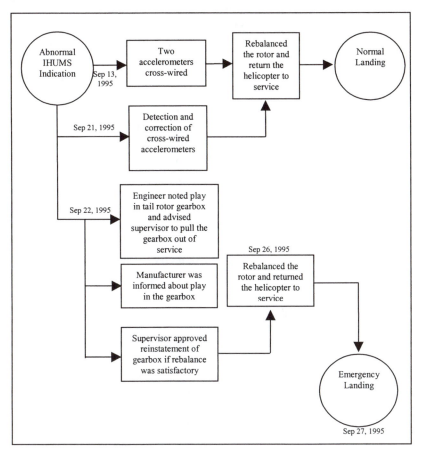

Figure 9-3: **The chain of events in the Super Puma accident**

Over the weekend, the manufacturer was informed of the gearbox shaft play. Without waiting for a response from the manufacturer, the shift supervisor determined that the gearbox could remain in service if the vibration could be reduced by rebalancing the rotor. The incident report did not have any information regarding how the shift supervisor arrived at this judgment. The supervisor asked another engineer to reassemble the rotor. Following the re-assembly, the rotor passed duplicate inspections. The reassembly and the first inspection were carried out during the night shift and the second of the duplicate inspections was carried out by a third engineer, possibly on the day shift.

Following the re-assembly, the tail rotor was rebalanced and the vibrations had reduced to an acceptable level. During this elaborate process of disassembly, reassembly, and inspections, no regulations or maintenance procedures were violated. The only issue here is whether it was appropriate to compensate for a play in the gearbox by rebalancing the rotor. It was great that somebody (either the supervisor or the original engineer who diagnosed the problem to the gearbox) decided to seek the manufacturer's opinion on this dilemma (an idea consistent with the CAP model discussed in Chapters 3 and 4). It was unfortunate that (a) they did not wait for the manufacturer's response (which in fact was to withdraw the gearbox from service) and (b) it was possible to compensate for the gearbox's deficiency by rebalancing the rotor. It is interesting, and noted by AAIB that nobody questioned why the tail rotor needed balancing if it had not sustained any damage or repair.

Causal Analysis

The incident report indicates that the defective flap needle-roller bearing led to an abnormal cyclic loading and contributed toward fretting corrosion. This corrosion resulted in the fracture of the tail rotor flapping hinge. The fractured flapping hinge induced the severe airframe vibration—the ultimate reason for the emergency landing.

It seems like there were several maintenance interventions established; however, they were ineffective. The accelerometers attached to the tail boom were cross-wired resulting in inappropriate correction of the vibration; visual inspection technique that was recommended to determine the presence of a crack in the tail rotor flap hinge retainer was inadequate; and the ground staff was unable to use the IHUMS data effectively because of the vast volume of data collected by the unit as well as its tendency for false alarms. Moreover, the maintenance crew was not able to isolate the cause of the vibration, but they were able to compensate by repeatedly rebalancing the rotor system. This strategy of applying standard solutions (rebalance) to standard problems (vibrations) resulted in *Normalized Risk*, which was discussed in Chapter 6, because nobody really tried to investigate the cause of those vibrations.

Figure 9-4 illustrates the causal diagram for this incident. The issue in this case is that the maintenance interventions that were in place were ineffective in detecting the crack.

In order to prevent such an incident/accident in the future, the U.K. AAIB made the following six systemic recommendations: (1) Aerospatiale should revise the maintenance manual and servicing recommendations to require periodic detailed inspection of the tail rotor shaft flapping hinge retainers for crack indication during the 50 hour inspections; (2) the CAA should review the integrity of helicopter public address systems and determine the most satisfactory way of significantly improving the reliability of such systems in conditions of severe vibrations; (3) the CAA should review the function and trigger thresholds of the ground based IHUMS software with the aim of introducing procedures which will be able, routinely and without substantial operator intervention, to highlight adverse trends; (4) the CAA should consider means by which ready access could be provided to fleet-wide trend data which would identify abnormal trends on a particular aircraft against an operator's whole fleet; and (5) in order to maximize the effectiveness of IHUMS through proper integration with the maintenance programs of existing helicopter types, the CAA should require all group "A" helicopters on the U.K. register to be subject to evaluation against the latest BCAR/JAR rotor and transmission Design Assessment requirements.

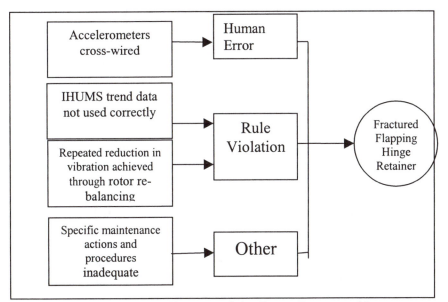

Figure 9-4:   Causal diagram of the Super Puma accident

Case Number 3: Turboprop Airplane (NTSB Case Number AAR 92/04, Continental Express 2574)

On September 11, 1991, Continental Express Flight 2574 (N33701), an Embraer 120, operating under 14CFR § 135, experienced a structural breakup in flight and crashed in a cornfield near Eagle Lake, Texas. All the passengers aboard the aircraft were fatally injured.

Probable Cause

The probable cause of this accident was determined to be the failure of Continental Express maintenance and inspection personnel to adhere to proper maintenance and quality assurance procedures for the airplane's horizontal stabilizer deice boots that led to the sudden in-flight loss of the partially secured left horizontal stabilizer leading edge and the immediate severe nose-down pitch over and breakup of the airplane. Contributing to the accident was the failure of the Continental Express management to ensure compliance with the approved maintenance procedures, and the failure of the FAA surveillance to detect and verify compliance with approved procedures.

The Chain of Events

This is a case of both poor communication practices among maintenance groups as well as failure of defenses. The ultimate structural failure occurred because the airplane was released into service with all the deice boot attachment screws from the top left hand side of the horizontal stabilizer missing. Nobody detected the missing screws because it was a high-tail airplane and so the top part of the stabilizer was not visible from the ground. Also, this specific maintenance action was not considered to be a required inspection item by Continental Express.

Now, let us take a look at why those screws were missing in the first place. You can follow along Figure 9-5. The night before the accident, the maintenance control office scheduled the removal and replacement of both deicer boots on the accident aircraft. The second shift supervisor had some extra time so he decided to help out the third shift. He asked two of his mechanics and one inspector to work on the deicer boot job. The two mechanics removed most of the screws from the bottom half of the right side of the stabilizer while the inspector removed screws from the top half of both left and right sides of the stabilizer. That was all they could do before their shift ended.

Continental Express used a written turnover system to help two maintenance shifts communicate the status of their work. The outgoing shift was expected to write what they had accomplished and the incoming shift was expected to review such write-ups. This process was approved by the FAA. Third-shift inspector reviewed the written turnover sheets before the second shift inspector had a chance to write the turnover. Consequently, the third shift inspector never received a turnover from the second shift inspector. Even if he had received the written turnover, the usefulness of that turnover is questionable because the second shift inspector simply wrote, 'helped the mechanic remove the deice boots'. Also, neither the third shift supervisor nor any of his mechanics were informed about the screws that were removed from the top half of the left hand side stabilizer. To make matters worse, since the original job card was intended for the third shift, the second shift never made an entry on the card regarding the status of their work.

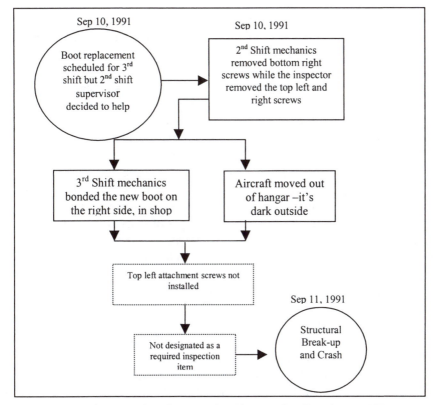

Figure 9-5:   The chain of events leading to the Continental Express accident

While operating with limited information regarding the status of the deicer boot job, the third shift mechanics proceeded to remove the right hand side leading edge assembly. They took it to the shop and bonded the new deicer boot to it. While they were gone to the shop, the hangar mechanics needed to bring in another aircraft, so they pushed out the accident aircraft—out in the dark. The mechanics returned with the right stabilizer leading edge and installed it on the aircraft. They never looked at the left hand side because apparently there was no need to do so. The third shift supervisor noticed that he was running out of time and so he decided to do the left hand side boot another time. Ultimately, the aircraft was delivered to the gate with all the top left hand side deicer boot attachment screws missing. The copilot did not notice the missing screws in his walk-around because they were not visible from the ground.

Causal Analysis

The causal analysis of this accident is illustrated in Figure 9-6. In this case, the maintenance work was intended for the third shift. Remember the Hawkins-Ashby model? If you try to apply that model to this case, you will soon discover that multiple changes were made to the system and hence the risk compounded. For example, the software element was placed out of the system when the third-shift task was initiated by the second shift. They did not take any special precautions to compensate for this variation. Then, the environment element was placed outside the system when the hangar mechanics decided to push the aircraft out in the dark, making it difficult for the original mechanics to work on the airplane and also causing them to lose focus. Again, neither the hangar mechanics nor the third-shift mechanics working on the aircraft compensated for this variation.

From the perspective of the different types of risks discussed in Chapter 6, the second shift supervisor took the *Good Samaritan* risk by trying to help the third shift. Of course, the thought was noble but additional precautions should have been taken to manage this risk. For example, the second shift supervisor probably recognized that there would be no record of the status of this job on the job card because the job was assigned to the third shift (third shift's cards would not be available to the second shift). Additionally, the second shift inspector took *Blatant* risk by not writing a complete and clear turnover for the third shift inspector. The accident report does not indicate whether or not there was an adequate amount of time for turnovers between shifts. This information would have been helpful to understand why the two inspectors did not talk about the job face-to-face.

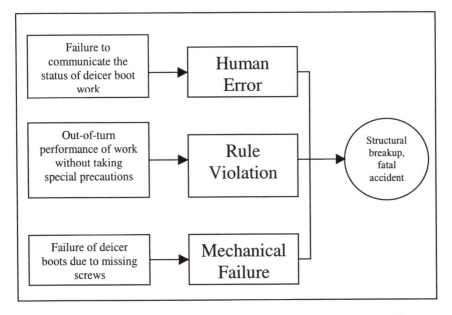

Figure 9-6:   Causal diagram of the Continental Express accident

One of the very essential behaviors that every mechanic must practice all the time is to make special efforts to notify others about partially completed jobs. There are several levels of dynamics that go on in a maintenance environment. For example, the people who are assigned to a particular lead mechanic or a supervisor or an engineer may be different every shift or may change within the shift. Similarly job priorities change all the time. When you start the shift, one job may be the top priority and halfway into that job, something else might arise as top priority. Consequently, the maintenance environment is constantly changing. The most reliable way to keep track of the developments, is to refer to the paperwork. If the paperwork/paper trail is incomplete or wrong, the risk of making an error increases exponentially.

Case Number 4: Turboprop Airplane (NTSB Case Number AAR-96-06)

On August 21, 1995, an EMB-120 RT, N256AS, operated as Atlantic Southeast Airlines flight 529, experienced the loss of a propeller blade from the left engine propeller while climbing through 18,100 feet. The airplane then crashed during an emergency landing near Carrollton, GA. The captain and four passengers sustained fatal injuries. Three other passengers died of injuries in the following 30 days. The first officer, the flight attendant and

11 passengers sustained serious injuries, the remaining 8 passengers sustained minor injuries.

Probable Cause

The NTSB determined that the probable cause of this accident was the in-flight fatigue fracture and separation of a propeller blade resulting in distortion of the left engine nacelle, causing excessive drag, loss of wing lift, and reduced directional control of the airplane. The fracture was caused by a fatigue crack from multiple corrosion pits that were not discovered by Hamilton Standard because of inadequate and ineffective corporate inspection and repair techniques, training, documentation, and communications.

Contributing to the accident was Hamilton Standard and the FAA's failure to require recurrent on-wing ultrasonic inspection for the affected propellers.

The Causal Chain of Events

The inflight failure of the Hamilton Standard (HS) propeller blade was caused due to an undetected crack in the taper bore of that blade. Based on two other blade separation accidents known to HS, they developed an ultrasonic inspection program to detect potentially dangerous blades. Based on the high volume of false alarms regarding these tests, HS concluded that if there was any visible mechanical damage such as that found on shot-peened blades, it could be blend-repaired. Although the intent of HS engineers (as stated in the NTSB report) was to simply use the blended repair to clear any superficial damage that may be causing the false indication of a crack in the ultrasonic inspections, their actual instructions were ambiguous. It was not clear if all seemingly mechanical damage, whether the blade was actually shot-peened or not, could be blended out. So the technicians inspecting such blades were left on their own to make the best judgment. In the case of the accident blade, the technician was able to validate the rejectable ultrasonic reading, but was not able to find the actual crack in his visual inspection.

The accident report does not indicate why the shop tracking form for the accident blade was not signed-off by a repairman when it had a column for the repairman's approval. Yet the blade received an airworthiness tag and was forwarded to the next HS facility for pre-shipping preparation. Figure 9-7 illustrates the chain of events leading to the crash of this Atlantic Southeast Airlines aircraft.

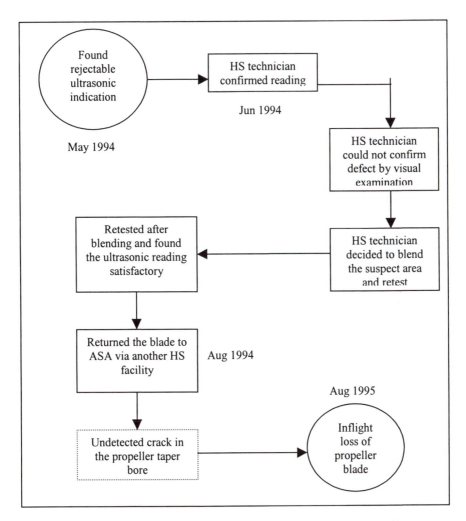

Figure 9-7:   The chain of events in the Atlantic Southeast accident

Causal Analysis

The most significant failures occurred at the rule level. There is no knowledge of how the HS technician decided that it was okay to blend the unshot-peened blade (besides his understanding) because there was no clear documentation available to substantiate his judgment. In this sense, he used the wrong rule to make his decision. As you might recall from our discussion regarding the use of CAP (Chapters 3 & 4), the ambiguity in documented instructions presented an opportunity to seek *external validation*. Additionally, there was a systemic rule-based failure because someone tagged the blade as airworthy when it had no evidence of passing an inspection by a repairman. It is plausible to consider that the HS technician was not able to recognize the crack when he looked for it under white light. This would be a human error. The mechanical failure, obviously, is the in-flight separation of the propeller blade. Figure 9-8 illustrates the causal diagram.

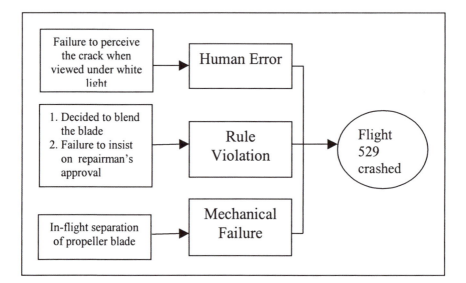

Figure 9-8:   Causal diagram of the Atlantic Southeast accident

Case Number 5: Turbojet Airplane (NTSB Case Number AAR 95-04, Learjet 35A)

On December 14, 1994, a Phoenix Air Learjet 35 crashed in Fresno, California. The flightcrew had declared an emergency inbound to Fresno Air Terminal due to engine fire indications. The flightcrew was heard on Fresno tower frequency attempting to diagnose the emergency conditions and control the airplane until it crashed, with landing gear down, on an avenue in Fresno. Both pilots were fatally injured. Twenty-one persons on ground were injured, and twelve apartment units in two buildings were destroyed or substantially damaged by impact and fire.

Probable Cause

The NTSB determined that the probable causes of this accident were as follows: (1) improperly installed electrical wiring for special mission operations that led to an in-flight fire that caused airplane systems and structural damage and subsequent airplane control difficulties; (2) improper maintenance and inspection procedures followed by the operator; and (3) inadequate oversight and approval of the maintenance and inspection practice by the operator in the installation of the special mission systems.

The Chain of Events

A series of Special Mission Power Wiring installations were initiated in 1989. Since such work was considered to be a major alteration, an FAA Form 337 was filed to document the scope and details of this alteration. According to the regulations (14CFR §43.13, Appendix B), the Form 337 should be filed within 48 hours after the aircraft is approved for return to service. Interestingly enough, an approved Form 337 is used by an authorized inspector as his basis for the approval of an aircraft for return to service. So, in reality, the Form 334 should be filed prior to undertaking the repair/alteration and it must be approved prior to the inspector's release of the aircraft back into service. The FAA inspector approving the Form 337 needs to ensure that the data provided in this form does not compromise airworthiness or the safety of the aircraft. The inspector approving the return of aircraft to service needs to ensure that the actual repair is consistent with the data provided in the Form 337. For some reason, these procedures were not adhered to by the mechanics and the inspectors associated with the alteration of Phoenix Air's aircraft. Consequently, 15 aircraft were wired incorrectly. Theoretically, there were 15 independent opportunities to identify the discrepancy between the actual work and the Form 337; however, none of the mechanics or the inspectors challenged the original work. By assuming that the first job was done correctly, they took the *Blatant* risk and endangered all 15 aircraft.

Then why did the first mechanic make an error in performing this alteration? This alteration was to be performed in the confines of the tail cone. So, he asked another mechanic where the wires were to be connected. Due to the miscommunication between these two mechanics, the wires were connected directly to the battery charging bus rather than to the generator bus. Due to this error, the 300 Amp DC power circuit did not have any over-current protection.

Figure 9-9 illustrates the chain of events for the Phoenix Air accident and Figure 9-10 illustrates the corresponding causal diagram.

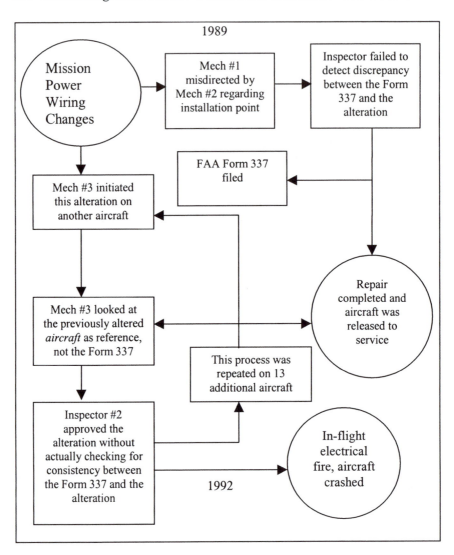

Figure 9-9:   The chain of events in the Phoenix Air accident

The NTSB report does not specify how many mechanics or inspectors were actually involved in this accident; however, it seems like multiple mechanics and inspectors may have fallen prey to the error made by the first mechanic who did the original alteration. Also, note the time-frame: the original alteration was completed in 1989 and the alteration on the accident aircraft was completed in 1992. So, for three years, nobody thought of validating the alteration with its documentation. If we were to say that mechanic # 1 led the rest of the mechanics astray by making an error, we must also concede that the rest of the mechanics did not provide adequate back-up to mechanic #1 when he needed it the most!

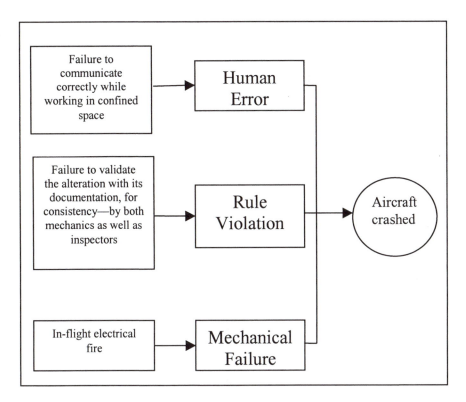

Figure 9-10:   The causal diagram of the Phoenix Air accident

Case Number 6: Domestic Air Carrier (NTSB Case Number AAR 96/03, ValuJet Flight 597)

On June 8, 1995, a DC-9-32, operated as ValuJet Airlines Flight 597, was scheduled to operate from Atlanta, Georgia to Miami, Florida. As it began its takeoff roll, an uncontained engine failure resulted in severance of the right engine main fuel line and an associated fire. The take-off was rejected and all occupants were evacuated. Two flight attendants and five passengers were injured. The pilots, the third flight attendant, and 52 passengers were not injured. The airplane's fuselage was destroyed.

Probable Cause

The NTSB determined that the probable cause of this accident was the failure of Turk Hava Yollari maintenance and inspection personnel to perform a proper inspection of a 7th stage high pressure compressor disk, thus allowing the detectable crack to grow to a length at which the disk ruptured, under normal operating conditions, propelling engine fragments into the fuselage; the fragments severed the right engine main fuel line, which resulted in a fire that rapidly engulfed the cabin area. The lack of an adequate recordkeeping system and the failure to use process sheets to document the step-by-step overhaul/inspection procedures contributed to the failure to detect the crack and, thus, to the accident.

The Chain of Events

An uncontained failure of the right engine occurred at low speed, early in the takeoff roll. The NTSB concluded that the engine failed due to the rupture of the 7th stage high-pressure compressor disk. This disk ruptured because of a radial crack that was not detected in the previous overhaul opportunity. In general, the crack was not detected because of poor inspection process and ambiguous procedures at the Turkish repair station where this engine was overhauled (4 years ago). The NTSB accident report indicates that there were several factors contributing to the ambiguity of the overhaul and inspection procedures at the repair station. First, the engine maintenance manual *was not clear* whether the SR hole (the location of the crack) was to be inspected when the tierod holes were being inspected. (Nobody sought validation like one would using the CAP.) Second, the engine maintenance manual *was in English*, while the *workforce was more fluent in Turkish*. Language difficulties increased the risk level. As per the Hawkins-Ashby model (Chapter 1), the liveware was placed out of the system because the technicians were not as fluent in English as the technical writers had expected. One could also view this situation as software was placed out of the system because the manuals were not meant for non-English-speaking users. Either way, one element of the SHELL model was placed out of the system and it was not compensated for by the organization or the users. The engine manufacturer had conducted an audit of the facility and recommended that specific process sheets delineating the inspection procedures, standards, and equipment be prepared in Turkish. No such process sheets were prepared. Third, there was no clear way of

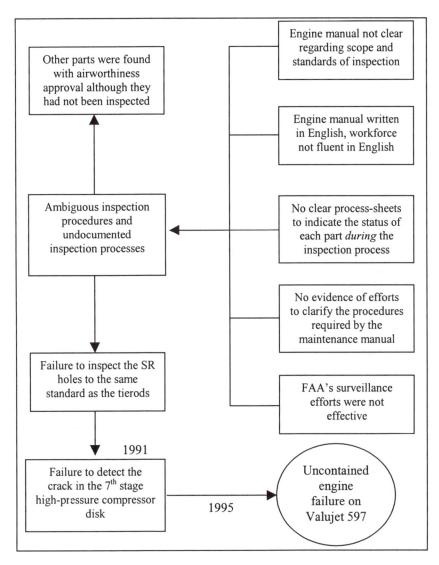

Figure 9-11: **The chain of events in the Valujet accident**

identifying the inspection status of the parts while they were being inspected. Consequently, it was possible for un-inspected parts to be released as airworthy. Finally, the FAA's surveillance of this foreign repair station was marginal. Therefore, there was no reliable way of knowing that all the parts of an engine that was overhauled by this facility had in fact received appropriate level of inspection. Figures 9-11 and 9-12 illustrate the chain of events leading to this accident and the causal factors responsible, respectively.

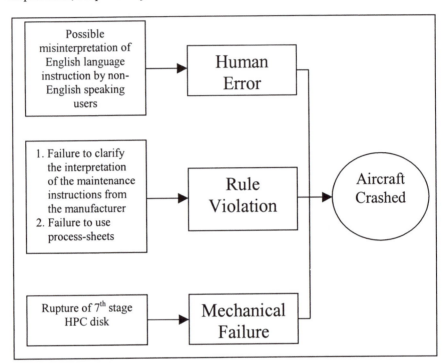

Figure 9-12:   The causal diagram of the Valujet accident

Case Number 7: Domestic Air Carrier (U.K. AAIB Case Number 3/96 EW/C95/2/3)

On February 23, 1995, a British Midlands Airways Boeing 737-400 experienced a loss of oil quantity as well as pressure on both engines. The crew diverted to Luton Airport and shut-down both engines during the landing roll. There were no injuries or damage in this incident.

Causal Factors

The AAIB investigation identified the following causal factors: (1) although the borescope inspection was signed-off as complete, the high-pressure rotor drive covers on both engines were not installed; (2) the engines were not run at ground idle after the inspection, as required by the Aircraft Maintenance Manual; (3) the Quality Assurance department failed to correct known deviations, over a significant period of time, by Company engineers; and (4) the Civil Aviation Authority, failed to withhold the JAR-145 approval of the Company in spite of the known deficiencies in their quality assurance system.

The Chain of Events

This accident is a glaring example of how workplace distractions, self-imposed pressures, and deviation from prescribed procedures can mutate into catastrophic combinations.

A British Midland Boeing 737-400 was scheduled for a dual borescope inspection during a night shift. A borescope inspection, in itself, is a demanding task. When combined with the fatigue issues of night shift work, the potential for error is higher. In the case of this aircraft, several additional complications were present.

The Line Engineer who was assigned this task, was short on help so he decided to tackle the borescope inspection job early in the shift. In fact, he may have even started the job prior to his official shift time. He prepared the number. 1 engine for inspection and walked over to the Base Maintenance hangar to obtain the borescope. There he asked the Base Maintenance Controller for the borescope and someone to assist him by turning the HP rotor while he examined the engine through the borescope.

The Base Maintenance Controller was also swamped with work and short-handed; however, he convinced the Line Engineer to allow him to help—the Controller wanted to do this job himself so that he could satisfy the currency requirements for his license. The Line Engineer obliged.

When the Line Engineer walked over to the Base Maintenance hangar, he had no intention of delegating the borescope inspection to someone else; consequently, he did not make any notes regarding the status of his pre-inspection work. He did verbally explain to the Controller that he had prepared the number 1 engine for inspection.

The Controller was distracted/pre-occupied by the following issues: (a) he was returning from a week's leave; (b) he had to go back and forth between the aircraft and other maintenance tasks in the hangar; (c) he was low on staff; (d) his storekeeper was absent, and (e) he needed these two inspections to satisfy the currency requirements of his license. Procedurally, he delegated most of the assembly/disassembly tasks to his fitter and he interrupted the fitter's workflow several times. Also, since the borescope inspection was originally intended for Line Maintenance, the associated paperwork did not have all the cross-checks and inspection steps that were familiar to the Controller.

As a result of these dynamics, the Controller failed to examine the engine thoroughly prior to releasing it to service. When the next shift's Line Engineer picked-up the airplane, he saw that the aircraft was outside the hangar and presumed that a ground test run might have been performed. The flight crew, in their preflight walk-around, discovered that the hydraulic as well as ignition circuit breakers were deactivated and the E/E bay hatch was open. They expressed their dissatisfaction to the Line Engineer prior to accepting the aircraft. The Line Engineer could not determine how the previous shift could have performed a ground test run when the ignition circuit breakers were off. He released the aircraft.

Figures 9-13 and 9-14 illustrate the chain of events and the causal factors, respectively.

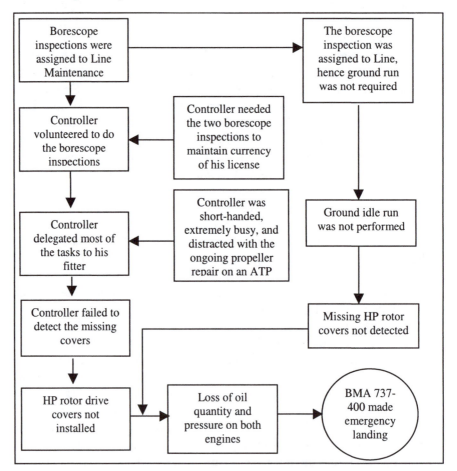

Figure 9-13:   The chain of events in the British Midland accident

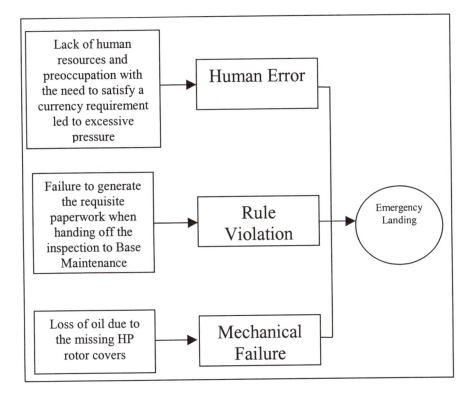

Figure 9-14:   The causal diagram of the British Midland accident

In this case, the human resources were very limited—both the Base Maintenance Controller as well as the Line Engineer knew that they were working with fewer than necessary personnel, but instead of finding creative means to compensate for this deficiency (per the Hawkins-Ashby model), they compounded it. They did not recognize the full implications of their deviation—although the Controller recognized the difference in the paperwork associated with approving the borescope inspection, he did not consult with the Engineer about the reason for the difference or think if he may be missing an essential step (as discussed under the CAP section in Chapters 3 and 4). From a systemic perspective, it seems like the U.K.-CAA was aware of the inconsistencies in the maintenance practices, but it failed to take corrective actions.

Case Number 8: International Air Carrier (NTSB Case/U.K. AAIB Report Number: 5/2000 (EW/C98/1/3), United B-767-322ER)

On January 9, 1998, a United Airlines Boeing 767-322ER was enroute from Zurich to Washington, DC (this was an extended twin engine operation—ETOPS—flight). The crew noticed abnormal warnings on the flight deck instrumentation and circuit breakers began to trip. The Captain consulted with the Company's maintenance control at London Heathrow Airport (LHR) and decided to divert and land at LHR. Upon landing, several abnormalities occurred: the right thrust reverser did not deploy completely; there was some smoke in the cabin; in the emergency evacuation process, one of the escape slides jammed; and because of some miscommunication between the crew and the LHR tower, the tower controllers claimed that they did not know that the aircraft was landing with technical problems—this delayed the response by emergency vehicles on the ground.

Causal Factors

The U.K. Air Accident Investigation Board's (AAIB) investigation identified the following causal factors: (1) the circuit breakers tripped because of an electrical arcing near the forward galley chiller unit within the Electronic & Equipment (E&E) bay; (2) prior damage to the wiring loom insulation adjacent the aft/upper corner of the chiller unit had occurred due to contact with such units during associated removal and installation; this chiller unit had been replaced on the day before the accident; (3) aluminum alloy shavings were present within the E&E bay prior to the accident and had probably assisted the onset of arcing between adjacent damaged wires in the loom; (4) incorrect installation of the chiller unit, with its heat exchanger exhaust fitted with a blanking plate, would have caused warm exhaust air to discharge from an alternative upper vent which was capable of blowing any aluminum shavings around the wiring looms; (5) the crew were unaware of the potentially serious arcing fire in the E&E bay during the flight due to failure of the bay smoke warning system to activate on the flight deck, because the density of smoke emitted by the arcing wiring in the bay was not apparently sufficient to be detected by the only smoke sensor; and (6) the jamming of a severely worn latch, associated with the right off-wing slide compartment, prevented that escape slide from operating during the evacuation.

The Chain of Events

The United Airlines aircraft was on an ETOPS flight from Zurich to Washinton, DC. The crew noticed abnormal warnings on their instrument panel. They consulted the Company's maintenance control center at Heathrow airport and decided to divert and land at Heathrow. It is not clear whether the crew notified the Heathrow tower that they were coming in due to a technical problem; however, it is difficult to imagine that when the crew asked for clearance to land at LHR, the tower did not enquire about their status and intention; after all, the flight was *diverted* to LHR. Anyway, there were no further problems until the flight touched down. During the landing roll, the right thrust reverser failed to deploy and there was smoke in the forward section of the cabin. So, the captain called for an emergency evacuation. Then, one of the escape slides did not deploy. The passengers and crew suffered some minor injuries in the evacuation process.

In the Figure 9-15, if you follow the chain of events leading to the warning messages in the cockpit, it is interesting to note that in an attempt to force-fit a wrong chiller unit, someone damaged the neighboring wires. Additionally, there was some conductive debris such as metal shavings, coins, safety wire pieces, and copper wire pieces. With the hot exhaust from the chiller unit blowing in the wrong direction, the presence of conductive debris in close proximity to a damaged wiring loom, it was no surprise that arcing took place.

Figure 9-16 illustrates the causal factors associated with this incident. This incident goes to illustrate one more time that aviation is a complex and tightly coupled system. As we discussed in Chapter 7 under the normal accident theory, a change in any one of its components can lead to unforeseen consequences, rapidly.

Additionally, an important point to note in this case is that this was an ETOPS flight. According to an article in *Aerospace Engineering* (1999), an ETOPS flight is subjected to a thorough examination, held to higher maintenance and performance standards, and maintained by specially qualified technicians. Under such conditions of improved maintenance practices, it is surprising that (a) the wrong chiller was installed, (b) the escape slide latch was jammed, and (c) the right-side thrust reverser failed to deploy completely.

The *Aerospace Engineering* (1999) article mentions how 'dual maintenance errors' are being minimized by avoiding identical multiple maintenance actions to ETOPS-critical systems. According to this system, the British Midlands aircraft would never have been scheduled for dual borescope examination in the same shift. And even if it was scheduled, the two borescope examinations would have been performed by two different people.

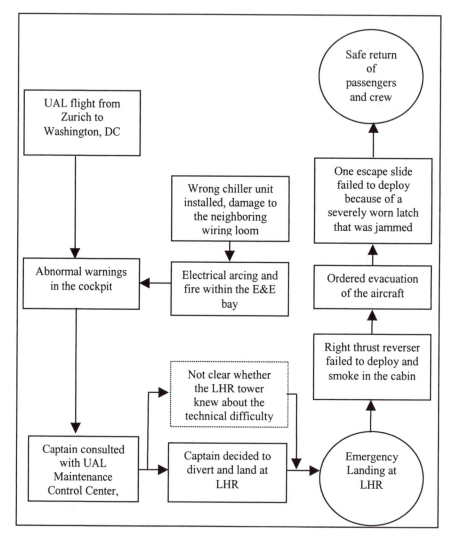

Figure 9-15: **The chain of events in the emergency landing by a United Airlines ETOPS flight**

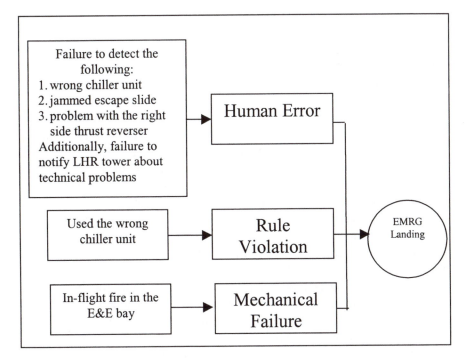

Figure 9-16: **The causal factors in the emergency landing by a United Airlines ETOPS flight**

Chapter Summary

The eight maintenance-related cases presented in this chapter illustrate some of the typical errors and risks that are associated with maintenance actions. The Cessna 210 case is an example of *Good Samaritan* risk. It showed how repetitive maintenance actions can lead to complacency as well as increase risk of an error due to the increased level of exposure. The Super Puma case is an example of *Normalized* Risk. It showed how rebalancing the tail rotor masked the cracked hinge—they kept addressing the vibration issue with rebalancing, without considering that perhaps something else may be wrong. In the case of the Continental Express EMB-120, poor communication between shifts resulted in the release of the aircraft with all the de-icer boot attachment screws missing from the top half of the right horizontal stabilizer. It is a combination of *Good Samaritan* and *Blatant* risks. Furthermore, it is a good example wherein the Hawkins-Ashby model could have been helpful in understanding the risks. In the fourth case, another EMB 120, the Hamilton Standard technician decided to blend-out the suspect area even though he was not sure whether such an action was permitted. Consequently, although unintentionally, he masked the crack in the taper bore which ultimately resulted in in-flight separation of the blade. This case illustrates the importance of external validation, an essential step in the Concept Alignment Process. In the case of the Learjet accident, the mechanic assumed (thereby taking *Blatant* risk) that a similar repair on another aircraft was correct and decided to replicate the repair on his aircraft. The inspector did not verify that the repair conformed to the drawing associated with the FAA Form 337 (thereby taking *Blatant* risk). So, both the mechanic as well as the inspector based their judgment on incorrect data. The Valujet case resulted from incorrect maintenance practices at a foreign repair station. The maintenance instructions were ambiguous, the technicians may not have been fluent in English so as to clearly understand the maintenance instructions, and ultimately there was no clear way to determine the inspection status of a part resulting in several un-inspected parts being released as airworthy. This case obviously had several compounding factors making it almost impossible for the workers or the inspectors to know the exact status of any part. The British Midlands accident was a classic case of lack of resources and individual distractions forming a catastrophic combination. Neither the Line Engineer nor the Base Maintenance Controller made any efforts to control the risks due to distractions when they knew that they were short-handed (resources were limited and time pressure was high). Finally, in the case of the United Airlines flight, seemingly minor error—wrong chiller unit—resulted in an in-flight fire. This incident, in particular, illustrates the potential of seemingly minor sloppiness in maintenance actions causing unprecedented damage.

In closing, we would like to emphasize that accident reports as well as self-reports such as the ASRS or CHIRP reports are most likely to emphasize the compliance elements of safety because that is the only area of legal accountability. We hope that in the next generation of MRM programs, we are able to focus on open communication and interpersonal trust.

Review Question

1. The above cases illustrate that a unique combination of human errors and rule violations results in catastrophic consequences. List the generic rules that you would incorporate in your work habits so as to minimize the probability of a deadly combination of human errors and rule violations.

Chapter 10

Resources

Introduction

In this chapter, we will provide information about Internet-based as well as paper-based resources in the overall aviation safety domain. Government sources such as the FAA, NTSB, and the Bureau of Transportation Statistics have reliable quantitative data at the system level. Such data will tell you the overall trend in aviation safety and you will be able to compare these data across different modes of transportation. If you are interested in causal analysis, you will have to read through each accident report in great detail and manually analyze the data. If you are interested in understanding whether a particular safety course in your organization is effective, you will need to do some detailed data collection. The bottom line is that there are plenty of sources that provide the general, systemic data; but few that can provide reliable, consistent data at a microscopic level.

Government-sponsored Data Sources

Aviation Safety Reporting System (ASRS)

The Aviation Safety Reporting System is located at http://asrs.nasa.gov/. This program is administered by NASA. As you know from previous chapters, NASA Forms or ASRS Forms are used by both pilots as well as mistakes or to report on systemic problems that they have encountered. These reports are de-identified and the data are compiled in the form of a variety of reports that would be of interest to the entire aviation community. Additionally, individuals as well as the FAA can request specific type of data. ASRS also offers a purchase option, whereby you can purchase a CD containing all the ASRS reports and then search them (manually at this time) to meet your specific needs.

This is a great source of archival data for research purposes. One important aspect to remember, however, is that the data are biased. The two basic problems with ASRS data are as follows:

1. The system is entirely voluntary—certain individuals who are more likely to report a problem submit reports; consequently, an area of large number of reports is likely to be simply a reflection of reporters' bias
2. Only about 20% of the incoming reports are coded/recorded by ASRS due to staffing constraints.

In spite of these deficiencies, the ASRS reports provide reasonable data regarding systemic problems. We would encourage you to use ASRS reports to substantiate your research problem, but not depend on these data alone to recommend or test possible solution or intervention strategies.

British Airways Safety Information System (BASIS)

The BASIS system is owned and operated by British Airways. This system is available to member-companies through a password-protected web access. BASIS seems to be more focused on the technical aspects of data sharing rather than human error. Additional information about BASIS can be found at http://www.basishelp.com/#. You can also request a demo CD from the BASIS site.

Confidential Human Factors Incident Reporting Programme (CHIRP)

CHIRP is located at http://www.chirp.co.uk/. This program is quite similar to the U.S.-based ASRS program in terms of type of data that are being solicited. However, the issues of immunity from prosecution, level of participation from the various professional groups in aviation, and the sources of funding are quite different among ASRS and CHIRP. Nonetheless, these two sources serve as interesting resources for comparison of systemic issues.

Transport Canada's Incident Reporting System And Other Safety Efforts

Transport Canada has developed an online incident reporting system. The reporting form can be accessed at http://www.tc.gc.ca/CivilAviation/ SystemSafety/caco/report.asp. Whether ASRS-type immunity is available to the reporter is not known at the time of this writing. Transport Canada has also developed a safety culture scoring system that will help you assess your organization's vulnerability to accidents. You can try it at the following address:

http://www.tc.gc.ca/civilaviation/systemsafety/tp13844/menu.htm

Additionally, they have an excellent publication called *Introduction to Safety Management Systems*. It can be accessed at the following address: http://www.tc.gc.ca/aviation/syssafe/tp13739/english/index_e.htm

Human Factors in Aviation Maintenance and Inspection, FAA

Since 1988, the FAA has sponsored numerous research projects to identify problems in the maintenance and inspection segments of the industry. As a result of these research efforts, tremendous amount of reports, papers, and presentations are available in the public domain. Additionally, the FAA's Office of Aviation Medicine joined forces with the UK-CAA and Transport Canada to host an annual conference on Human Factors in Aviation Maintenance and Inspection. Each organization, the FAA, CAA, and TC, takes turn hosting it in their respective country. Therefore, it is a great forum of international collaboration, in terms of learning from each other's success stories and challenges. Their website is located at http://hfskyway.faa.gov/. Starting September 2003, this conference series will be renamed to *Safety Management Systems* conference.

The National Aviation Safety Data Analysis Center (NASDAC), FAA

NASDAC is located at http://nasdac.faa.gov/. This database provides both qualitative and quantitative data on a variety of subjects and from a variety of sources. This is a very useful resource for students, practitioners, and researchers. For example, you can search accident and incident reports by State, Date, N-number (registration number), Airline, Aircraft Model, and Operation Type.

The National Transportation Safety Board (NTSB)

The NTSB is located at http://www.ntsb.gov. Recently, the NTSB has started offering courses to the general public through their NTSB Academy. If you are interested in areas such as accident investigation, crash site management, or assistance to families of accident victims, the NTSB Academy offers some excellent courses.

The NTSB is responsible for investigating accidents in Aviation, Railroads, Highways, Pipelines, and Marine. Additionally, it also provides guidance on Hazardous Materials.

Initially, you may want to focus on the aviation accidents database so that you are familiar with the typical contents of such reports. However, some of you might find it interesting to note the accidents in other modes of transportation. As you might guess, there are several lessons to be learned among the various transportation modes. For example, issues such as fatigue, probability of detection of a failure, layout of control panels, quality of information, etc. are common across the modes.

U.S. Military Data

Military transport aircraft accident data are available through the Air Safety Network website at http://aviation-safety.net/database/other/.

Additionally, The U.S. Navy offers exhaustive links to a wide variety of websites that provide both military as well as civilian (limited) aviation safety information (http://vislab-www.nps.navy.mil/~avsafety/#hotlists).

The branch-specific sites are as follows:
1. The U.S. Army Safety Center
   (http://safety.army.mil/home.html)
2. The U.S. Naval Safety Center
   (http://www.safetycenter.navy.mil/)
3. The USMC Safety Division
   (http://www.hqmc.usmc.mil/safety.nsf)
4. The United States Coast Guards Marine Safety
   (http://www.uscg.mil/hq/g-m/gmhome.htm)
5. The U.S. Air Force Safety Center (http://www-afsc.saia.af.mil/)

The U.S. military, beyond doubt, has tremendous operational experience. Safety is a critical aspect of every operation--whether on surface, above the surface, or below the surface! From a research perspective, military facilities have been the "breeding ground" for experimental research because the organizational conditions are a lot more conducive to experimental research. Nonetheless, applications of such research findings to the civilian world are difficult to implement.

Non-government Sources

Besides the NTSB and the FAA websites, certain other websites my be useful to you in your quest for specific accident reports, particularly foreign air carriers or U.S. air carrier accidents in a foreign territory. Some such websites are as follows:

1. Aviation Safety Network (http://aviation-safety.net/index.shtml)
2. FlightSafety Foundation (http://www.flightsafety.org/home.html)
3. AirSafe, Inc. (http://www.airsafe.com/index.html)
4. General Aviation Accidents/Incidents Reports and Information (http://www.landings.com/)

Specific Accident Investigation Boards

1. Australian Air Transport Safety Board (ATSB) (http://www.atsb.gov.au/)
2. Transport Canada (http://tsb.gc.ca/ENG/)
3. United Kingdom's Air Accidents Investigation Branch (AAIB) (http://www.aaib.dft.gov.uk/)

As you read a variety of accident reports, you will soon realize that different reports cite information in different formats as well as from different perspectives. Also, as you track one particular organization's reports over a decade or so, you will realize that the reporting format and content focus have changed.

Excellent Additions To Your Reference Library

We present the following collection of books as an excellent resource for theoretical as well as practical aspects of aviation safety and risk management information.

1. ATA—U.S. Air Transport Association (2001). *Spec 113: Maintenance human factors program guidelines.* Retrieved January 15, 2002, from http://www.airlines.org/public/publications/display1.asp?nid=938.
2. Collins, J. C., and Porras, J. I. (1997). *Built to last: Successful habits of visionary companies.* New York, NY: HarperCollins Publishers, Inc.
3. FAA (1998). *Aviation human factors guide* (v3.0) [CD-ROM]. Washington, DC: Federal Aviation Administration.
4. FAA (1999). *FAA Maintenance Resource Management handbook.* Washington, D.C.: Federal Aviation Administration.
5. FAA (2001). *Advisory Circular 120-72 Maintenance Resource Management training.* Washington, DC: Department of Transportation.

6. Helmreich, R., and Merritt, A. (1998). *Culture at work in aviation and medicine: National, organizational, and professional influences*. Aldershot, U.K.: Ashgate Publishing Limited.
7. McDonald, N., Johnston, N., and Fuller, R. (Eds.) (1995), *Applications of psychology to the aviation system*. Aldershot, U.K.: Ashgate Publishing Limited.
8. Phillips, J. (1997). *Return on investment in training and performance improvement programs*. Houston, TX: Gulf Publishing Company.
9. Reason, J. (1997). *Managing the risk of organizational accidents*. Aldershot, U.K.: Ashgate Publishing Limited.
10. Taylor, J.C. and Christensen, T.D. (1998). *Airline Maintenance Resource Management: Improving communication*. Warrendale, PA: Society of Automotive Engineers.

References

AAIB (n.d). *Report on the accident to Aerospatiale AS332L Super Puma, G-TIGK, in North Sea 6 nm South West of Brae Alpha Oil Production Platform on 19 January 1995* [Aircraft Accident Report No: 2/97 (EW/C95/1/1)]. Air Accidents Investigation Branch. Retrieved February 2, 2001 from http://www.aaib.dtlr.gov.uk.

AAIB (n.d.). *Report on the incident to a Boeing 737-400, G-OBMM on Daventry on 25 [sic 23] February 1995* [Aircraft Accident Report No: 3/96 EW/C95/2/3]. Air Accidents Investigation Branch. Retrieved February 2, 2001 from http://www.aaib.dtlr.gov.uk.

Ackoff, R., and Emery, F. (1972). *On purposeful* systems. Chicago: Aldine-Atherton.

Aerospace Engineering (1999, November). Maintenance lessons from ETOPS, 29-31.

Allen, J., and Marx, D. (1994). Maintenance Error Decision Aid project. In *Proceedings of the Eighth International Symposium on Human Factors in Aircraft Maintenance and Inspection*. Washington, DC: Federal Aviation Administration, 101-115.

Ashby, W. R. (1956). *Introduction to cybernetics*, (pp. 202-218). New York: John Wiley & Sons.

ATA (1999). *SPEC 113: Maintenance Human Factors Program Guidelines*. Washington, DC: Air Transport Association.

ATA (2002). *Safety record of U.S. airlines*. Retrieved December 16, 2002 from http://www.airlines.org/public/industry/display1.asp?nid= 1036.

Badaracco, J. (1997). *Defining Moments: When managers must choose between right and right*. Boston, MA: Harvard Business School Press.

Beaumont, G. (1995). Achieving organizational attachment through resource management. In N. McDonald, N. Johnston, and R. Fuller (Eds.), *Applications of psychology to the aviation system* (pp. 69-74). Aldershot, U.K.: Ashgate Publishing Limited.

Bethune, G., and Huler, S. (1998). *From worst to first: Behind the scenes of Continental's remarkable comeback*. New York: John Wiley & Sons.

Bovier, C. (1998, February). Debriefs: removing the veil of silence. *Flying Careers*, 8-13.

Chandler, J. (1996, February). Experts offer tips on outsourcing. *Aviation Equipment Maintenance*, 26-28.

Clark, P. (2002). *Ramp safety revisited: Chaos or concerto?* Presented at the United Kingdom Flight Safety Committee Annual Seminar. Retrieved February 21, 2003 from http://www.ukfsc.co.uk/Attachments%20for%20Priv%20Info/Paul%20Clark%20Seminar%202002.pdf

Collins, J., and Porras, J. (1997). *Built to last: Successful habits of visionary companies.* New York: HarperCollins Publishers, Inc.

Dismukes, K., Jobe, K., and McDonnell, L. (1997, March). *LOFT debriefings: an analysis of instructor techniques and crew participation.* Moffett Field, CA: NASA- Ames Research Center.

Drury, C. (1998) Work design. In M. Mattox (Ed.), *Human factors guide for aviation maintenance* Retrieved August 20, 2002 from http://hfskyway.faa.gov/HFAMI.

Drury, C., and Rangel, J. (1996). Reducing automation-related errors in maintenance and inspection. *Human Factors in Aviation Maintenance—Phase VI: Progress Report* (Vol. II, pp. 281-306). Washington, DC: Federal Aviation Administration/Office of Aviation Medicine.

Drury, C., Wenner, C., and Murthy, M. (1997). A proactive error reporting system. *Human Factors in Aviation Maintenance-- Phase VII: Progress Report* (pp. 109-121). Washington, DC: Federal Aviation Administration/Office of Aviation Medicine.

Durkin, J. (1994). *Expert systems: Design and development.* New York: Macmillan.

Emery, F., and Trist, E., (1965). The causal texture of organizational environments. *Human Relations*, Vol 18, pp. 21-31.

FAA (1997). *Advisory Circular No. 120-66, Aviation Safety Action Programs (ASAP).* Washington, DC: Federal Aviation Administration.

FAA (1999). *Advisory Circular No. 120-66A, Aviation Safety Action Programs (ASAP).* Washington, DC: Federal Aviation Administration.

FAA, (2002). *Human Factors in Aviation Maintenance and Inspection Training.* Retrieved December 3, 2002 from http://hfskyway.faa.gov/training_toc.htm

Fotos, C. (1991, August 26th). Continental applies CRM concepts to technical, maintenance corps, training in stresses, teamwork, self-assessment techniques. *Aviation Week & Space Technology*, 32-35.

Freiberg, K., and Freiberg, J. (1996) *Nuts! Southwest Airlines' crazy recipe for business and personal success.* Austin, TX: Bard Press.

Gertman, D., and Blackman, H. (1994). *Human reliability and safety analysis data handbook.* New York: John Wiley & Sons.

Goglia, J., Patankar, M., and Taylor, J. (2002). Lack of error mitigation tools: The weakest link in maintaining airworthiness? In *Proceedings of the 55ʰ Annual International Air Safety Seminar (Dublin, Ireland).* Washington, DC: Flight Safety Foundation.

Goldsby, R. (1996, January). Training and certification in the aircraft maintenance industry: Technician resources for the twenty-first century. In W. Sheperd (Ed.), *Human Factors in Aviation Maintenance—Phase Five Progress Report.* Washington, DC: Federal Aviation Administration/Office of Aviation Medicine.

Grandjean, E. (1980). *Fitting the task to the man: An ergonomic approach* (3rd ed.). London: Taylor & Francis, Inc.

Gregorich, S., Helmreich, R., and Wilhelm, J. (1990). The structure of cockpit management attitudes. *Journal of Applied Psychology, 75,* 682-690.

Havard, S. (1996). Why adopt a human factors program in engineering? In B. J. Hayward and A. R. Lowe (Eds.), *Applied aviation psychology: Achievement, change and challenge* (pp. 394-399). Aldershot, U.K.: Ashgate Publishing Limited.

Hawkins, F. H. (1987). *Human factors in flight.* Aldershot, U.K.: Ashgate Publishing Limited.

Hays, W. (1963). *Statistics for psychologists*, New York: Holt, Rinehart & Winston.

Hayward, B. (1995). Organisational change: the human factor. In N. McDonald, N. Johnston, and R. Fuller (Eds.), *Applications of psychology to the aviation system* (pp. 63-68). Aldershot, U.K.: Ashgate Publishing Limited.

Helmreich, R., and Merritt, A. (1998). *Culture at work in aviation and medicine: National, organizational and professional influences.* Aldershot, U.K.: Ashgate Publishing Limited.

Helmreich, R., and Wilhelm, J. (1991). Outcomes of Crew Resource Management training. *International Journal of Aviation Psychology, 1*(4), 287-300.

Helmreich, R., Fouchee, C., Benson, R., and Russini, W. (1986). Cockpit Resource Management: Exploring the attitude-performance linkage. *Aviation Space & Environmental Medicine 57*(12), 1198-1200. Aerospace Medical Association.

Helmreich, R., Merritt, A., Sherman, P., Gregorich, S., and Wiener, E. (1993). The Flight Management Attitude Questionnaire (FMAQ), *NASA/UT/FAA Technical Report 93-4*, Austin, TX: The University of Texas.

Hertzberg, F. (1968). One more time: how do you motivate employees? *Harvard Business Review, 46*, 53-62. Boston, MA: Harvard Business School Press.

Hobbs, A. and Robertson, M. (1996). Human factors in aircraft maintenance workshop report. In B.J. Hayward and A. R. Lowe (Eds.), *Applied aviation psychology: Achievement, change, and challenge* (pp. 468-474). Aldershot, U.K.: Ashgate Publishing Limited.

Hofstede, G. (1984). *Culture's consequences: International differences in work related values (Abridged Edition).* Beverly Hills, CA: Sage.

Hutchinson, C.R.III. (1997). Aviation speedometers: Metrics on the hangar floor. *Ground Effects, 2* (1, January/February), 1-5.

Jian, J., Bisantz, A., and Drury, C. (2000). Foundations for an empirically determined scale of trust in automated systems. *International Journal of Cognitive Ergonomics, 4*(1), 53-71.

Johnston, N. (1993). CRM: Cross-cultural perspectives. In E.L. Wiener, B. G. Kanki, and R.L. Helmreich (Eds.) *Cockpit Resource Management.* San Diego: Academic Press.

Kanki, B., Walter, D., and Dulchinos, V. (1997). Operational interventions to maintenance error. In *Proceedings of the Ninth International Symposium on Aviation Psychology.* Columbus, OH: The Ohio State University, 997-1002.

Kantowitz, B., and Sorkin, R. (1983). *Human factors: Understanding people-system relationships.* New York: John Wiley & Sons.

Kirkpatrick, D. (1975). Techniques for evaluating training programs. *Evaluating Training Programs*, Alexandria, VA: American Society for Training and Development, 1-17.

Komarniski, R. (2000, November). No small talk. *Aircraft Maintenance Technology*, 60-61.

Lipnack, J., and Stamps, J. (2000). *Virtual teams: People working across boundaries with technology* (2nd ed.). New York: John Wiley & Sons.

Lopp, D. (1997). Human Factors in maintenance: an awareness discussion. *ATEC Journal, 18*(2), 4-6.

Lynch, K. (1996). Management systems: A positive, practical method of Cockpit Resource Management. In *Proceedings of the 41st Corporate Aviation Safety Seminar.* Orlando, FL: The Flight Safety Foundation, 244-254.

Marx, D. (1997). Moving toward 100% error reporting in maintenance. In *Proceedings of the Eleventh International Symposium on Human Factors in Aircraft Maintenance and Inspection.* Washington, DC: Federal Aviation Administration.

Marx, D. (1998). Learning from our mistakes: A review of maintenance error investigation and analysis systems. In *Proceedings of the Twelfth International Symposium on Human Factors in Aviation Maintenance and Inspection.* Retrieved December 6, 2002 from http://hfskyway.faa.gov/HFAMI.

Marx, D. (2000). *The causation trainer* (v.1.0) [Computer-based training program]. Retrieved August 28, 2001 from http://www.causationtrainer.com.

Marx, D., and Graeber, R. (1994). Human error in aircraft maintenance. In N. Johnston, N. McDonald, and R. Fuller (Eds.), *Aviation psychology in practice* (pp. 87-104). Aldershot, UK: Ashgate Publishing Limited.

Mathews, S. (2000, April). *Safety—an essential ingredient for profitability.* Paper presented at the SAE Advances in Aviation Safety Conference, Daytona Beach, FL.

Maurino, D. (1996). Eighteen years of the CRM wars: A report from headquarters. In B. J. Hayward and A. R. Lowe (Eds.), *Applied aviation psychology: Achievement, change and challenge* (pp. 99-109). Aldershot, U.K.: Ashgate Publishing Limited.

Maurino, D., Reason, J., and Johnston, N. (1997). *Beyond aviation human factors.* Aldershot, U.K.: Ashgate Publishing Limited.

McDonald, N. (1994a) Applied psychology and aviation: Issues of theory and practice. In N. Johnston, N. McDonald, and R. Fuller (Eds.) *Aviation psychology in practice.* Aldershot, U.K.: Ashgate Publishing Limited.

McDonald, N. (1994b) The management of safety on the airport ramp. In N. Johnston, N. McDonald, and R. Fuller (Eds.) *Aviation psychology in practice.* Aldershot, U.K.: Ashgate Publishing Limited.

NBAA (2002, June). *NBAA Aircraft ground damage prevention: Best practices for preventing business aircraft ground damage events.* Retrieved February 21, 2003 from http://www.nbaa.org/safety/ NBAAAircraftGroundDamagePrevention.ppt

NTSB (n.d.). *NTSB Report No. SEA95FA213.* Retrieved February 2, 2001 from www.ntsb.gov/ntsb/.

NTSB (1992, July). *Britt Airways, Inc. d/b/a Continental Express Flight 2574 in-flight structural breakup, EMB-120RT, N33701, Eagle Lake, Texas, September 11, 1991* [NTSB/AAR-92/04]. Washington, DC: National Transportation Safety Board.

NTSB (1995, August). *Crash during emergency landing, Phoenix Air, Learjet 35A, N521PA, Fresno, California, December 14, 1994* [NTSB/AAR-95/04]. Washington, DC: National Transportation Safety Board.

NTSB (1996, July). *Uncontained engine failure/fire, Valujet Airlines Flight 597, Douglas DC-9-32, N908VJ, Atlanta, Georgia, June 8, 1995* [NTSB/AAR-96/03]. Washington, DC: National Transportation Safety Board.

NTSB (1996, November). *In-flight loss of propeller blade, forced landing, and collision with terrain, Atlantic Southeast Airlines, Inc., Flight 529, Embraer EMB-120RT, N256AS, Carrollton, Georgia, August 21, 1995* [NTSB/AAR-96/06]. Washington, DC: National Transportation Safety Board.

Patankar, M., and Taylor, J. (1998).   The multi-party world of aircraft maintenance: a case for systemic management and human factors education.   In *Proceedings of the SAE Airframe/Engine Maintenance and Repair Conference* [SAE Technical Paper Number 983103]. Daytona Beech, FL.

Patankar, M., and Taylor, J. (1999a).   Professional and organizational barriers to implementing macro human factors based safety initiatives: a comparison between the airlines of the United States and India.   In *Proceedings of the SAE Airframe/Engine Maintenance and Repair Conference* [SAE Technical Paper Number 1999-01-2979]. Vancouver, BC.

Patankar, M., and Taylor, J. (1999b). *Corporate aviation on the leading edge: systemic implementation of macro-human factors in aviation maintenance* Paper No. 1999-01-1596. SAE General, Corporate & Regional Aviation Meeting & Exposition, Wichita, KS.

Patankar, M., and Taylor J. (2000a).   Corporate aviation on the leading edge: systemic implementation of macro-human factors in aviation maintenance. *SAE Transactions: Journal of Aerospace*, *1*(108), 305-310.

Patankar, M., and Taylor, J. (2000b).   Targeted MRM programs: setting ROI goals and measuring results. In *Proceedings of the SAE Advances in Aviation Safety Conference* [SAE Technical Paper Number 2000-01-2127]. Daytona Beach, FL.

Patankar, M., and Taylor, J. (2001). *Analysis of organizational and individual factors leading to maintenance errors* [SAE Technical Paper Number 2001-01-3005]. Warrendale, PA: Society of Automotive Engineers.

Patankar, M. and Taylor, J. (In Press). Posterior probabilities of causal factors leading to unairworthy dispatch of a revenue flight. *Journal of Quality in Maintenance Engineering*, Bradford, U.K.: MCB Publishing.

Perrow, C. (1984). *Normal accidents: Living with high-risk technologies*. New York: Basic Books.

Phillips, J. (1997). *Return on investment*. Houston: Gulf Publishing.

Pidgeon, N., and O'Leary, M. (1995). Organisational safety culture and aviation practice. In N. McDonald, N. Johnston, and R. Fuller (Eds.), *Applications of psychology to the aviation system* (pp. 47-52). Aldershot, U.K.: Ashgate Publishing Limited.

Rankin, B., and Allen, J. (1996, April-June). Boeing introduces MEDA, Maintenance Error Decision Aid, *Airliner,* 20-27.

Reason, J. (1997). *Managing the risks of organizational accidents*. Aldershot, U.K.: Ashgate Publishing Limited.

Resnik, M. (1997), *Choices: An introduction to decision theory*. Minneapolis, MN: University of Minnesota Press.

Roberts, K. (1990). Some characteristics of one type of High Reliability Organization. *Organization Science, 1*(2), 160-173.

Robertson, M., Taylor, J., Stelly, J., and Wagner, R. (1995). A systematic training evaluation model applied to measure the effectiveness of an aviation maintenance team training program. In *Proceedings of the Eighth International Symposium on Aviation Psychology*. Columbus, Ohio, The Ohio State University, 631-636.

Sagan, S. (1993). *The limits of safety: Organizations, accidents, and nuclear weapons*. Princeton, NJ: Princeton University Press.

Scoble, R. (1994). Recent changes in aircraft maintenance worker relationships. *Proceedings of the Eighth International Symposium on Human Factors in Aircraft Maintenance and Inspection*. Washington, DC. Office of Aviation Medicine, 45-59.

Seidenman, P., and Spanovich, D. (1995, November). Heavy-iron repair shops fight for survival. *Aviation Equipment Maintenance*, 23-28.

Seidenman, P., and Spanovich, D. (1996, August). Startups and air cargo mods drive heavy-iron repair shops. *Aviation Equipment Maintenance*, 20-25.

Skyrme, D. (2001). The virtual corporation. *Management Insight* (2). Retrieved on June 29, 2001 from http://www.skyrme.com/insights/1virtorg.htm.

Smith, D. (2001). *Reliability, maintainability, and risk: Practical methods for engineers including reliability centred maintenance safety-related systems (6th ed.)*. Oxford: Butterworth-Heinemann Ltd.

Stelly, J., and Taylor, J. (1992). Crew coordination concepts for maintenance teams. In *Proceedings of the Seventh International Symposium on Human Factors in Aircraft Maintenance and Inspection*. Washington, DC: Federal Aviation Administration.

Taggart, W. (1990). Introducing CRM into maintenance training. In *Proceedings of the Third International Symposium on Human Factors in Aircraft Maintenance and Inspection.* Washington, DC: Federal Aviation Administration, 93-110.

Taylor, J. (1991). Maintenance organization. In *Human Factors in Aviation Maintenance Phase 1: Progress Report.* Washington, DC: Federal Aviation Administration, Office of Aviation Medicine.

Taylor, J. (1994). *Using focus groups to reduce errors in aviation maintenance* (Original title: Maintenance Resource Management [MRM] in Commercial Aviation: Reducing Errors in Aircraft Maintenance Documentation, Technical Report—10/31/94) Los Angeles: Institute of Safety & Systems Management, University of Southern California. Available at http://hfskyway.faa.gov.

Taylor, J. (1994). *Maintenance Resource Management (MRM) in commercial aviation: reducing errors in aircraft maintenance documentation* (Technical Report). Los Angeles, CA: University of Southern California.

Taylor, J. (1995). Effects of communication and participation in aviation maintenance. In *Proceedings of the Eighth International Symposium on Aviation Psychology.* Columbus, Ohio: The Ohio State University, 472-477.

Taylor, J. (1996). Participative culture and safety in airline maintenance. In *Human Factors in Organizational Design and Management—V: Proceedings of the Fifth International Symposium on Human Factors ODAM.* Amsterdam: North-Holland, 589-594.

Taylor, J. (1998a). *Evaluating the effects of Maintenance Resource Management (MRM) interventions in airline safety* (Report of research conducted under FAA Grant #96-G-003). Los Angeles, CA: Institute of Safety and Systems Management, University of Southern California. Available at http://hfskyway.faa.gov, and on the FAA distributed CD-ROM, *Human factors in Aviation Maintenance and Inspection,* 1999.

Taylor, J. (1998b). Evaluating The Effectiveness of Maintenance Resource Management (MRM). In *Proceedings of the Twelfth International Symposium on Human Factors in Aircraft Maintenance and Inspection, Gatwick, UK,* 85-99.

Taylor, J. (1999). *Some effects of national culture in aviation maintenance.* SAE Paper 1999-01-2980. SAE Advances in Aviation Safety Conference, Daytona Beach, FL.

Taylor, J. (2000). Reliability and validity of the Maintenance Resources Management, Technical Operations Questionnaire (MRM/TOQ). *International Journal of Industrial Ergonomics, 26,* 217-230.

Taylor, J., and Christensen, T. (1998). *Airline Maintenance Resource Managemet: Improving communication*, Warrendale, PA: Society of Automotive Engineers.

Taylor, J., and Felten, D. (1993). *Performance by design: Sociotechnical systems in North America*. Englewood Cliffs, NJ: Prentice Hall.

Taylor, J., and Patankar, M. (1999). Cultural factors contributing to the success of macro human factors in aviation maintenance. In *Proceedings of the Tenth International Symposium on Aviation Psychology*. Columbus, Ohio: The Ohio State University.

Taylor, J., and Patankar, M. (2001). Four generations of MRM: An analysis of the past, present, and future generations of MRM programs. *The Journal of Air Transportation World Wide, 6* (2), 3-32.

Taylor, J., and Robertson, M. (1994). Successful communication for maintenance. *The CRM Advocate*. October, 4-7.

Taylor, J., and Robertson, M. (1995). *The effects of Crew Resource Management (CRM) training in airline maintenance: Results Following Three Years Experience*. NASA Contractor Report 196696, Washington, DC: National Aeronautics and Space Administration.

Taylor, J., and Thomas, R. (In Press a) Written communication practices as impacted by a Maintenance Resource Management training intervention. Accepted for publication in *The Journal of Air Transportation*.

Taylor, J., and Thomas, R. (In Press b). The structure of trust in aviation maintenance. Accepted for publication in the *International Journal of Aviation Psychology*.

Taylor, J., Robertson, M., and Choi, S. (1997). Empirical results of Maintenance Resource Management training for aviation maintenance technicians. In *Proceedings of the Ninth International Symposium on Aviation Psychology*. Columbus, Ohio: The Ohio State University, 1020-1025.

Taylor, J., Robertson, M., Peck, R., and Stelly, J. (1993). Validating the impact of maintenance CRM training. In *Proceedings of the Seventh International Symposium on Aviation Psychology*. Columbus, Ohio: The Ohio State University, 538-542.

Thom, M. (1997). Industry inputs for better communications training for aviation maintenance students. *ATEC Journal, 19*(1), 8-10.

Thurber, M. (1999, September). Dial M (Maintenance) for murder. *Aviation Maintenance*, p. 4.

Vaughan, D. (1996). *The Challenger launch decision: Risky technology, culture, and deviance at NASA*. Chicago: University of Chicago Press.

Weick, K. (1987). Organizational culture as a source of high reliability. *California Management Review 19*(2), 116-124.

Wenner, C., and Drury, C. (1996). A unified reporting system for maintenance facilities. *Human Factors in Aviation Maintenance— Phase VI: Progress Report* (Vol. II, pp. 191-242). Washington, DC: Federal Aviation Administration/Office of Aviation Medicine.

Westrum, R. (1995). Organisational dynamics and safety. In N. McDonald, N. Johnston, and R. Fuller (Eds.), *Applications of psychology to the aviation system* (pp. 75-80). Aldershot, U.K.: Ashgate Publishing Limited.

Wickens, C. (1984). *Engineering psychology and human performance*. Boston: Addison Wesley.

Wiener, E., Kanki, B., and Helmreich, R. (1993). *Cockpit Resource Management*. San Diego, CA: Academic Press.

Wulle, B. and Lapacek, M. (1997) Effective Pilot/Technician Communication Aids Troubleshooting. *Ground Effects*, 2 (3, May/June), 10-11.

Index